SAGE was founded in 1965 by Sara Miller McCune to support the dissemination of usable knowledge by publishing innovative and high-quality research and teaching content. Today, we publish over 900 journals, including those of more than 400 learned societies, more than 800 new books per year, and a growing range of library products including archives, data, case studies, reports, and video. SAGE remains majority-owned by our founder, and after Sara's lifetime will become owned by a charitable trust that secures our continued independence.

Los Angeles | London | New Delhi | Singapore | Washington DC | Melbourne

Women in School Leadership

Women in SCHOOL LEADERSHIP

N. MYTHILI

Los Angeles | London | New Delhi
Singapore | Washington DC | Melbourne

Copyright © N. Mythili, 2019

All rights reserved. No part of this book may be reproduced or utilized in any form or by any means, electronic or mechanical, including photocopying, recording, or by any information storage or retrieval system, without permission in writing from the publisher.

First published in 2019 by

SAGE Publications India Pvt Ltd
B1/I-1 Mohan Cooperative Industrial Area
Mathura Road, New Delhi 110 044, India
www.sagepub.in

SAGE Publications Inc
2455 Teller Road
Thousand Oaks, California 91320, USA

SAGE Publications Ltd
1 Oliver's Yard, 55 City Road
London EC1Y 1SP, United Kingdom

SAGE Publications Asia-Pacific Pte Ltd
18 Cross Street #10-10/11/12
China Square Central
Singapore 048423

Published by Vivek Mehra for SAGE Publications India Pvt Ltd. Typeset in 10.5/13 pt Berkeley by Zaza Eunice, Hosur, Tamil Nadu, India.

Library of Congress Cataloging-in-Publication Data

Name: Mythili, N., author.
Title: Women in school leadership/N. Mythili.
Description: New Delhi, India: SAGE Publications India Pvt Ltd, 2019. |
   Includes bibliographical references and index.
Identifiers: LCCN 2019004903 (print) | LCCN 2019008422 (ebook) | ISBN
   9789353283803 (E-Book) | ISBN 9789353283780 (print: alk. paper) | ISBN
   9789353283797 (epub)
Subjects: LCSH: Women school administrators—India. | Women in
   education—India. | Educational leadership—India.
Classification: LCC LB2831.826.I4 (ebook) | LCC LB2831.826.I4 M96 2019
   (print) | DDC 371.2—dc23
LC record available at https://lccn.loc.gov/2019004903

ISBN: 978-93-532-8378-0 (HB)

SAGE Team: Abhijit Baroi, Safia Hassan and Rajinder Kaur

To My Mother
She does not know about gender or leadership
Yet she is sensitive to gender and is a leader for us all

She does not question the patriarchy
But has not succumbed to it either

She does not assert her leadership
Yet leadership embraces her

She does not lead from the front
But others look up to her, keeping in the front

She is the shelter to get solace and guidance
To boost confidence and morale

She does not behold modernization
But modernity beholds her

She is my mother
To whom I dedicate this work

Thank you for choosing a SAGE product!
If you have any comment, observation or feedback,
I would like to personally hear from you.

Please write to me at **contactceo@sagepub.in**

Vivek Mehra, Managing Director and CEO, SAGE India.

Bulk Sales

SAGE India offers special discounts
for purchase of books in bulk.
We also make available special imprints
and excerpts from our books on demand.

For orders and enquiries, write to us at

Marketing Department
SAGE Publications India Pvt Ltd
B1/I-1, Mohan Cooperative Industrial Area
Mathura Road, Post Bag 7
New Delhi 110044, India

E-mail us at **marketing@sagepub.in**

Subscribe to our mailing list
Write to **marketing@sagepub.in**

This book is also available as an e-book.

CONTENTS

List of Illustrations   xi
List of Abbreviations   xv
Preface   xvii

1. **School Leadership of Women in Developing Countries: Perspectives and Practices**   1
   The Third Billion in Development Discourse   1
   Factors Influencing Women's School Leadership in Developing Countries   3
   School Leadership of Women in India   10
   Swirl of Structure–Agency Interaction: A Threat   12
   Overview of the Book   17

2. **Career and Human Development**   19
   Structure–Agency Interaction and Human Development   19
   Life-Course Approach and Human Development   20
   Ecology of Human Development   22
   The 'Whole' and the 'whole' Relationship for Human Development   23
   Agency of Women School Leader and Human Development   24
   Power, Authority and Power Differentials   25
   Central Argument and Its Relationship to Research Question   27
   Methodological Approach for the Study   28

3. **Participation of Women in School Leadership Positions in India: Opportunities and Outcomes** — 33
   Representation of Women in School Leadership Positions in Developing Countries — 33
   Equal Opportunities and Outcomes Influencing the Participation — 34
   Examining Opportunities for School Leadership Positions in Education System — 37
   Representation of Women in School Leadership Positions across Different School Categories — 43
   Other Factors Influencing the Representation of Women in School Leadership Positions — 62
   Conclusions — 72

4. **Ladder of School Leadership of Women** — 81
   Emergent Property of School Leadership of Women: Process and Outcomes — 81
   Narratives — 85
   Agency of Women — 107

5. **Determinants of School Leadership of Successful Women in India** — 112
   Conceptual Framework for Structure–Agency Interaction: Threefold Matrices — 112
   Studying a Fivefold Structure–Agency Interaction — 117
   Tracing the Path of School Leadership of Women — 143

6. **Legitimization of School Leadership of Women** — 151
   Legitimacy of School Leadership of Women in India: Constructing a Conceptual Model — 151
   Legitimization Process of Women School Leaders — 160
   A Continuum of Interaction for Legitimacy between Leadership-Focus Behaviour and Gender Perspective — 176

7. **Theorizing School Leadership of Women in the Indian Context** — **182**
   Looking through the Lens of Social Ontology — 182
   An Overview of the Process of Theorization of School Leadership of Women in the Indian Context — 184
   Path-Wise Exposition to Theorization of School Leadership of Women in the Indian Context — 188
   Quest for Success — 205
   Defining School Leadership for Women in the Indian Context — 210
   Policy Implications — 211

References — 219
Index — 229
About the Author — 234

LIST OF ILLUSTRATIONS

FIGURES

3.1	Opportunities Available for the Participation of Women in School Leadership Positions and Other Influencing Factors	36
6.1	Legitimization Process of Women School Leaders in the Indian Context	157
7.1	Path of School Leadership Traversed by Women School Heads in the Indian Context	186
7.2	Theorizing School Leadership of Women in India	187

TABLES

3.1	Proportion of School Categories: All India	39
3.2	Proportion of Different School Categories	40
3.3	Representation of Women in School Leadership Positions and Women Teachers in Different School Leadership Positions: All India (in Percentage)	43
3.4	Women in School Leadership Positions: Representation Pattern of States/UTs	45
3.5	Representation of Women in School Leadership Positions in the Eastern Region (in Percentage)	50
3.6	Representation of Women in School Leadership Positions in the Western Region (in Percentage)	52

3.7	Representation of Women in School Leadership Positions in the Northern Region (in Percentage)	54
3.8	Representation of Women in School Leadership Positions in the Southern Region (in Percentage)	57
3.9	Consolidated Regional-Level Results on Representation of Women as A-HMs in India (in Percentage)	58
3.10	Representation of Women in School Leadership Positions at the Regional Level: An Aggregate Scenario (in Percentage)	59
3.11	Aggregate Trend at the State Level: Representation of Women in Four Leadership Positions (in Percentage)	61
3.12	Emerging Pattern of Women in School Leadership Positions in States/UTs Having HR	63
3.13	Recruitment Criteria and Process Adopted by the Government School Heads in Indian States/UTs	64
3A.1	Distribution of School Categories in States/UTs and at All-India Level	75
3A.2	Distribution of Women Teachers in Different School Categories at the State Level (in Percentage)	78
4.1	Emergent Themes, Their Characteristics, Ladder of School Leadership and Predominant Structure Associated for School Leadership of Women in the Indian Context	83
4.2	Basic Profiles of Women School Heads	86
5.1	Capacity–Agency Interaction to Study Structure and Agency Interaction	113
5.2	Relationship between Nature and Magnitude of Different Structures Influencing School Leadership	114
5.3	Interaction between Structure and Agency for Identifying Determinants of School Leadership of Successful Women in the Indian Context	116
5.4	Interaction between Diversity in School Contexts (Chrono Structure) and Agency of Women School Head for Identifying Determinants of Successful School Leadership for Women	120

5.5	Interaction between Education System (Macro Structure) and Agency of Women School Head for Identifying Determinants of Successful School Leadership for Women	124
5.6	Interaction between Family (Micro Structure) and Agency of Women School Head for Identifying Determinants of Successful School Leadership for Women	130
5.7	Interaction between School (Meso Structure) and Agency of Women School Head for Identifying Determinants of Successful School Leadership for Women	133
5.8	Interaction between Community (Exo Structure) and Agency of Women School Head for Identifying Determinants of Successful School Leadership for Women	142
5.9	Determinants of Successful School Leadership of Women in the Indian Context: Consolidation of Results	146
5.10	Path of School Leadership of Women in the Indian Context: Role of Determinants	150
7.1	Leadership Attributes, Processes and Functions Determining the Success of Women School Leaders in the Indian Context	189

LIST OF ABBREVIATIONS

AASA	American Association of School Administrators
A-HM	acting headmistress/headmaster
BA	Bachelor of Arts
BEd	Bachelor of Education
BRC	Block Resource Centre
CRC	Cluster Resource Centre
CTE	College of Teacher Education
D	deterministic (determinant for structure–agency interaction)
DEd	Diploma in Education
DElEd	Diploma in Elementary Education
DEO	District Education Officer
DIET	District Institutes of Educational Training
DPEP	District Primary Education Programme
ER	equal representation
FYP	Five-Year Plan
GAD	gender and development
GDP	gross domestic product
GOI	Government of India
HM	headmistress/headmaster
HR	higher representation
HS	higher secondary (level of schooling)
HS-only	higher secondary only (school category)
HT	head teacher

JNV	Jawahar Navodaya Vidyalaya
M	mediated (determinant for structure–agency interaction)
MEd	Master of Education
MHRD	Ministry of Human Resource Development
MLA	Member of Legislative Assembly
NUEPA	National University of Educational Planning and Administration (current abbreviation NIEPA, National Institute of Educational Planning and Administration)
P	primary (level of schooling)
P-only	primary only (school category)
PhD	Doctor of Philosophy
PSC	Public Service Commission
QNA	quantitative narrative analysis
RMSA	Rashtriya Madhyamik Shiksha Abhiyan
S	secondary
S-only	secondary only
SCERT	State Council for Educational Research and Training
SLDP	School Leadership Development Programme
SMC	School Management Committee
SSA	Sarva Shiksha Abhiyan
U-DISE	Unified-District Information on School Education
UEE	universalization of elementary education
UNESCO	United Nations Educational, Scientific and Cultural Organization
UP	upper primary
UP-only	upper primary only
UPSC	Union Public Service Commission
UR	under-representation
UT	union territory
V	voluntary (determinant for structure–agency interaction)
VP	vice-principal
WID	women in development

PREFACE

As I began my journey by reading the literature on women school leaders, it was surprising to learn that they were considered along with women teachers without making any distinction between teachers and school heads in the Indian context. As such, women's leadership in schools did not attract the attention of scholars or practitioners as it should have been. It was also not known to what extent they were represented in school leadership positions in India, be it at elementary, secondary or senior secondary schools as acting headmistresses, head teachers, vice-principals or principals. This observation received further impetus when it became certain that the entire area of school leadership was least explored and understood in India's school education system. Interestingly, several studies on women leaders are available in the context of Arab countries, Israel, Pakistan and Africa, which are also traditional societies, and most of them are developing countries like India. It was amply clear that women's school leadership is an unexplored area in Indian context. So I decided to pursue my interest on women holding school leadership positions as a category that is distinct from teachers.

The second aspect that was increasingly becoming certain from international literature, especially in developing country contexts, is that gender discrimination and barriers to women's school leadership were often researched. But they fell short of explaining how these women succeeded as leaders where teaching profession is dominated by men and context is that of traditional society. What has enabled them now to talk about discrimination and barriers they faced? Hence, the focus got narrowed down to investigating how women actually succeeded as leaders.

Third, while trying to develop a conceptual framework for the study, I recognized that these studies largely fell into the domains which were either gender and feminist studies or sociology of education. If the focus is women, then often a feminist perspective was adopted. If the studies pertained to sociology, they largely discussed about the agency of women. The predominance of these two approaches gave raise to choosing a feminist perspective and/or sociology of education to dwell on structure–agency interaction for many researchers. But neither of these approaches when considered exclusively or together could convince me to get the answers for the research question I was trying to answer. This is because of the reason that leadership, which is the central theme, would be lost if I have to restrict myself to feminism, gender and/or structure–agency interaction. Nonetheless, these approaches are not unimportant either. Studying the participation of women in school leadership positions using secondary data also needs a different perspective because neither feminism nor sociology of education was adequate to explain the reasons and results. The search in this direction suggested that perspective on opportunities and outcomes in economics can explain the phenomenon related to secondary data. As I was progressing in the journey on women's school leadership, it was also clear that success is a gradual process over time and space. It is also dependent on the individual aspirant and her family, career and professional development. It called for looking into life course perspective as well. Last but not least, all this study and discussion is about women leaders who are in schools deeply immersed in the teaching–learning process, school administration and management. Hence, education studies is another crucial perspective to be included to know how women as head teachers, vice-principals or principals succeeded. As a result, adopting a multidisciplinary approach emerged for studying women's school leadership. So, in this book, I intend to present before the readers the status of women's participation using secondary data; voices of women working in school leadership positions from the field; the process of interaction between structure and agency to systematically identify the determinants of school leadership of women, thereby tracing the path they traversed to succeed; and the interactive processes between school leadership and gender perspective exploring into the unfamiliar areas of legitimization of women's school leadership even in the international context. In fact, for any leadership to succeed, acquiring legitimacy of leadership is an important step. For women school leaders, acquiring legitimacy is a process of interaction between their leadership behaviour and gender perspective. The results obtained were nested together and further studied to arrive at a theory on school leadership of women by applying the tenets of social ontology. Policy suggestions followed at the end.

This book makes a humble beginning and aims to generate a discourse among the academia, practitioners, education officials and decision-makers in the government at the state and national levels about women school leaders in India. It assumes increased importance especially in today's context when school leadership development is considered as an important variable by the Ministry of Human Resource Development for improving the quality of education. This book can be considered as a way of recognizing the women school leaders whose efforts, at times, are very high, working amid challenges in urban, rural, semi-rural and isolated terrains of difficult geographies in the Himalayas in the far-flung areas in Sikkim and Himachal Pradesh.

Here, I must acknowledge that these women were willing to share their experiences that are subtle and sensitive in nature by trusting me. This was indeed heartening and a unique experience for me as a researcher. My special thanks and due acknowledgement goes to them in the first and foremost instance. My due acknowledgements also to the National Institute of Educational Planning and Administration (NIEPA), where I am currently working, with its rich library and National Centre for School Leadership (NCSL) for the institutional support received. I thank all my colleagues and also those retired from NIEPA. My respectful acknowledgements to SAGE, the publisher, who agreed to take a stab at this unexplored area in the Indian context and publish this book. It was indeed a rich experience working with SAGE India's team members. I consider walking the path to reach this milestone, navigating uncertainties and challenges, indeed a new form of empowerment for me.

FACTORS INFLUENCING WOMEN'S SCHOOL LEADERSHIP IN DEVELOPING COUNTRIES

Different factors influence women's school leadership roles in varied forms with varying effects. It is also true that a kind of tension arises due to the interaction between opposing sets of dyadic factors which are unique to women's leadership. Some of them are discussed herewith.

Masculinity–Femininity Syndrome

The specific attributes of feminine leadership styles are attributed to socialization, cultural origin and organizational culture at the macro socio-political level, the meso organizational level and micro level related to individual-self which influence women to attain leadership positions (Cubillo & Brown, 2003). Women teachers are mostly confined to women's ghetto at lower classes, often made to engage in non-teaching works such as making tea, cleaning classroom, and fetching water, resulting in the perception 'women are less able to work professionally', professional isolation, divide between men and women teachers and less respect from students (ibid., p. 99).

Women's leadership is discussed using different bi-polarities. The popular among them are 'fitting-in' the traditional roles of masculine-dominated leadership styles and 'giving-in' opportunities for women to practice their own leadership styles; daring to openly reveal feminine leadership behaviours as 'silent cries' for social justice and to assert a place of their own in the organization versus conformity to social norms and orthodox stereotypes; task-oriented vis-à-vis relationship-oriented leadership behaviour; and associating femininity with incompetence and masculinity with competency (Trinidad & Normore, 2005).

'Fitting-in' refers to expectations about women school heads to learn the ways that is generally used by men to lead the schools and hence accept and follow masculine-dominated leadership styles. 'Giving-in' opportunities refers to women giving up of their own inherent feminine strengths as leaders and yielding to the pressure to follow the popular masculine approach to leadership. If the woman school head refuses to give up her feminine strengths as a leader and asserts clandestinely her inherent strengths to lead the school, it is called 'silent cries'. When the women asserts not to 'fit-in', not to 'give up' but influence the school processes through her 'silent cries', she is also asking for recognition of her feminine leadership qualities to be on par with those of masculine leadership qualities. From a social justice point of view, it refers to women's aspiration for gender equality in the roles as school leaders. During the process of attaining gender equality, women encounter contradictions and tensions, created due to the dynamics of interactions between herself and community and society through multiple identities and positions in families, communities, classrooms and schools. All these influence the ways in which women teachers reconcile these different positions and identities. Walkerdine (1990) calls these as 'impossible fictions'.

Covert Compulsions to Assume Male Persona

Research evidence on gender issues in school leadership in a few developing countries converge on a number of planks: under-representation of women in school leadership positions; family, community and social constraints (Addi-Raccah, 2002; Addi-Raccah & Ayalon, 2002; Arar, 2010); orthodox and gender stereotypes (Fitzgerald, 2003); and perception that school leadership is a male domain with low participation from women (Brinia, 2012; Panigrahi, 2013; Miller, 2013; Kyriakoussis & Saathi, n.d.). Notwithstanding these notions, a woman school head in northern Pakistan demonstrated herself as a 'different' person, combining conformity to cultural patriarchal values with her role as school leader, negotiating and renegotiating 'multiplicities of self' drawing inspiration from the 'persistent flow of water in a stream outside her village without stopping in its course' (Ashraf, 2008, p. 51). There is a covert compulsion for women to maintain a male persona while practising female community-building skills (Martin, 2011).

Socio-Cultural Effect

Since long, women have faced the glass-ceiling and glass-wall effects as school leaders (Metz & Neely, 1998), which continues even now.

Women school leaders are affected by sexual orientation (Shakeshaft, 1987), gender discrimination (Dorsey, 1989; Makura, n.d.), gender identity (Ozga, 1993; Abu-Tineh, 2012), mono-culturalism of power (Blackmore 1999), inequality in the opportunities to work (Mc Lay & Brown, 1999; Lugg & Tooms, 2010), marginalization of ethnic minority (Coleman, 2003), low self-esteem (Monari, 2008; Chabaya, Rembe, & Wadesango, 2009), notion about the ethics of care as the sole responsibility of women as one who inherits naturally the ability to take care of children (Popescu & Gunter, 2011), break in the career due to the responsibilities of child care (Sperandio & Kagoda, 2011) and passive racism (Preciurumantuntu & Bolt, 2012). Women principals were ignored by the education system when they tried to develop Arab schools in Israel (Shapira, Arar, & Azaiza, 2011). Educated and employed women in Pakistan face the pressure of maintaining harmonious relationships with family and community (Kurshid & Saba, 2018).

Thwarted Opportunities

Male teachers are promoted as secondary school heads, whereas women are given primary school headship to fulfil the affirmative action policy requirement (Marshall, 1985). Women teachers also have a negative perception regarding leadership roles, fearing excess work (Limerick & Lingard, 1995). Training and education for women are given with a view to come up to the level of men, which fills the deficits in their capabilities disregarding the strengths which they might bring into the profession on their own (Cubillo & Brown, 2003). Women hesitate to participate actively in professional organizations (Srivastava, 2008) and often lack formal and informal networks among themselves, which men have (National College of School Leadership, UK, n.d.).

In Nepal, Pakistan and Afghanistan, women have meagre chances to pursue education beyond the school level (Kirk & Winthrop, 2008). Male teachers continue to dominate the teaching profession in developing countries (Jane, Akao, Kilavanwa, & Warsal, 2010). Women are discouraged from obtaining university-level education, necessary for securing a principal's position in Bangladesh (Sperandio, 2011). They continue to experience overt and covert discouragement to take up leadership roles within the society's culture (Limerick & Lingard, 1995; Gaus, 2011). These have caused lack of leadership preparation (Mutopa, Maphosa, & Shumba, 2006; Sperandio & Kagoda, 2011), resulting in misrecognition and non-recognition of women as school leaders (Fuller, 2013).

Patriarchy

A 'public patriarchy' (Walby, 1990) at the macro level arising from hegemonic traditions and cultures, religious customs, beliefs and norms force women to oblige and bind them to familial roles of caring. In India, there is an impact of social norms, family mores, social class, socialization and caste on women's career aspirations (Gupta, 1991), choice of profession (Banerjee, 2002) and income in the employment (Khetrapal, 2003). Formal education alone is not adequate to empower women and neutralize the accumulated distortions of the past. This is because the content of education and the context in which it is imparted and the intangible inputs play a deeper role in the lives of women, which are more important than just formal schooling (Ramachandran, 2008). It is due to the fact that women are generally constrained by social class, norms and family mores about the choice of jobs (Jandhyala, Mehrotra, & Ramachandran, 2014). It especially affects the economic status of the family as most of these women come from lower income families (Shenoy-Parker, 2014, p. 63).

Drawing a Parallel between Home and School

The teaching profession gets less specific as compared with other professions as family roles diffuse into teacher's roles. Teaching occupation is such that tasks expected of a teacher are specific and clearly defined both in terms of time and space requiring planning. This is the conflict between congruence and compatibility, even though women express satisfaction about their role, which is mainly due to new economic roles acquired in the family yet continuing to be good wives and mothers (Nair, 1988). Women's inability to enter into well paid but culturally inappropriate jobs further reinforces perceptions about teaching as a culturally appropriate profession for women (Ashraf, 2008), as one which can provide an additional source of income for the family without disturbing patriarchy (Jandhyala et al., 2014; Jandhyala & Ramachandran, 2015).

For instance, Ashraf (2008) narrates the woman teacher's life in the northern Pakistan. Women's traditional roles according to that region are child care and using 'innate' love and affection. It also constitutes the basis for division of tasks in the school. It resonates with a 'family-like life' in schools too. Their real homes are located also mostly within the close proximity of the real schools. Elders in the family keep a watch on their women to protect the 'vulnerability' of their women who are teachers from interacting with 'outside men', that is, men who are teachers in the same school. In this way, ascribed familial responsibilities of women are harmonized with roles in the schools as teachers.

These women in Pakistan, who had tremendous pressure to maintain harmonious relationships with family and community, showed marked agility to cope with it without compromising on their jobs or careers (Kurshid & Saba, 2018). In Nepal, although financial motivation appears strong, the incentive of long holidays, staying close to home to run the family life in parallel and short working hours were stronger among women teachers (Bista, 2008). Interestingly, parents in Nepal perceive these advantages preferred by women teachers as limiting factors as it does not provide the necessary exposure to the outside world, which is important for the children's total development (Kirk, 2008, p. 98).

Mediating Agency

Agency is the ability of the women school head to address the challenges, while leading the school, negotiating through different structures and identities as an individual and performing different roles in a relational framework to achieve her goals as the head of the school. Nonetheless, agency of the women school head is also influenced and shaped by different people who come in contact with her and interact with her, different circumstances influenced by cultural and social moorings, economic and political situations in the society and the like.

Hence, agency in the present study is not only about the capacity to act independently but also influenced by other people and different structures while making such choices to act freely. It is also not just agency but mediating agency for women school heads. Therefore, agency is not a bare-bone, but a socio-culturally mediated one, having control over one's behaviour, producing actions that affect other entities as well as self and producing actions which are objects of evaluation (Lantolf & Poehner, 2008). Despite inequalities and constraints, factors such as vocational anticipatory socialization (Jablin, 1985), confidence and beliefs in abilities (Bandura, 1982, 1997), contextual affordance (Lent, Brown, & Hackett, 1994) and institutional agencies like socialization pressures and cultural norms (Watt & Eccles, 2008; Eccles, 2014; Symonds, Maurice, & Linda, 2014) positively influence the career of women. For example, a woman head teacher in rural Pakistan made the 'inappropriate' behaviour of walking alone in public places into 'appropriate' behaviour to reach the school. Some behaviours of women in rural Pakistan are considered inappropriate despite the fact that there is nothing wrong in those behaviours and that she has the ability to do so. In this study, the women school head walked alone to reach the school despite being aware of people's attention that she was drawing towards her while walking alone. However, while travelling alone to district headquarters to meet education officials using a public or private transport, she took the help of her uncle who would accompany her to the bus stand and speak to the fellow travellers and the driver casually to let them know that she is his niece who is travelling on official work to the district. So, at times, she conformed to the dominant gender norms strategically to avoid unnecessary attention but never let conformity govern her social movements (Ashraf, 2008, p. 47). It is an example for mediating agency.

Gender: Making a Difference for Successful Leadership

Bargaining with the patriarchy (Kandiyoti, 1997), women school heads use parallel strategies of both conformity to dominant attitudes and resistance to patriarchy (Ashraf, 2008). Trinidad and Normore (2005) in their review of studies observe that women adopt democratic and participative leadership styles. They prefer transformational leadership style, which closely relates to female values developed through socialization processes. Some transformational leadership practices which women practice include relationship building, consensus building, power as influence and working together for a common purpose. Successful women school leaders exhibit certain unique leadership behaviours similar to those used in transformational leadership style.

Successful women school leaders adopt democratic and participative leadership styles, prefer relationship building and consensus building, see power as influence and share power, work together for a common purpose, engage in interactivity, enhance self-worth, substitute self-interests for overall good, use effective communication, care about individual differences and motivate others (Cubillo & Brown, 2003; Trinidad & Normore, 2005). Women's style is characterized by people-based style, role-modelling, clear expectations and rewards (Mckinsey & Company, 2009). Thus, effective school leadership of women is about being more relationship-oriented, intuitive, future-oriented, flexible, passionate, loyal, reasonable, collaborative and empathetic (Gerzema, 2013). Capturing the gender differences, Patel (2013) observes that there is no difference in the ability of men and women, but women bring a different perspective to their strategic decision-making by being sensitive to others; taking initiative; practising self-development, integrity and honesty; and driving others for results. Women also show a democratic/participative leadership style and are less directive/autocratic, more inclined to transformational leadership styles of being more intent on rewarding others, less hierarchical, more cooperative and collaborative and willing to enhance self-esteem of others. Women principals in Israel dealt with managerial prowess to ensure professional success and repressed personal emotional expression, but reported extreme stress, frustration and helplessness in their early career stage. In their mid-career, they promoted pedagogy and assisted in the growth of their staff, and felt strength and self-confidence arising from accumulated deep professional experience that was accompanied with a sense of relief in their work and moved away from authoritarian style stemming from their expertise as pedagogic leaders (Arar, 2017).

SCHOOL LEADERSHIP OF WOMEN IN INDIA

In India, Durga Bai Deshmukh Committee (GOI, 1959) emphasized on setting up placement services in all teacher training institutions for women to get employment which would also give one-time grant or loan for enabling them to attend the interview. It also suggested part-time employment for women to have a work–life balance. The emphasis on women's education with a focus on girls' education began in 1974 from the fifth Five Year Plan (FYP). It continued in the sixth FYP initiating the appointment of women teachers from 1980 onwards. It saw the shift in 2012 through the 12-th FYP emphasizing to create greater 'freedom' and 'choice' to reduce violence, improve employability and work participation to overcome institutional and structural barriers to mainstream gender. The National Policy on Education (GOI, 1986), Programme of Action (GOI, 1992) and the National Curriculum Framework for Teacher Education (GOI, 2009) also emphasized bringing about basic changes in women's basic status by fostering new values to eliminate sex stereotyping and promoting women's participation in non-traditional occupations and in emerging technologies as well as empowerment as the key means. These policies also endeavoured and implemented the appointment of women in single- or two-teacher primary schools. Regardless of these efforts, problems seem to multiply, issues remain unresolved and gender inequality and discrimination perpetuate as the system continues to function in gender-blind alleys. Therefore, interest in this field persists as issues reopen in the changing social, economic, cultural and educational contexts from time to time.

Studying the proportion of men and women teachers since the 1950s, Agarwal and Aggarwal (1995) observe that there are fewer women compared with men at all levels of education and the proportion of women teachers in low-literacy states is extremely poor, especially at primary and middle levels constituting only 21 per cent and 23 per cent, respectively. Further, the number of women teachers even decreases as the level of education increases. This is due to a shortage of women teachers in rural areas, which has a background linkage to low availability of post-primary/secondary education facilities for rural girls who therefore do not fulfil the essential entry criteria for teacher training courses (Nair, 2001). The annual rate of growth of women teachers from 1959–1960 to 2004–2005 shows an increment of 3.79 per cent as against 0.83 per cent for male teachers at the primary level. The corresponding figures are 7.39 per cent and 5.29 per cent in upper primary schools and 6.32 per cent and 3.41 per cent in high schools, respectively (Kumar, 2011). Kumar concludes that even though there is a positive growth rate of teachers over the years, representation of women teachers continues to be lower than that of male teachers and administrators in India. Several externally funded projects such as District Primary Education Programme (DPEP) and its allied programmes also took up recruitment of women teachers in a mission mode in the 1990s to boost the participation of women teachers, especially in Karnataka, Maharashtra and Andhra Pradesh (before division). A few other states such as Rajasthan provided part-time employment for women teachers to facilitate them to manage responsibilities between home and school. Some of these states also provided financial support for women to undergo teacher training. Nonetheless, there is a relative decline in the popularity of the teaching profession among women who tend to move to other professions and occupations with the expansion and diversification of education in India and Sri Lanka (Nair, 2001).

As the burning issues were to address teacher shortage in the schools, ensure continuation of girls' schooling and undertake mass recruitment of teachers with special emphasis on women teachers as necessary in India, much attention was not paid at that time to the recruitment of women school heads. Research studies referred above also have hardly attempted to make a distinction between women teachers and women school heads. Therefore, today in India, discussions on women in school education are primarily focused on women teachers, providing only an indirect insight into the status of women school heads. These indirect insights serve as useful means to understand issues related to women school heads who were teachers for a long time earlier.

Manjrekar (2013) observes that the wider structural determinants, ideologies and practices defining and regulating women teachers within the domestic sphere and paid workforce are historically related and socially reproduced. Women are constrained by social class, norms and family mores about the choice of jobs (Jandhyala et al., 2014) due to the complex gendered hierarchy and relationship of economic exigencies, cultural norms, community loyalty and religiosity (Belliyappa & De Souza, 2017). Anglo-Indian women teachers are circumscribed by gender and community identity despite showing marked agency (ibid.). In this sense, a wider approach to the teaching pedagogy to address the diverse contexts including that of students is missing in teacher education (Batra, 2009).

Nevertheless, these studies leave a vacuum in understanding school leadership of women, as their impact is not the same as that of women teachers. Indian studies generally discuss the impact of social norms, family mores, social class, socialization and caste on women's career aspiration, choice of profession and income from employment. They highlight the role conflict among women teachers or discuss the stereotyped practices that inhibit the impact women teachers can make. Earlier studies by Govinda (2002), NUEPA (2010), Sujatha (2011), European Union, Save the Children and NUEPA (2013) and the 12th FYP (GOI-Planning Commission, 2013) also overlooked the gender equality aspect in school leadership despite recognizing the importance of school leadership for school quality. Due to the paucity of studies on women school leaders in India and South Asia, a discussion on women teachers will serve as a useful backdrop for the present book.

SWIRL OF STRUCTURE–AGENCY INTERACTION: A THREAT

Since long, discourses on women in education have been held under the single large umbrella of women's empowerment in South Asia including India, disregarding women as career-seeking individuals in school leadership positions having their own individual capabilities, strengths and aspirations to be leaders. This has resulted in the under-recognition of women as school leaders who are distinct from teachers. Practising school leadership is influenced by the dyads of agency and submission, experiencing power and powerlessness, searching for possibilities and impossibilities, identifying the doable and non-doable, navigating between official truths and women's realities and negotiating subjectivities and identities, all of which change the dynamics of power in becoming and being school heads. The impossible fiction of a woman school head is that she is expected to achieve the goals under the given circumstances of extremely limited powers and autonomy for decision-making and school governance. This systemic constraint is smeared with implied expectations of nurturing and caring behaviours while having an obligation to efficiently manage the subordinate men and women.

Though these studies show deep concern regarding the related socio-cultural contexts and barriers, they do not discuss the influence of opportunities for school leadership positions available within the education system and to what extent does this availability influence women's participation in India. It is an area that largely remains untouched in the Indian context for understanding school leadership of women.

Despite these accumulated past and present hardships, some women do succeed as school leaders. It is imperative to shift the perception about women to recognize them as intellectual leaders with an ability to influence and change situations and circumstances at this juncture, which changes the semi-professional status accorded to teaching profession and school leadership to suitably position women with due professional identity. Studies have failed to capture the complexity in becoming and being successful school leaders. This gap may be attributed to adopting a singular approach that has rendered limited scope till date. Due to this, the core meaning of women's leadership is also not addressed satisfactorily so far.

Further, the limitation of the present conceptual contexts curtails the understanding of the dynamics of interaction within different structures on the one hand and between different structures and agencies on the other hand, which pose serious restrictions and threats on how to overcome the barriers on the path of successful school leadership. It also makes a systematic identification of the determinants of successful school leadership across different structures unclear as different structures influence leadership in different ways, not only to address challenges but also to utilize the advantages provided by various structures to excel as school leaders, depending on circumstances and abilities. All this falls short of a robust conceptualization that can throw light on the core nuances that help the agency of women to interact with structures to succeed as school leaders.

An important fact overlooked in Indian policy measures (discussed earlier) is that the school head is not seen as a leader requiring special leadership attributes unique to educational processes. Till recently, a school head was considered as a teacher and popularly called 'head teacher' (HT), thus missing the critical distinction between a school head, teacher and school leader throughout the educational discourses in India. A ripple effect of this is obvious in the form of overlooking women as leaders in school education. Further, most of the educational discourses in education with respect to women were brought under the single umbrella of women's empowerment or women's education, referring to them as women teachers despite studying women school heads in their research. Thus, women suffer from the misrecognition and non-recognition of their professional identity as school leaders. It is further exacerbated due to the impact of social norms, family mores, social class, socialization and caste on women's career aspirations, choice of profession and income from employment for women to pursue their aspirations in developing country contexts characterized by traditional societies. Consequently, women suffer from covert and overt non-acceptance, invariably pointing towards the lower legitimacy accorded to them as school leaders and to women's school leadership.

Different perceptions and practices regarding leadership of women in fact indicate a low legitimacy accorded to them as leaders. The above review indicates diverse ways in which low legitimacy is implied in these gendered stereotypes, orthodox practices and perceptions in the family, school, community and education system. These are as follows: male teachers promoted as secondary school heads that is above the position of primary school head to which women teachers are promoted; women to be educated to fill up the deficits for gaining equality in abilities with men; discouraging women from entering university education, which is a pre-requisite to apply for school leadership positions; misrecognition and non-recognition of leaders; family roles forming the basis for creating task divisions in the school to create family-like schools, to insulate from interacting with 'outside men'; a brother-like male school head overseeing the activities of the women teachers in the school; treating teaching as a culturally appropriate job for women and so on. So, the teaching profession at large and women's school leadership in specific lack requisite legitimacy, which includes lack of studies carried out in the Indian context specifically on women school heads. While teacher empowerment discourses focused on gender sensitization for men and women, they disregarded the focus of the professional status of teaching and school leadership of women. All these have created a kind of situation wherein women as heads of schools need not expect the same level of dignity and leadership excellence as their men counterparts. In general, school leadership of women does not enjoy as much legitimacy as that of men does. This aspect has remained largely unexplored in traditional and developing country contexts.

Women in the education sector are treated as a single category, making no distinction between school heads, teachers, educational administrators and women's education in the Indian context. Research in the area of school leadership of women is relatively new, and hardly any studies are found in the Indian context. Studies are mostly in the area of empowerment of women teachers in general or women's education. Even in the international context, studies especially in the developing and traditional societies delve into gender issues and challenges faced, which indeed is a deficit approach. Some studies that focus on successful women refer to certain attributes rather than the processes by which they succeed, which are especially crucial in developing country contexts. Therefore, in the present study, review of literature focused on the tension between mutually opposing factors or the dyads influencing the leadership of women in schools.

The dilemma arises in attempting to understand whether it is the structure alone, agency alone, structure–agency interaction or structure–structure interactions. Or is it the power, authority and leadership without considering structure or/and agency? Or is it the agency of women leader alone or agency of others such as family or education system and community members? Is it gender or leadership with gender? The question is also about who are those women who consider teaching as a profession and perform their roles in a professional manner? How do the fundamental or inherent capacities and core competencies of women school heads get revealed through the layers of belief systems and gendered notions? How do these women cross the threshold level to excel as leaders? What are the ways in which they navigate between different structures while interacting simultaneously with them? What is the process by which women leaders negotiate their roles and identities to assert their professionalism as school leaders? Finally, what is meant by school leadership of women in the Indian context? These dilemmas coexist and interact in a dynamic environment between the coordinates of structure–agency, equity–equality, power–power differentials, authority–legitimacy, gender–leadership, negotiate–navigate, representation–participation and so on. All these constitute the swirl of threat that leads to the question: How do some women school heads succeed as leaders in the schools despite constraints and consequences of gendered notions? What is the path women traverse to succeed as school leaders in the Indian context?

In addition to raising the research question, two other significant gaps also came to the fore. It arose from a deep dissatisfaction about the methods adopted in the studies reviewed, which could not reveal the process by which women succeeded as leaders. Instead, these frameworks and studies stopped at highlighting challenges and issues. These gaps are (a) to identify the critical dimensions to answer the research question on how women succeed; and (b) the need for developing distinct conceptual frameworks for each of these dimensions based on relevant theories for a fine-grained analysis drawing from multiple disciplines and adopting a multi-disciplinary approach. Accordingly, four objectives for the study were formulated, which are dealt with separately in different chapters. These objectives are as follows:

- To study the extent to which opportunities available in the education system influence women's participation in school leadership positions in India.
- To discover the trajectory of the path traversed by women to succeed as school leaders in the Indian context.

- To identify the determinants of school leadership of successful women in the Indian context.
- To investigate the process of legitimization of school leadership for women in the Indian context.

OVERVIEW OF THE BOOK

The first chapter deals with a variety of studies on school leadership of women especially focusing on developing countries and traditional societies that are relevant to the Indian context. The second chapter has two sections. The first attempts to position the discourse on women's school leadership within the theoretical discourse in a multi-disciplinary approach to understand human development and women's career using theoretical underpinnings from structures, agency, life-course perspective, power, status, authority and ecology of human development. The second section of the same chapter presents a detailed description of the methodology adopted. The third chapter analyses the extent of participation of women in school leadership positions using secondary data for all of India and state levels by applying economic theories of equality of opportunity. It seeks to investigate on how different factors influencing the opportunities have an impact on the representation of women in school leadership positions in India. From the fourth to the sixth chapters, a detailed analysis of the qualitative data is made from three different angles referring to the path traversed by women school heads, determinants of women's school leadership and legitimization of school leadership of women. The fourth chapter presents a detailed note of the narratives and the emergence of the path traversed by women leaders, considering all aspects from diverse dimensions including many structures, agencies, in-school processes and so on. The agency of the women is also discussed in relation to their interaction with the structures. In the subsequent two chapters, that is, the fifth and the sixth chapters, these narratives are further studied, adopting a nuanced approach to discover the role of women's leadership as they traverse the path especially in terms of how they interact with various structures, exercising agency in which they exhibit leadership-focused behaviours in diverse ways and seek to gain legitimacy as leaders. The seventh and final chapter attempts to synthesize all the findings for theorizing on school leadership of women in the Indian context. The central argument of the study raised is covered from Chapter 4 onwards, and the related research is attempted to be covered comprehensively in the final chapter.

Career and Human Development

STRUCTURE–AGENCY INTERACTION AND HUMAN DEVELOPMENT

Ecology of human development takes place across five sub-systems nested together, namely micro, meso, exo, macro and chrono (Bronfenbrenner, 1994). There is a complex relationship between these five sub-systems as they interact with people and processes, structures and agency and systems and sub-systems, giving rise to specific groups of people with 'social structure power'. These social structure powers are entities or wholes having emergent properties or causal powers distinct from human individuals (Elder-Vass, 2010). Nevertheless, they depend on the contributions of individuals. In other words, social practices are shaped by officially sanctioned structures and institutions that also enforce certain other social practices (Ostrom, 1986). Thus, social structure powers which are wholes or entities and human individuals are interdependent at macro, meso and micro levels or sub-systems to set a historical context to frame large-scale realities (Everett & Charlton, 2014) and tend to be reproduced through other social actions by empowering or constraining (Sewell, 1992, p. 19). In this way, social actions framing the experiences of human individuals are built over time and ideated through large-scale realities (Sawyer, 2005).

In the Indian educational context, ecological environment for women's leadership development can be considered as the sites of nested structures through which the socio-educational reality is constructed. Construction of woman's professional identity as a school leader is influenced by different actors in these sub-systems.

The familial support by parents and husband as a specific group of people constitutes the micro system. In the school, which is the meso system, the content and structure of women's school leadership is formed due to the relationship and interactions with teachers, staff and students, who form the specific group. The exo system composed of School Management Committee (SMC) and parents as the specific group indirectly influences the content and process of women's school leadership. Education system characterized by its hierarchical layers and education functionaries as the specific group is the macro system. The chrono system refers to the diversity in a larger context of the society as reflected in the school's social, political, cultural, economic, geographical and religious moorings for its educational and schooling processes. The social structure power present in these specific groups of people across the five sub-systems has causal powers to form the wholes or entities arising from complex relationships between them and interactions with each other in multiple ways.

LIFE-COURSE APPROACH AND HUMAN DEVELOPMENT

According to the life course theory, the individuals living the lives are also a formative process of interactions (Elder, Johnson, & Crosnoe, 2004) in the ever-changing socio-historical contexts that not only provide a setting for the human development but also make people who they are. Such a development happens through repeated interactions over time in multiple situations and relational contexts. Accumulation of such experiences during people's life's course results in diverse pathways and outcomes for all individuals irrespective of gender (Ridgeway & Correll, 2004). But then, pathways of women differ significantly from those of men as they perceive skills, values and competencies differently. They may also opt for different belief systems for making occupational choices and attainments on account of the significantly different subjective importance attached to values and goals (Eccles, 2009) when compared with that of men. Possibly this distinction is due to social reproduction of socialization processes and gendered perceptions about women's own capabilities and interests although career goals are crucial for their lives. According to Jablin (1985), vocational anticipatory socialization also influences women's career. Zikhali and Perumal (2016) emphasize on the educational background of women leaders, which they use as a tool to empower themselves. Notwithstanding, there is also a linkage between structural constraints and individuals' values, attitudes, capabilities and career choices (Schoon & Eccles, 2014).

The type of work women do is also affected due to occupational sex segregation, referring to participation of men and women in different occupations, and job-level sex segregation, referring to positions held within a single company, allowing for differentiation in the levels between companies for the same job or different jobs (Ryle, 2015). These two segregations are multi-layered with perpetual reciprocation, involvement and renegotiation for working women in India. Both are internally juxtaposed, having a multi-directional process, which is a new normal for Indian working women (Shenoy-Parker, 2014). Choice of occupation for women is shaped by socialization and negotiating changes in gender roles when women choose jobs that are explained by social learning (Ryle, 2015).

Bronfenbrenner (1994) describes human development as one that is progressive and spanning throughout life. The developmental process involves changes in the form, content, power and direction of development. It arises from the complex interaction between different human beings; human beings and objects; and human beings and symbols. These interactions take place within the environment, which may be either remote or immediate to the human beings. Therefore, outcomes of human development also vary with changes in the developing person and environment. Such enduring forms of interactions in the environment are referred to as 'proximal processes'. Proximal processes reduce or buffer against environmental differences in the developmental outcomes, resulting in variations in the pathways of men and women to construct life's courses and developmental outcomes (ibid.). In the context of the present study, there is a lot of similarity between proximal processes and structure–agency interaction. Hence, these two are not seen as different from each other as processes of women's leadership.

ECOLOGY OF HUMAN DEVELOPMENT

Human development is characterized by six properties spread across five sub-systems, namely micro, meso, exo, macro and chrono sub-systems (Bronfenbrenner, 1994). These are as follows: a person must engage in an activity on a fairly regular basis over an extended period of time for effective development to occur; to be developmentally effective, activities must continue long enough to become 'increasingly more complex' without mere repetition; and developmentally effective proximal processes are not unidirectional and that initiatives do not come from one side. There must be some degree of reciprocity in the exchange which is not limited to interactions with people but involves objects and symbols; for reciprocal interactions to occur in the latter circumstances, objects and symbols in the immediate environment must invite attention, exploration, manipulation, elaboration and imagination; and the powerful moderating factors such as form, content, power and direction of proximal processes produce substantial changes in the content, timing and effectiveness of proximal processes to provide for future realization of evolving potentials involving significant others (Bronfenbrenner & Moris, n.d., pp. 810–813).

'Proximal process' deals with developmentally generative dispositions to understand actions and reactions that women school heads receive from different systems and actors, who, in turn, assess the impact of experiences and respond suitably to change the nature and scope of those actions. It empowers women to meta-cognize school leadership through abstracting experiences into a new educational reality and for creating an identity for oneself. It is a process in which 'significant others' in the family also take part in countering gendered practices and notions to impact content and structure of school leadership of women. Interaction between different sub-systems constitute the ecology in which different proximal processes are interwoven. This interweaving of proximal processes takes place between creating an identity and abstracting experiences into a new educational reality for school leadership of women. Significant others in the family act as a connecting link counteracting the gendered notions and stereotype practices shaping the developmentally generative dispositions. All sub-systems constitute specific groups of people having social structure powers to form the ecology of school leadership in India in which women school heads comprise one such specific group of people. Therefore, all educational processes, social practices, leadership knowledge and actions regarding women's school leadership are also interconnected, operating through different structures across different sub-systems and structures in the ecology of school leadership of women.

The overarching influence of chrono system (diversity in school context referring to a larger society in the vicinity of the school) on macro (education system) and exo systems (community) constitutes a critical space that shapes the school's psycho-social environment, the meso system. The education system draws socio-cultural values, traditions and belief systems from the chrono system to interact with processes and interpret roles and responsibilities of individuals to create a unique culture of leadership by women school heads. The exo system mediates between macro education system and meso school system by providing need-based support, resisting or showing indifference arising from ignorance and knowledge. Family, the micro system, perceived as an intimate structure that connects with the school by way of influencing and guiding daughter/wife, thereby, interacting indirectly with the education system and community, all of which have their roots in the chrono system. Women derive their values, strengths and beliefs from the family to negotiate, navigate, influence, direct, empower and change their life course as leaders. Some women have been able to step aside from the overwhelming influence of chrono, macro and exo systems on their school leadership to succeed a little more than others, whereas others try to balance between successes and failures. The nuanced details of how women lead and succeed as school heads are explored further in different chapters.

THE 'WHOLE' AND THE 'wHOLE' RELATIONSHIP FOR HUMAN DEVELOPMENT

The causal power of social structures is understood through 'emergent properties' referring to the 'whole' or 'entity' that explains how an entity can have a causal impact on the world in its own right that is not just the sum of its parts would have if they were not organized into this kind of whole. The capability of having such an impact is the 'causal power' of the entity or 'whole' concerned (Elder-Vass, 2010). Here, for the purpose of presenting in the book, the whole or entity is written as 'Whole' with capital 'W' to refer to the causal power of the entity representing the entirety of the emergent property. The emergent property is one that is not possessed by the sum of its parts, that is, the 'wholes', individually in the absence of structuring of relations between them. Emergence refers to synchronic relationship between properties of a Whole (entity) and its parts at a particular moment in time. Emergent power only exists when parts concerned are organized into the type of a whole that has these powers. Hence 'wholes', that is, the parts, are powers of the 'Whole', not of the parts within themselves. Complex theorists stress the point that 'emergence' above all is an outcome of coupled as well as context-dependent interactions. Technically, these interactions and the resulting systems are non-linear (Holland, 1998, pp. 121–122).

In the context of the present book, the emergence of the 'Whole' is school leadership of women and how they succeed. The emergent power of school leadership of women, the Whole, exists as a result of four 'wholes', which are also organized into different types having distinct powers of the 'Whole'. These 'wholes' are as follows: availability of opportunities for participation of women in school leadership positions; determinants of successful school leadership in case of women; path traversed by women school heads to succeed as leaders; and legitimization of women as school leaders.

AGENCY OF WOMEN SCHOOL LEADER AND HUMAN DEVELOPMENT

In the lived experiences of people, the causal power of the 'Whole' is intercepted and deflected to cause issues, challenges and problems. In case of school leadership in traditional and developing societies, women leaders suffer from diverse challenges arising from social, traditional cultural, systemic, family and such other sub-systems and structures setting a historical context across micro to chrono sub-systems. These may take the form of monoculture of power arising out of orthodoxy, gender stereotypes, gender discrimination, etc., resulting in a lack of leadership preparation and discouragement of women to take up leadership roles and negative perceptions about women as leaders. It has caused under-representation of women in leadership positions, career break due to child care, ethics of care, passive racism and marginalization of ethnic communities. These challenges and problems indicate subtle contradictions, inherent challenges and overwhelming complexities for women to navigate and negotiate to succeed as school leaders. Therefore, it is crucial to study how different sub-systems/structures interact with the agency of women school head, causing emergence of school leadership of women in the Indian context.

Notwithstanding, interaction between different structures and agency is not without the exercise of power, authority and gender. It is important to understand how women deal with power and authority and perceive power differentials (the wholes) while carrying out their roles and responsibilities in leadership positions as school heads at elementary/secondary or senior secondary levels (the Whole). In other words, the process by which women establish their legitimacy as leaders using power, authority and status by negotiating the power differentials while working with teachers in the school is a crucial area of investigation. Legitimate power is the ability to exert power that is derived from the position of authority one holds. Legitimacy for the leader comes from the willingness of subordinates to accept the leadership even though legitimate power comes because of the position of authority. Therefore, perception of power differentials arises between leaders and subordinates if the subordinates do not totally accept leadership. Different perceptions cause varying degrees of compliance of subordinates to the authority or overcome resistance to the exercise of authority by the administrator. These establish varying degrees of acceptance for legitimacy of leadership.

POWER, AUTHORITY AND POWER DIFFERENTIALS

An individual achieves 'power' by exercising his/her own will despite resistance from others in any social relationship. It is different from 'power relations', which refers to the dominance creating a binary relationship—the dominant and subordinate. Power relation characterizes obedience or voluntary compliance or belief in the action of the dominant person as legitimate. Weber (1968) views legitimate actions as actions of those who obey having an interest in doing so or at least believe that they have such an interest (pp. 212–215).

When dominance of the person is accepted, the very acceptance gives authority to that person, and it is legitimate. Any leadership by position meant for a specific purpose characterizes such authority in a bureaucratic system. It automatically lends legitimacy to the leader who is in that position, to which subordinates attribute legitimacy by accepting leadership. However, the degree of acceptance may vary from person to person as subordinates or followers. This creates variations in the legitimacy of leadership of the dominant person.

Legitimacy of the person and his/her authority also depends upon the nature and quality of motives. Solidarity-based interests and advantages for material gains between leader and subordinate are always unstable relationships. Even though emotions and ideals may supplement such interests, it is not reliable for basing authority. So, legitimacy of authority of the dominant person, that is, the leader, is dependent on the belief of the subordinates rather than on the qualities of the leadership, however significant they may be (Weber, 1968).

An authority can be traditional, charismatic or rational in an organization or a system. In educational bureaucracy, rational or legal authority is more suitable than the other two as it rests on rules and rights of the authority or the leader to issue commands for influencing the behaviour of subordinates. In case of woman leaders, legitimacy is also intercepted by gendered notions that creep into the education system, drawing from social and cultural contexts of the larger society. Different women leaders respond differently with varying intensity as they perceive differently.

Notwithstanding, legitimacy is the greatest for individuals in leadership positions if their appointments are made based on prescribed qualifications with requisite expertise; or if the legitimacy is allocated by someone on the top of the authority structure (Read, 1974). Hence, leadership positions, leaders' expertise and qualification in that position, their gender and behaviour legitimize them as leaders in the organization (Walker & Zelditch, 1993). The authority or leadership's legitimacy in education can be of two types, which are competing in nature. First, the base of authority for administrations is dependent on their status in the organization. Second, base of the authority for teachers arises from their personal resources in the form of their deep content knowledge and pedagogy that are closely related to students' learning (Ogawa & Bossert, 1995).

CENTRAL ARGUMENT AND ITS RELATIONSHIP TO RESEARCH QUESTION

The present book argues that women succeed because they practice those leadership values drawn from life that are not limited to school leadership alone and make the most of their inherent capacity. They choose to do so because it yields positive results to reach successive milestones identified in their journey as leaders, which boosts their morale to look ahead, to take courage to ignore racing against the tide of gendered notions and to question stereotypes overtly or covertly for achieving success in the way they wish to define for themselves as school leaders. Therefore, it is important to investigate not just into how women succeeded but the path which they traversed to succeed.

In and through the interactions and processes between different structures/sub-systems, agencies and legitimization processes, leadership of women remains the connecting thread. The related leadership theories, functions, principles and processes have to be suitably applied and explained to discover the leadership attributes and leading processes of women school heads in the Indian context. For all these, the existing scenario on the participation of women in school leadership positions provides an apt beginning. Hence, the methodology involves a mixed method quantitative and qualitative data analyses, which provides a holistic approach for the study.

METHODOLOGICAL APPROACH FOR THE STUDY

The study is multi-disciplinary in nature and characterizes a unique methodological rigour by developing suitable conceptual frameworks to address each objective, separately. Theories from economic, sociology, gender, leadership, psychology, life course and education are applied to answer the research question. Economic theories were used on availability of opportunity to study participation of women in school leadership positions. The ecological model of development from psychology, life-course perspective on career of women and agency of women from sociology were applied to interpret the narratives to identify the path traversed. In identifying the determinants, the interaction between five structures and agency of women was studied by identifying the explicit and implicit cues for studying the situational strength of the structures interacting and opportunity for agency using sociological theories. While investigating legitimization, theories on leadership-focus and gender perspective besides sociology were applied to school and family structures to assess status attribution, perception of power differentials, degrees of negotiation and acceptance. The conceptual frameworks and results obtained from data analysis were weaved together to build a theory at the end. The task of integrating the findings derived from the application of conceptual frameworks in building the theory on school leadership of successful women in the Indian context is intended to advance the scholarship on school leadership of women.

Multi-disciplinary approach serves several functions: broadening the perspective; perceiving and analysing social life through different disciplinary lenses, filters and angles; relating cross-disciplinary boundaries to find multiple connections between phenomena and explanations; contributing to knowledge base and cognitive resources for qualitative data analysis and interpretation; and enhancing the ability to transfer the findings from local and particular to more generalizable settings and contexts (Saldana, 2015, p. 96). What we are examining is the values in her socio-cultural contexts and conflicts (ibid., p. 107). Besides adopting a multi-disciplinary approach to qualitative data, secondary data analysis on women's participation partially adopted the intent of quantitative narrative analysis (QNA).

It is a simple linguistic structure of subject–action–object or actor–action–actor with their respective modifiers such as number of actors involved, types of actors, time and space of action, reason and outcome (Franzosi, 2012, p. 85).

Quantitative Approach to the Study

The study was designed to investigate both the macro-level secondary data on school leadership of women using basic quantitative analysis and complement it with in-depth qualitative data study of a few women from different states. Analysing the secondary data was done on the basis of all-India- and state-level studies. It considered all states and union territories (UTs). Unified-District Information on School Education (U-DISE) data (NUEPA-MHRD, 2016–2017) was used for the purpose. School leadership positions and school categories were considered to study the representation of women in different leadership positions in the Indian context to understand the participation of women in school leadership positions at all-India and state levels. Economic theories referring to the equality of opportunities and outcomes were used. Following the secondary data analysis, nature, processes and factors influencing the success of women, school heads were studied through qualitative data.

Qualitative Approach to the Study

Narrative inquiry was carried out to discover the emergent pattern reflecting the nuanced interactions between different structures and agency of women school heads. The inquiry was focused on bringing forth the hidden subtle contradictions, explicit challenges inherent in the system which are complex and overwhelming for women school heads. These are also developmentally generative dispositions in the life course that defined school leadership of women in the Indian context by juxtaposing contrasts and varying manifestations of leadership roles as lived realities to effectively present paradoxes to move beyond the mutually opposing binaries of masculinity–femininity, subjectivity–objectivity, competitiveness–submissiveness, relationship oriented–task oriented and so on.

The stories of these women school leaders were problematized for studying in three ways: the interaction of women with different structures exercising agency; how women navigated between different multiplicities of self to understand gender perspectives which influenced their leadership behaviour; and the various ways in which women negotiated different status attributions and power differentials. They paved the way for deriving the determinants of school leadership of successful women, their legitimization as school leaders and the path traversed for success. Findings related to determinants and legitimization of school leadership of women were juxtaposed and positioned within the core concepts of leadership and gender. In this process, some of the small yet significant details which could not be covered in the main narratives were aptly utilized to provide deeper insights that filled the gaps arising from larger themes used in the narratives. Sometimes some instances were also repeated, but with a different purpose using a different lens for nuanced analysis adopting a multidisciplinary approach to examine the objectives set forth for the study. In this way, the present research attempts to move beyond the rhetoric by trying not to be caught up in the flurry of discussions related to gender stereotypes, leadership styles and gender differences, yet not keeping them out entirely from the study.

Method of Study

The case study was carried out considering 10 states in India for the purpose of collecting qualitative data. Twenty women participated in the interviews from different states. These states include Delhi, Haryana, Rajasthan, Uttar Pradesh and Himachal Pradesh in the northern region; Telangana in the southern region; Madhya Pradesh from the central region; and Sikkim in the northeastern region of India. A twofold rationale was adopted to select women leaders: they should be working as school heads in government schools as designated leadership positions at elementary, secondary and senior secondary levels; and they should have been nominated for school leadership development programme (SLDP) as members of state resource group to implement SLDP by the respective state governments. Usually, these nominations are done especially at the national level on the basis of their contributions for school improvements, unique contributions in different areas of teaching–learning processes to improve student learning, community participation as well as having a proven record of excellence at least for some length of time. The data were collected on individual profiles of women school heads using a schedule that sought basic details of the women. Individual and focus group interviews were held using semi-structured questionnaires. While individual interviews provided essential information, focused group interviews and discussions were rich with insights. These interviews were conducted between June 2014 and November 2015.

Though interviews began with formal questions, the free flow of conversation during the interviews added richness to the data especially in the natural settings of informal conversations. Identifying myself as one with them by relating my previous experience as a school teacher helped in significantly reducing the interviewer–interviewee dichotomy in the perception which invariably positions 'we' the teachers teaching in schools, 'she' the faculty teaching in university.

It was not easy to obtain the data on sensitive issues and concerns of women leaders through traditional methods except through trust building with them by spending longer hours and interacting with them on various aspects of schooling. It was possible to build the initial familiarity with the respondents and later into trust as many of them attended the 1-month residential programme on school leadership. It was obligatory for them to stay away from home and workplace while attending the 1-month programme.

Though the themes were largely fluid, they primarily were centred around basic profiles; familial background and support; gendered notions about leadership of women and agency of women school head; and leading school administration and management. Those who were not part of the 1-month programme were invariably members of state resource groups who had an opportunity to interact with the researcher closely for a year in various capacities and engagements on leadership building in their respective states.

Generally, the women preferred talking and discussing in groups apparently out of a firm conviction that what they were saying was generally valid and not just their own ideas. They were careful not to personalize any of the challenges faced in school. Hence, a unique methodology is used here. I wish not to label it under any specific method, except to say that a focus group interview was held. The richness of the data can be attributed as their contributions to the knowledge on Indian women's school leadership because they willingly shared these and trusted me as a researcher.

Participation of Women in School Leadership Positions in India

Opportunities and Outcomes

REPRESENTATION OF WOMEN IN SCHOOL LEADERSHIP POSITIONS IN DEVELOPING COUNTRIES

There are fewer women compared with men at all levels of education in general. In India, the proportion of women teachers in low-literacy states is extremely poor especially at primary and middle levels, constituting only 21 per cent and 23 per cent, respectively, since the 1950s (Agarwal & Aggarwal, 1996). The proportion of women teachers even declined as the level of education increased due to shortage of women teachers in rural areas. This is because of low availability of post-primary/secondary education facilities for rural girls who could not fulfil the essential entry criteria into teacher training courses (Nair, 2001). In Saudi Arabia, even if the teaching profession is female-dominated with 75 per cent women teachers, only 28 per cent of them are elementary school principals and 14 per cent are high school principals (Addi-Raccah, 2002; Addi-Raach & Ayalon, 2002). Representation of women in secondary schools as principals is only 12.7 per cent in Tanzania, 8 per cent in Vanuatu and 2.9 per cent each in Solomon Islands and Papua New Guinea (Jane et al., 2010). Chances of men becoming head teachers (HTs) at the primary level are twice higher compared with women (DfE, 2011). Though the

United States shows an impressive trend in the rise of women leaders, American Association of School Administrators (AASA) reveals that only 21 per cent of women rise to superintendent levels (Grogan & Shakeshaft, 2011). In the Indian context, studies pertaining to the representation of women school heads in different school leadership positions are not yet explored. General observations recorded for women's employment by Pande and Ford (2011) are also applicable to women's school leadership that mainly indicate women's attitude influencing their representation. These are as follows: women want to be leaders and that there is no significant difference in the aspirations of women who have children and those who do not; economic development does not beget female leadership; women's broadening career paths have not led to a proportional increase in female leaders; further, women begin to aspire to leadership position only if they see other women filling similar positions; an aversion to competition or preference for non-competitive environments may limit women from occupying leadership positions (ibid., p. 4). It is also not known to what extent opportunities are available in the education system so as to influence their participation in school leadership positions. The present chapter explores these two aspects.

EQUAL OPPORTUNITIES AND OUTCOMES INFLUENCING THE PARTICIPATION

Actual opportunities are dependent on formal opportunities such as structural availability of access, participation and other outside socio-cultural and economic factors (Halsey, Heath, & Ridge, 1980). Educational outcomes judge the relative merit and individual fairness as that which can provide equal life chances, open competition for scarce opportunities, equal cultivation for different capacities or/and independence of educational attainments from social origins (Wood, 1987). From this perspective, attainment of higher educational levels is also a form of opportunity for gaining entry into leadership positions as professionals. Education levels imply person's capabilities for achieving valuable goals. In this sense, higher the educational level, higher the capability of that individual. It means that opportunity rather than outcome or achievement is more appropriate (Cohen, 1993) for studying participation. This is because what a person is not responsible for are his/her opportunities. But, s/he is responsible for transforming available opportunities into outcomes even though s/he may not be entirely responsible for his/her preferences (Roemer, 1993, p. 148). People also exercise different degrees of responsibility for two reasons. First, their circumstances may cause them to in a way that is beyond their control; second, some will try harder than others (ibid.). The degree to which a person makes use of his/her capacities to actually function is crucial, even if capabilities are equalized by providing equal access to equal opportunities (Sen, 1992). Therefore, it is crucial to establish the influence of opportunities on outcomes, efforts and exogenous circumstances (Ferreira & Peragine, 2015).

In the context of school education system in India, opportunities are distributed in a hierarchical manner across different school categories in which school leadership positions are located. Education system being hierarchical in nature, school leadership positions are predominantly influenced by the schooling pattern, recruitment policies in different states and parallel leadership positions available as alternate choices to school leadership positions. As discussed above, capabilities are yet another form of opportunity. So, the representation of women in school leadership positions is not merely a matter of comparing with men in those positions, but an outcome of different types of opportunities available in the system that influence the acquisition of leadership positions in the system. These opportunities are of four types. They are as follows: distribution of school categories, schooling pattern and school leadership positions, which are interdependent; recruitment policies and processes; capabilities of women as school heads; and alternate choices in parallel leadership positions in the education system (Figure 3.1).

'Distribution of opportunities' refers to the spread of different school leadership positions across different school categories for which leadership positions are assigned. This depends on the schooling pattern adopted in states. 'Recruitment policies' refer to the manner in which teachers are promoted to school leadership positions directly on the basis of merit or seniority-based promotion or a combination of both in suitable proportion. 'Capabilities' of women

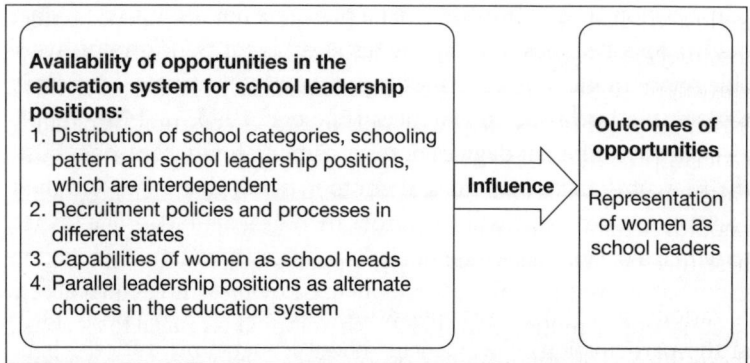

Figure 3.1 *Opportunities Available for the Participation of Women in School Leadership Positions and Other Influencing Factors*

teachers influence in ascending to school leadership positions. These capabilities can be categorized into 'achieved' and 'ascribed' capabilities for the present study. 'Achieved capabilities' of a person are nothing but attainments in educational and professional qualifications that are essential to be eligible for competing to acquire school leadership position, and 'ascribed capabilities' are those inherited socially in terms of caste and chronologically in terms of age by the women. 'Location of work' in terms of rural or urban positing is decided by higher officials technically. Hence, the location of work is an ascribed capability.

In some states, school heads have an opportunity to work in programmatic structures such as Sarva Shiksha Abhiyan (SSA) and Rastriya Madhyamic Shiksha Abhiyan (RMSA) without compromising their pay or grade, salary or service. This can be on deputation or transfer or promotion to a higher level. These are the alternate choices to that of school leadership positions in the education system referred to as 'parallel leadership positions'. These positions are mostly located in SSA and RMSA offices as programme officers at the district level, District Institutes of Educational Training (DIET) as lectures, College of Teacher Education (CTE) as lecturer, State Council of Educational Research and Training (SCERT) as faculty, Block Resource Centres (BRC) as BRC coordinator and/or Cluster Resource Centres (CRCs) as cluster resource coordinator. The last two are equivalent to that of school leadership at elementary level, whereas the rest are mostly equivalent to secondary school headmistress/headmaster (HM). Principals of senior secondary schools mostly do not opt for parallel leadership positions as they have greater autonomy and decision-making powers regarding the school's activities when compared with school leadership positions at secondary and elementary levels. All these together refer to 'availability of opportunities'.

Various forms of opportunities discussed so far have an impact on the participation of women in school leadership positions. It is measured in terms of the proportion of women school heads vis-à-vis men for the same leadership position. So, 'outcome of opportunities' refers to the representation of women in school leadership positions. It is a function of opportunities available with respect to school categories, school leadership positions assigned to these school categories, schooling patterns, capabilities of women, recruitment and promotion policies and alternative choices as parallel leadership positions available in the education system.

EXAMINING OPPORTUNITIES FOR SCHOOL LEADERSHIP POSITIONS IN EDUCATION SYSTEM

All 36 states and UTs have been considered for the study. Secondary data from U-DISE (2016–2017) have been used for the purpose (NIEPA-MHRD, 2016–2017). Percentage analysis was carried out in which the proportions of men and women were calculated and compared. Representation of women teachers was also studied to suitably position the results of representation of women in school leadership positions. Based on the results, states were categorized into three types. First, states having below 50 per cent of women are referred to as states with Under-Representation (UR) of women in school leadership positions. Second, those having above 50 per cent women were categorized as states with Higher Representation (HR) of women in school leadership positions. Third, states which had exactly 50 per cent were labelled as states with Equal Representation (ER) of women in school leadership positions.

Matching School Categories with School Leadership Positions

The analysis begins by matching the school categories with school leadership positions. The pattern of school education being not uniform in all states, matching school categories with relevant school head's positions constitutes an essential step to study representation. There are four school leadership positions, namely acting HM (A-HM), Head teacher (HT or secondary school HM), vice-principal and principals, across all states for senior secondary schools. A-HMs are in-charge heads in the school. It is neither a designated school head's post nor sanctioned post nor refer to a vacancy. In the absence of a designated school head occupying the position to lead the school, a person is put in charge to take care of the duties. Usually the senior most teacher is nominated as the A-HM. Most of the primary schools (I–V standards) are managed by A-HMs as they do not carry designated HM's post in most states. But, in case of large-sized elementary schools (P+UP school category) having student enrolment of 150 or more, a designated HM is appointed. Even though A-HMs are usually meant for the primary level, it is also found in all other school categories wherever regular/designated school head is not present. HT is a regular appointment assigned to secondary level such as P+UP, UP+S and P+UP+S school categories. Vice-principal and principal positions are also designated school leadership positions at senior secondary level in P+UP+S+HS and UP+S+HS school categories. Appointments for these regular positions are made through an open selection process or on promotion basis or both. Appointment through promotion basis depends on seniority in which the number of years of experience is a significant criterion. Direct recruitment requires eligible candidates who are already working in the education system to compete by passing the examination and interview conducted for the purpose. Usually a combination of both is adopted by the states.

Availability of Opportunities in Different School Categories

There are 10 school categories in India. Out of them, 54.7 per cent are P-only schools, 18.7 per cent are P+UP schools, 3.9 per cent are

P+UP+S schools, 3.3 per cent are UP+S schools, 3.2 per cent are P+UP+S+HS schools and 2.2 per cent are UP+S+HS schools. These school categories constitute 60 per cent of the total school categories, and they also have designated school leadership positions except in P-only schools. Hence, they were considered in the present study. Remaining 40 per cent of the schools are stand-alone schools mostly without a designated school leadership position and hence not considered in the study. These school categories are UP-only, HS-only, S+HS, S-only and HS-only (Table 3.1). But some states such as Mizoram and Meghalaya have these school categories predominantly, for which designated HMs are appointed. Because the proportion of such states is too less and also due to the low viability of these stand-alone schools, they were not considered. However, P-only schools are considered despite not having a designated leadership position as they are essential to achieve universalisation of elementary education (UEE)

Table 3.1 *Proportion of School Categories: All India*

S. No.	School category[a]	Percentage of schools	Common names used[a]
1	P-only	54.7	Primary (1–5 standards)
2	P+UP	18.7	Elementary (1–8 standards)
3	P+UP+S+HS	3.2	Higher secondary (1–12 standards)
4	UP+S+HS	2.2	Higher secondary (6–12 standards)
5	P+UP+S	3.9	Primary to secondary (1–10 standards)
6	UP+S	3.3	Composite high school or secondary school (6–10 standards)
7	UP-only	9.6	Upper primary (6–8 standards)
8	S-only	2.2	Secondary or high school (9–10 standards)
9	S+HS	1.5	Higher secondary or senior secondary schools (9–12 standards)
10	HS-only	0.7	Higher secondary or senior secondary schools (11–12 standards)

Source: U-DISE, NUEPA-MHRD (2016–2017).
Notes: [a]Henceforth, standard forms such as P+UP will be used while referring to school categories.

through which the child begins schooling. So, opportunity for school leadership is available only in 50 per cent of the school categories at the national level (Table 3.1).

It is interesting to note that even though P+UP+S, P+UP+S+HS and UP+S+HS school categories ensure complete schooling stage, they constitute only 3.9 per cent, 3.2 per cent and 2.2 per cent at the national level, respectively. Nonetheless, each of these school categories are present in 97 per cent of states and UTs in India (Table 3.2). These three school categories are the ones which ought to have designated school leadership positions in all states. By contrast, stand-alone schools such as UP-only, S-only, S+HS-only and HS-only

Table 3.2 *Proportion of Different School Categories*

School category	No. of states/UTs	Percentage of states/UTs	States/UTs without school category
P-only	36	100.0	
P+UP	36	100.0	
P+UP+S+HS	35	97.2	Mizoram
UP-only	32	88.9	Andhra Pradesh, Andaman and Nicobar Islands, Telangana, Sikkim
UP+S+HS	35	97.2	Mizoram
P+UP+S	35	97.2	Mizoram
UP+S	33	91.7	Mizoram, Dadra & Nagar Haveli, Daman and Diu
S-only	25	69.4	Andaman and Nicobar Islands, Arunachal Pradesh, Delhi, Haryana, Himachal Pradesh, Lakshadweep, Puducherry, Rajasthan, Sikkim, Telangana, Uttarakhand
S+HS	29	80.6	Uttarakhand, Tripura, Telangana, Sikkim, Mizoram, Goa, Andhra Pradesh
HS-only	30	83.3	Andaman and Nicobar Islands, Andhra Pradesh, Lakshadweep, Rajasthan, Sikkim, Telangana

at secondary and senior secondary levels without a designated school head constitute as high as 17 per cent of the total schools (Table 3.1). School categories such as P-only and P+UP which cater to address the vicinity from home for the very young children are present in all states. They constitute 54.7 per cent and 18.7 per cent of the total schools in the country, respectively. These usually do not have a designated school leadership position unless the enrolment of total students in the school is equal to or greater than 150 students.

Altogether, about 72 per cent of the schools do not have designated school leadership positions that accounts for 60 per cent of the total school categories. These school categories are: P-only, P+UP, UP-only, S-only, HS-only and S+HS. A mere 40 per cent of school categories constituting only about 22 per cent of the total schools, approximately, have designated school leadership position with regular vacancies. These are medium and large school categories. Only four school categories definitely belong to the group having designated school leadership positions. These are as follows: P+UP+S, UP+S, P+UP+S+HS and UP+S+HS. Thus, there is an abysmally low opportunity for teachers to become school heads occupying school leadership positions in India. Within this acute shortage of opportunities, the representation of women in school leadership position has to be examined. In other words, opportunities available for school leadership positions in terms of school categories and its distribution are grossly inadequate for both men and women teacher aspirants.

The fact that 60 per cent of the school categories have no designated school leadership position indicates the system's dysfunctional nature. Even when all three designated leadership positions are filled with regular appointments and all vacancies are filled, their proportion would still remain below 30 per cent of the total schools. Therefore, stand-alone school categories, such as S-only, HS-only, S+HS, UP-only and P-only, which are mostly without the sanctioned posts for designated leadership positions, demand a wider debate in terms of their relevance, social and economic viability and contribution for achieving universal goals of education. Such debates also need to address the confusion arising from a large number of school categories without designated leadership positions severely affecting the availability of opportunity for appointing school heads.

P-only and P+UP school categories are present in the entire India across all states and UTs. All states and UTs have P+UP+S+HS, UP+S+HS and P+UP+S school categories except Mizoram. In 33 states and UTs, UP+S school category is present. A significant number of states/UTs do not have S-only, S+HS-only and HS-only school categories ranging from nearly about 69.4 per cent to 83.3 per cent of total states and UTs in India. So, these three school categories have not been considered in the study for any leadership position. It is also acknowledged here that these states either do not have these school categories or they may be scanty (Table 3.2).

The most popular schooling pattern in many states is a combination of P-only or P+UP schools with that of P+UP+S, P+UP+S+HS, UP+S and UP+S+HS schools. Each state has a predominant pattern of schooling. For example, in Karnataka and Kerala, the predominant pattern of schooling is P-only, P+UP and P+UP+S schools. So, Karnataka and Kerala have a higher opportunity for HT's post rather than principal's or vice-principal's. By contrast, Uttar Pradesh has all types of school categories, and opportunities may be spread across all types of schools. This situation provides more opportunity to acquire school leadership positions. But with a wider spread of all school categories without emphasizing on a few relevant school categories with designated school leadership positions, no single category will have HR of women.

In Mizoram, predominant school categories are S-only, HS-only and S+HS, which are rarely seen in other states. By contrast, the popular school categories of other states such as P to HS and UP to HS are not present in Mizoram. Though Mizoram has regular school heads appointed in these stand-alone schools due to the schooling pattern, the representation of women does not get reflected in the analysis as the study is not considering the stand-alone schools. In Andhra Pradesh, the predominant school pattern is P-only and UP+S schools. It is obvious that there may be more HTs than principals. These differences in schooling pattern considering the combination of school categories imply that opportunities for school leadership depend upon the school category in the states/UTs. Hence, the representation of women in different leadership positions is influenced by the pattern of schooling in that state. Refer to Appendix 3A.1 for more details on school categories in the states/UTs.

REPRESENTATION OF WOMEN IN SCHOOL LEADERSHIP POSITIONS ACROSS DIFFERENT SCHOOL CATEGORIES

All-India Scenario

All-India-level analysis indicates women have a mixed representation across different leadership positions and school categories. Table 3.3 indicates that there is an encouraging trend of HR of women with 55.9 per cent as women vice-principals in P+UP+S+HS schools. There is also a higher proportion of women teachers with 57.4 per cent in the same school category, that is, P+UP+S+HS. Representation of women principals in the same school category is 36.3 per cent. The trend in UP+S+HS school category shows that there are 27.9 per cent principals and 35.7 per cent vice-principals. It is definitely a positive trend for achieving gender equality especially at the higher level of school leadership positions, namely vice-principals (Table 3.3). In case of HTs at

Table 3.3 Representation of Women in School Leadership Positions and Women Teachers in Different School Leadership Positions: All India (in percentage)

School category	P-only	P+UP	P+UP+S+HS	UP-only	UP+S+HS	P+UP+S	UP+S
A-HM	33.6	38.4	42.7	25.6	29.6	38.4	26.2
HTs		33.1				32.2	27.4
Vice-principals			55.9		35.7		
Principals			36.3		27.9		
Women teachers	47.7	50.5	57.4	34.7	43.2	54.0	41.5

Source: Author's own calculations using raw data from UDISE, NUEPA-MHRD (2016–2017).

the secondary level of schooling in P+UP+S and UP+S, women are way below the cut-off mark of 50 per cent with only 32.2 per cent and 27.4 per cent, respectively. This is despite the HR of women as teachers with 54 per cent for P+UP+S school category, though not for UP+S school category, which has a lower representation with only 41.5 per cent. In case of P+UP+S schools, it may also be due to the recruitment policy where many states largely follow seniority-based promotion policies even today (more is discussed in the section on recruitment policies).

HR of women vice-principals in 55.9 per cent of the P+UP+S+HS school category may be accepted to be an eye opener counted with ER of women and men. Women teachers are higher represented in three out of seven school categories considered in the study, namely 50.5 per cent in P+UP schools, 57.4 per cent in P+UP+S+HS schools and 54.0 per cent in P+UP+S schools. It is indeed an encouraging trend which would eventually lead to HR of women in leadership positions as well.

Representation of Women in School Leadership Positions in Different States/UTs: A Consolidation

A comprehensive scenario considering all states is presented in this section by consolidating and studying the results of individual states/UTs regarding the three types of representation, namely UR, ER and HR. All four leadership positions have been considered for the purpose (Table 3.4).

A-HMs: Position of A-HMs or in-charge HMs is highly fleeting in nature as they can be rolled back as teachers within two or three days of appointment or retained for years without any substantial powers or authority. So, in-depth study of A-HMs is of less significance. Nonetheless, the representation of women is low as 69.8 per cent of the total states in India have UR of women even for A-HM's position from different school categories when considered together. Only 3.7 per cent of the states show ER of men and women as A-HMs and 26.4 per cent of states/UTs show HR of women as A-HMs. Though less, there is a presence of women as A-HMs in vacancies which are not filled at least in some states/UTs.

Table 3.4 Women in School Leadership Positions: Representation Pattern of States/UTs

Leadership Position	School Category	No. of states	UR No	UR %age	ER No	ER %age	HR No	HR %age
Acting HMs	Primary only (P only)	36	24	66.7	2	5.6	10	27.8
	Elementary (P+UP)	36	23	63.9	2	5.6	11	30.6
	Primary with Higher secondary (P+UP+S+HS)	35	18	51.4	2	5.7	15	42.9
	Upper primary only UP only	32	24	75.0	0	0.0	8	25.0
	Upper Primary with Higher Secondary (UP+S+HS)	35	30	85.7	1	2.9	4	11.4
	Primary with secondary (P+UP+S)	35	20	57.1	0	0.0	15	42.9
	Composite secondary (UP+S)	33	30	85.7	2	5.7	1	2.9
	Aggregate pattern	**242**	**169**	**69.8**	**9**	**3.7**	**64**	**26.4**
Designated HMs	Elementary (P+UP)	36	28	77.8	0	0.0	8	22.2
	Primary with secondary (P+UP+S)	35	25	71.4	3	8.6	7	20.0
	Composite secondary (UP+S)	33	31	93.9	0	0.0	2	6.1
	Aggregate pattern	**104**	**84**	**80.8**	**3**	**2.9**	**17**	**16.3**
Vice Principals	Primary with Higher secondary (P+UP+S+HS)	35	15	42.9	4	11.4	16	45.7
	Upper Primary with Higher Secondary (UP+S+HS)	35	28	80.0	2	5.7	5	14.3
	Aggregate pattern	**70**	**43**	**61.4**	**6**	**8.6**	**21**	**30.0**
Principals	Primary with Higher Secondary (P+UP+S+HS)	35	25	71.4	1	2.9	9	25.7
	Upper Primary with Higher Secondary (UP+S+HS)	35	32	91.4	0	0.0	3	8.6
	Aggregate pattern	**70**	**57**	**81.43**	**1**	**1.429**	**12**	**17.1**

Head Teachers: There is a clear trend of rise in the participation of women as HTs in P+UP+S schools as 8.6 per cent of the states/UTs (or in three states/UTs) have ER and 20 per cent of the states (or in seven states/UTs) have HR. It is also encouraging to see that 22 per cent of the states/UTs (or in eight states/UTs) have an HR of HTs in P+UP schools. This is a clear trend in the rise of women as HTs when ER and HR are considered together, which comes to 20 states/UTs. However, in terms of UP+S schools, there are more states/UTs where women HTs are under-represented.

Vice-Principals: In P+UP+S+HS schools, as high as 16 states/UTs show HR of women vice-principals which includes Madhya Pradesh (52.6 per cent) and Goa (100 per cent). This school category accounts for 45.7 per cent of states/UTs showing HR of women as vice-principals. There is also an HR of women teachers for the same school category ranging with 57.4 per cent at the national level. In the same school category, two UTs, such as Dadra and Nagar Haveli and Daman and Diu, and two states, such as Haryana and Jammu and Kashmir, have ER of men and women vice-principals, having 50 per cent each. These states/UTs can also be included under HR states.

P+UP+S+HS being the most comprehensive school category consisting of primary to higher secondary standards, HR of women vice-principals in this category is a significant indicator of greater participation of women in teaching and school leadership positions. This school category also demands qualified and competent men and women in leadership positions to manage, administer and lead teachers, staff, students, parents and community from primary to senior secondary classes for ensuring quality education. So, it is encouraging to see HR of women as vice-principals in this school category.

For UP+S+HS school category, there is HR of women vice-principals in five states/UTs. In two states/UTs, Daman and Diu and Tamil Nadu, there is an ER of men and women as vice-principals. These two states/UTs can also be considered under HR. The proportion of women teachers is 43.2 per cent in this school category. Among UR states, Madhya Pradesh, Karnataka, Chhattisgarh, Delhi and Jammu and Kashmir can be considered to be showing a definite movement towards a greater participation of women as vice-principals.

When compared between P+UP+S+HS and UP+S+HS school categories in all states and UTs, representation of women as vice-principals is predominantly higher in P+UP+S+HS school category than in UP+S+HS school category. This is because UP+S+HS schools cannot substitute or replace the importance of the full-fledged composite school category like P+UP+S+HS which also includes pre-primary schools in many states/UTs in the recent times. So, HR or UR of women in UP+S+HS school category obviously depends on the presence of P+UP+S+HS schools prevailing in the state/UT and the concentration of men and women vice-principals and teachers in it. In sum, there is HR of women as vice-principals and teachers at senior secondary levels, across many states and UTs, which is much higher when compared with representation of women as HTs in P+UP, P+UP+S and UP+S schools.

Principals: Nine states/UTs show HR of women principals, with Chandigarh showing the highest representation (76.1 per cent) and West Bengal with the lowest representation (52.1 per cent) of women principals in P+UP+S+HS schools. Remaining HR states in P+UP+S+HS school categories are: Uttarakhand (52.5 per cent), Karnataka (53.9 per cent), Tamil Nadu (59.4 per cent), Kerala (60.6 per cent), Punjab (63.7 per cent), Goa (66.7 per cent) and Delhi (72 per cent). Representation of women teachers in these HR states/UTs is also higher, for example, it is 68.2 per cent in Uttarakhand and 81.6 per cent in Chandigarh, a unique trend indeed. (For more details, refer to Table 3A.2 in the Appendix given at the end of this chapter). Only Diu and Daman has ER of men and women principals, which can also be considered under HR states/UTs. In case of UP+S+HS schools, women principals are higher represented only in three states/UTs, namely Kerala, Lakshadweep and Chandigarh with 53.4, 68.7, and 100 per cent, respectively. The latter two are UTs and also small in size. There are no states/UTs which have ER of men and women principals in this school category. In Kerala and Chandigarh, women teachers are also in higher proportion, with 70 per cent and 75 per cent, respectively. The percentage of women principals in UR states/UTs in UP+S+HS school category ranges from 0 per cent to 47 per cent. Percentage of women teachers in these UR states/UTs is also much lower. While there is a high participation of women in school leadership position and a much higher participation in case of teachers in P+UP+S+HS school category, it is far from satisfactory in UP+S+HS school category as 32 states show UR of women principals.

When representation of women in principal and vice-principal leadership positions along with women teachers is studied together, P+UP+S+HS school category clearly stands out as heading towards a faster and higher level of participation of women when compared with UP+S+HS schools. Also, in comparison with HTs and principals, the participation of women as vice-principals is far higher. It is especially true for P+UP+S+HS school category.

Region-Wise Analysis of Representation of Women in School Leadership Positions

In this section, the trend in the representation of women was studied across four educational regions of the country. All states and UTs were grouped under eastern, western, northern and southern regions. For this purpose, leadership positions related to A-HMs, HT, vice-principals and principals were studied for all regions, separately. However, for A-HMs, a consolidated regional-level study alone was taken up as it is not a designated leadership position. In the end, a consolidated region-wise analysis also has been carried out.

Eastern Region

HTs in the eastern region: By and large, women HTs are underrepresented in the eastern region. Only in Meghalaya, women are higher represented as HTs in P+UP schools and P+UP+S schools. In Tripura, 62.5 per cent of women are represented as HTs in UP+S schools, which refers to HR when compared with that of men HTs. The overall representation of women as HTs in the region is very low with only 23.5 per cent, 22.5 per cent and 22.0 per cent in P+UP, P+UP+S and UP+S schools, respectively.

Vice-principals in the eastern region: Five out of 12 states in the eastern region show HR of women as vice-principals in P+UP+S+HS school category. Jharkhand has 65.5 per cent of women vice-principals. Similarly, 70 per cent vice-principals are women in Meghalaya, 64.5 per cent in Nagaland, 60 per cent in Orissa and 53.3 per cent in West

Bengal. However, in UP+S+HS school category, only Meghalaya shows HR of women as vice-principals, which is 60 per cent.

Principals in the eastern region: Only West Bengal state shows HR of women principals in P+UP+S+HS schools with 52.1 per cent. No state in the eastern region shows HR of women as princi pals in UP+S+HS schools. However, there is an encouraging trend of women principals in Meghalaya and Nagaland in P+UP+S+HS schools, which show 42.9 per cent and 46.7 per cent, respectively. Similarly, in case of UP+S+HS schools, women vice-principals are moderately represented in Nagaland and West Bengal as their representation is 45.2 per cent and 40.9 per cent, respectively. However, the overall region shows under-representation of women as principals (Table 3.5).

Western Region

HTs in the western region: In P+UP category, Goa with 66.7 per cent is the only state showing HR of women as HTs in the western region. In P+UP+S school category, Dadra and Nagar Haveli shows 50 per cent representation of women as HTs and Goa also shows an HR of women with 62.9 per cent. In UP+S schools, no state or UT shows HR of women as HTs in the western region. Also, there is an encouraging trend in Gujarat with women HTs representing 45 per cent in P+UP+S school category. Similarly, Goa has 47.9 per cent of women HTs in UP+S school category. However, the overall trend in the representation of women as HTs is far lower in the western region.

Vice-principals in the western region: Five out of seven states in the western region show HR of women vice-principals in P+UP+S+HS schools. These states/UTs are Goa, Gujarat, Madhya Pradesh, Dadar and Nagar Haveli and Daman and Diu recording 100 per cent, 57.4 per cent, 52 per cent, 50 per cent and 50 per cent, respectively. Chhattisgarh is also on the path of HR with 45.4 per cent. In UP+S+HS schools, only Daman and Diu and Goa show an HR of women with 50 per cent and 60 per cent, respectively. Madhya Pradesh also is on the verge of reaching the 50 per cent mark with 48.1 per cent women principals in UP+S+HS school category.

Principals in the western region: In the western region, only two states/UTs show an HR of women principals in P+UP+S+HS schools.

Table 3.5 Representation of Women in School Leadership Positions in the Eastern Region (in Percentage)

Eastern region	HT						Vice-principal				Principal			
	Primary with upper primary		Primary with upper primary and secondary		Upper primary with secondary		Primary with upper primary and secondary/higher secondary		Upper primary with secondary/higher secondary		Primary with upper primary and secondary/higher secondary		Upper primary with secondary/higher secondary	
State/UT	Male	Female	Male	Female	Male	Female	Male	Female	Male	Female	Male	Female	Male	Female
Arunachal Pradesh	80.8	19.2	78.2	21.8	66.7	33.3	63.2	36.8	84.2	15.8	87.5	12.5	100.0	0.0
Assam	80.7	19.3	73.0	27.0	80.1	19.9	68.0	32.0	71.8	28.2	63.2	36.8	73.8	26.3
Bihar	84.9	15.1	90.7	9.3	86.6	13.4	82.6	17.4	86.7	13.3	82.3	17.7	94.7	5.3
Jharkhand	78.7	21.3	75.6	24.4	76.2	23.8	34.5	65.5	68.2	31.8	79.2	20.8	66.7	33.3
Manipur	78.5	21.5	79.3	20.7	66.7	33.3	91.2	8.8	90.9	9.1	75.0	25.0	72.2	27.8
Meghalaya	38.5	61.5	35.0	65.0	60.8	39.2	30.0	70.0	40.0	60.0	57.1	42.9	71.4	28.6
Mizoram	68.1	31.9	No school category											
Nagaland	76.5	23.5	75.0	25.0	74.3	25.7	35.5	64.5	65.2	34.8	53.3	46.7	54.8	45.2
Odisha	69.4	30.6	79.3	20.7	80.9	19.1	40.0	60.0	66.7	33.3	64.7	35.3	89.3	10.7
Sikkim	75.1	24.9	80.9	19.1	100.0	0.0	53.7	46.3	100.0	0.0	63.9	36.1	100.0	0.0
Tripura	79.9	20.1	79.8	20.2	37.5	62.5	75.0	25.0	0.0	0.0	66.7	33.3	100.0	0.0
West Bengal	79.4	20.6	68.9	31.1	71.9	28.1	46.7	53.3	71.4	28.6	47.9	52.1	59.1	40.9
Aggregate	76.5	23.5	77.5	22.5	78.0	22.0	53.6	46.4	72.1	27.9	66.1	33.9	75.3	24.7

Source: Author's own calculations using raw data from UDISE, NUEPA-MHRD (2016–2017).

These are Daman and Diu and Goa with 50 per cent and 66.7 per cent, respectively. Gujarat with 48.3 per cent is moving towards HR of women in the same school category. The overall percentage of women principals in the region is almost equal to that of men with 49.9 per cent. The situation reverses in case of UP+S+HS school category with no state showing HR of women as principals in the western region. The overall trend for the western region is not an encouraging one as the representation of women in school leadership positions is far lower than the cut-off point of 50 per cent in any school category (refer to Table 3.6).

Northern Region

HT in northern region: In elementary schools of P+UP category, women as HTs are represented higher in Chandigarh, Delhi and Punjab with 52.9 per cent, 78.2 per cent and 68.5 per cent, respectively. Similarly, in P+UP+S school category, women are represented higher again in Chandigarh, Delhi and Punjab with 61.4 per cent, 50.0 per cent and 68.6 per cent, respectively. However, in UP+S school category, all states and UTs show UR. Haryana, Himachal Pradesh and Uttarakhand are closer to the cut-off point of 50 per cent as women HTs' representation is at 43.6 per cent, 48.3 per cent and 46.3 per cent, respectively, in P+UP school category. Himachal Pradesh and Uttarakhand show similar trends with regard to women's representation with 40.6 per cent and 46.2 per cent in P+UP+S school category. Surprisingly, Delhi and Chandigarh show neither men nor women HTs in UP+S school category even though the data show that these two UTs have UP+S schools. The overall representation of women as HTs in the northern region is poor as it shows under-representation of women which does not cross 30 per cent in any of the three school categories.

Vice-principals in the northern region: The overall representation of women as vice-principals in the northern region in P+UP+S+HS schools is higher with 54.8 per cent. Only in Rajasthan and Uttar Pradesh, women vice-principals are under-represented. The highest representation of women vice-principals is in Chandigarh with 85.4 per cent. It is closely followed by Punjab with 71.1 per cent. In Jammu and Kashmir, the representation of men and women is equal. In UP+S+HS schools, women vice-principals are represented higher in

Table 3.6 Representation of Women in School Leadership Positions in the Western Region (in Percentage)

Western region	HT						Vice-principal						Principal				
	Primary with upper primary		Primary with upper primary and secondary		Upper primary with secondary		Primary with upper primary and secondary/ higher secondary		Upper primary with secondary/ higher secondary				Primary with upper primary and secondary/ higher secondary		Upper primary with secondary/ higher secondary	
State/UT	Male	Female	Male	Female	Male	Female	Male	Female	Male	Female			Male	Female	Male	Female
Chhattisgarh	60.6	39.4	64.2	35.8	89.4	10.6	54.6	45.4	57.9	42.1			58.7	41.3	66.4	33.6
Dadra & Nagar Haveli	55.0	45.0	50.0	50.0	No school category		50.0	50.0	0.0	0.0			60.0	40.0	100.0	0.0
Daman & Diu	66.7	33.3	100.0	0.0			50.0	50.0	50.0	50.0			50.0	50.0	100.0	0.0
Goa	33.3	66.7	37.1	62.9	52.1	47.9	0.0	100.0	40.0	60.0			33.3	66.7	75.0	25.0
Gujarat	72.8	27.2	54.8	45.2	65.5	34.5	42.6	57.4	78.6	21.4			51.7	48.3	85.4	14.6
Madhya Pradesh	67.3	32.7	62.8	37.2	78.6	21.4	47.4	52.6	51.9	48.1			64.9	35.1	70.7	29.3
Maharashtra	60.4	39.6	71.5	28.5	72.2	27.8	68.0	32.0	68.0	32.0			75.8	24.2	71.8	28.2
Aggregate	67.7	32.3	68.8	31.2	73.8	26.2	55.7	44.3	62.4	37.6			62.7	37.3	73.6	26.4

Source: Author's own calculations using raw data from UDISE, NUEPA-MHRD (2016–2017).

Chandigarh with 100 per cent and Punjab with 57.1 per cent. Delhi and Jammu and Kashmir show above 40 per cent representation, having 41.6 per cent and 40.0 per cent, respectively. Other states/UTs show a representation far below the cut-off point of 50 per cent. The overall percentage of women vice-principals is also far lesser in UP+S+HS school category with only 28.5 per cent.

Principals in the northern region: In P+UP+S+HS school category, women principals are higher represented in Chandigarh (76.1 per cent), Punjab (63.7 per cent) and Uttarakhand (52.5 per cent). Remaining states/UTs in the region show women's representation as principals far below the cut-off point. The overall representation of women principals in the northern region is only 30 per cent despite four states/UTs showing an HR in P+UP+S+HS school category. In UP+S+HS school category, an HR of women is seen only in Chandigarh with 100 per cent. Delhi and Punjab show 42.1 per cent and 47.3 per cent, respectively. But for these three states, other states in the region show under-representation of women as principals in UP+S+HS school category. So, the overall representation is also abysmally low with only 25.5 per cent for the northern region in UP+S+HS school category (refer to Table 3.7).

Southern Region

HT in the southern region: Representation of women HTs in P+UP schools is higher in three out of eight states/UTs in the southern region with Andaman and Nicobar Islands at the top of the list with 66.7 per cent and is followed by Tamil Nadu with 65.3 per cent and Kerala with 61.8 per cent. The overall percentage for the southern region regarding HTs in P+UP school category is also higher with 51.3 per cent. Karnataka shows 40.9 per cent, a positive trend indeed. In case of P+UP+S school category, Andaman and Nicobar Islands show ER of men and women HTs. Karnataka, Kerala and Tamil Nadu states show HR of women HTs with 56.6 per cent, 60.7 per cent and 69.2 per cent, respectively, for P+UP+S school category. The overall representation of HTs for the southern region in P+UP+S school category also shows an HR with 60.4 per cent. The rest of the states/UTs show no representation of women in P+UP+S school category. In UP+S school category, only

Table 3.7 Representation of Women in School Leadership Positions in the Northern Region (in Percentage).

Northern region	HT						Vice-principal						Principal					
	Primary with upper primary		Primary with upper primary and secondary		Upper primary with secondary		Primary with upper primary and secondary/ higher secondary		Upper primary with secondary/ higher secondary				Primary with upper primary and secondary/ higher secondary		Upper primary with secondary/ higher secondary			
State/UT	Male	Female	Male	Female	Male	Female	Male	Female	Male	Female			Male	Female	Male	Female		
Chandigarh	47.1	52.9	38.6	61.4	0.0	0.0	14.6	85.4	0.0	100.0			23.9	76.1	0.0	100.0		
Delhi	21.8	78.2	50.0	50.0	0.0	0.0	32.1	67.9	58.4	41.6			28.0	72.0	57.9	42.1		
Haryana	56.4	43.6	63.8	36.2	73.7	26.3	50.0	50.0	70.7	29.3			60.2	39.8	69.4	30.6		
Himachal Pradesh	51.7	48.3	59.4	40.6	77.4	22.6	34.5	65.5	70.3	29.7			60.5	39.5	77.0	23.0		
Jammu & Kashmir	68.5	31.5	68.8	31.2	75.4	24.6	50.0	50.0	60.0	40.0			73.6	26.4	84.6	15.4		
Punjab	31.5	68.5	31.4	68.6	54.7	45.3	28.9	71.1	42.9	57.1			36.3	63.7	52.7	47.3		
Rajasthan	81.0	19.0	79.0	21.0	69.4	30.6	77.3	22.7	85.7	14.3			81.2	18.8	72.2	27.8		
Uttar Pradesh	69.0	31.0	73.3	26.7	80.0	20.0	61.2	38.8	80.1	19.9			62.3	37.7	85.1	14.9		
Uttarakhand	53.7	46.3	53.8	46.2	88.3	11.7	34.4	65.6	82.2	17.8			47.5	52.5	86.3	13.7		
Aggregate	72.7	27.3	70.3	29.7	73.6	26.4	45.2	54.8	71.5	28.5			69.1	30.9	74.5	25.5		

Source: Author's own calculations using raw data from UDISE, NUEPA-MHRD (2016–2017).

Kerala has HR of women HTs with 67.7 per cent. All other states/UTs show under-representation, including Tamil Nadu with only 41 per cent. Puducherry, Telangana and Andhra Pradesh reveal no women HTs in any of the three school categories. Lakshadweep also shows no women HTs in P+UP+S and UP+S school categories. Rather than concluding that women are not present at all as HTs in these states, it can be assumed that data do not exist.

Vice-principal in the southern region: While Karnataka, Kerala and Tamil Nadu have HR of women vice-principals in the southern region showing 61.3 per cent, 77.4 per cent and 66.3 per cent and are being closely followed by Puducherry with 47.8 per cent, other states such as Andaman and Nicobar Islands, Andhra Pradesh, Lakshadweep and Telangana do not indicate the presence of even a single vice-principal. Even then, the overall representation of women vice-principals for the southern region is 68.2 per cent showing HR of women vice-principals in the region. In UP+S+HS school category also, women are represented higher only in Kerala with 68.3 per cent. Tamil Nadu has ER of men and women vice-principals in the same school category. Puducherry and Karnataka have 41 and 46.2 per cent of women vice-principals, respectively. Remaining four states show that there are no women vice-principals in UP+S+HS school category. Despite this, the aggregate representation of vice-principals in the southern region for UP+S+HS schools is higher with 60.2 per cent. It is possible that in states which show no vice-principals, there may not be a separate position for vice-principals and hence the zero percentage. Otherwise, it is unlikely that there are no women vice-principals at all in these states/UTs.

Principals in the southern region: Women are higher represented in Karnataka, Kerala and Tamil Nadu showing 53.9 per cent, 60.6 per cent and 59.4 per cent, respectively. The aggregate percentage of the southern region is boosted because of these three states as well as Puducherry which is close to the 50 per cent cut-off mark with 49.4 per cent. Remaining states/UTs show zero percentage of women as principals in P+UP+S+HS school category. In UP+S+HS school category, Kerala and Lakshadweep have an HR of women principals with 53.4 per cent and 66.7 per cent. By contrast, women are under-represented or not represented at all in the remaining states. Tamil Nadu inches closer to the cut-off mark of 50 per cent with 45.1 per cent of the principals being women in UP+S+HS school category. Despite the non-representation of women in some states/UTs, the aggregate percentage of women principals in the southern region is higher at 50.9 per cent (Table 3.8).

A-HMs in All Four Regions across All School Categories in India: An Aggregate Trend

A detailed state-wise discussion of results in all four regions is not necessary for A-HMs because this position is temporary and does not enjoy decision-making powers and people holding the charge can also change within a school. Hence, regional-level aggregate figures alone are considered to get an idea. Only in the southern region, the proportion of women A-HMs is higher in more school categories than in other regions. These school categories are P-only, P+UP, P+UP+S+HS and P+UP+S. Apart from the southern region, women A-HMs are found higher represented in the western region only in P+UP+S+HS schools which is about 49 per cent. In the eastern and northern regions, women A-HMs are not higher represented in any school category. Refer to Table 3.9 for detailed computation on the southern region.

Aggregate Trend across Four Regions of India

At the aggregate regional-level analysis (Table 3.10), it is evident that the representation of women vice-principals is higher in P+UP+S+HS school category in northern and southern regions. However, it is not less either, although it does not reach the cut-off point of 50 per cent in western and eastern regions as they indicate 44.3 per cent and 46.4 per cent, respectively. Out of all four regions, the overall proportion of representation of women vice-principals is the highest in the southern region with 68.2 per cent. It is followed by 54.8 per cent in the northern region. The least representation of women vice-principals is found in the western region with only 44.3 per cent. Only in the southern region, women as principals

Table 3.8 Representation of Women in School Leadership Positions in the Southern Region (in Percentage)

Southern region	HT						Vice-principal				Principal			
	Primary with upper primary		Primary with upper primary and secondary		Upper primary with secondary		Primary with upper primary and secondary/higher secondary		Upper primary with secondary/higher secondary		Primary with upper primary and secondary/higher secondary		Upper primary with secondary/higher secondary	
State/UT	Male	Female	Male	Female	Male	Female	Male	Female	Male	Female	Male	Female	Male	Female
Andaman & Nicobar Islands	33.3	66.7	50.0	50.0	0.0	0.0	0.0	0.0	0.0	0.0	0.0	0.0	0.0	0.0
Andhra Pradesh	0.0	0.0	0.0	0.0	0.0	0.0	0.0	0.0	0.0	0.0	0.0	0.0	0.0	0.0
Karnataka	59.1	40.9	43.4	56.6	72.8	27.2	38.7	61.3	53.8	46.2	46.1	53.9	76.2	23.8
Kerala	38.2	61.8	39.3	60.7	32.3	67.7	22.6	77.4	31.7	68.3	39.4	60.6	46.6	53.4
Lakshadweep	90.0	10.0	100.0	0.0	0.0	0.0	100.0	0.0	0.0	0.0	100.0	0.0	33.3	66.7
Puducherry	0.0	0.0	100.0	0.0	0.0	0.0	52.2	47.8	59.0	41.0	50.6	49.4	73.9	26.1
Tamil Nadu	34.7	65.3	30.8	69.2	59.0	41.0	33.7	66.3	50.0	50.0	40.6	59.4	54.9	45.1
Telangana	0.0	0.0	0.0	0.0	0.0	0.0	0.0	0.0	0.0	0.0	0.0	0.0	0.0	0.0
Aggregate	48.7	51.3	39.6	60.4	57.8	42.2	31.8	68.2	39.8	60.2	40.8	59.2	49.1	50.9

Source: Author's own calculations using raw data from UDISE, NUEPA-MHRD (2016–2017).

Table 3.9 Consolidated Regional-Level Results on Representation of Women as A-HMs in India (in Percentage)

Educational regions at all-india level	Primary only		Primary with upper primary		Primary with upper primary and second-ary/higher secondary		Upper primary only		Upper primary with second-ary/higher secondary		Primary with upper primary and secondary		Upper primary with secondary	
	Male	Female	Male	Female	Male	Female	Male	Female	Male	Female	Male	Female	Male	Female
Eastern region	71.7	28.3	76.3	23.7	65.3	34.7	78.4	21.6	77.1	22.9	77.5	22.5	78.4	21.6
Western region	64.6	35.4	59.2	40.8	51.0	49.0	74.1	25.9	70.4	29.6	60.2	39.8	65.6	34.4
Northern region	63.1	36.9	66.9	33.1	65.7	34.3	73.2	26.8	77.4	22.6	64.7	35.3	79.1	20.9
Southern region	42.1	57.9	42.7	57.3	23.3	76.7	28.3	71.7	50.2	49.8	29.0	71.0	53.1	46.9

Source: Author's own calculations using raw data from UDISE, NUEPA-MHRD (2016–2017).

Table 3.10 Representation of Women in School Leadership Positions at the Regional Level: An Aggregate Scenario (in Percentage)

Educational regions at all-India level	HT						Vice-principal						Principal					
	Primary with upper primary		Primary with upper primary and secondary		Upper primary with secondary		Primary with upper primary and secondary/higher secondary		Upper primary with secondary/higher secondary				Primary with upper primary and secondary/higher secondary		Upper primary with secondary/higher secondary			
	Male	Female	Male	Female	Male	Female	Male	Female	Male	Female			Male	Female	Male	Female		
Eastern region	76.5	23.5	77.5	22.5	78.0	22.0	53.6	46.4	72.1	27.9			66.1	33.9	75.3	24.7		
Western region	67.7	32.3	68.8	31.2	73.8	26.2	55.7	44.3	62.4	37.6			62.7	37.3	73.6	26.4		
Northern region	72.7	27.3	70.3	29.7	73.6	26.4	45.2	54.8	71.5	28.5			69.1	30.9	74.5	25.5		
Southern region	48.7	51.3	39.6	60.4	57.8	42.2	31.8	68.2	39.8	60.2			40.8	59.2	49.1	50.9		

Source: Author's own calculations using raw data from UDISE, NUEPA-MHRD (2016–2017).

shows HR in P+UP+S+HS and UP+S+HS school categories showing 59.2 per cent and 50.9 per cent, respectively. In other regions, women's representation as principals is far too lower. Among the HT's position, women are represented higher in P+UP and P+UP+S school categories with 51.3 per cent and 60.4 per cent, respectively. Woman's representation as HTs comes closer to 50 per cent cut-off mark with 42.2 per cent in UP+S school category in the southern region. The remaining regions show a very low representation of women in this leadership position. Another noteworthy trend is that women are higher represented as vice-principals, principals and HTs in the southern region except in case of UP+S school category for HT's position. This shows that the participation of women in leadership positions is significantly higher in the southern region.

Aggregate Trend in the Representation of Women in School Leadership Positions at the state Level

Representation of women school heads for all school leadership positions was studied by aggregating the total women school heads by considering the relevant school categories together. Table 3.11 gives a vivid scenario of states/UTs across all four school leadership positions.

According to Table 3.11, Chandigarh, Goa, Kerala, Punjab and Tamil Nadu show HR in all four school leadership positions, namely A-HMs, HTs, vice-principals and principals. Because A-HM's position is fleeting, we can consider these states as having women HR in three designated leadership positions which are stable, and appointments are made against regular vacancies.

Meghalaya shows HR in the leadership positions of A-HMs, HTs and vice-principals. In Andaman and Nicobar Islands, women are higher represented as A-HMs and HTs.

Similarly, Karnataka shows HR of women as A-HMs and vice-principals. Jharkhand and Madhya Pradesh show HR of women as vice-principals only. Haryana and Puducherry show HR of women as A-HMs only. A consolidated view of the emergent scenario is

Participation of Women in School Leadership Positions in India 61

Table 3.11 Aggregate Trend at the State Level: Representation of Women in Four Leadership Positions (in Percentage)

State/UT	A-HMs	HTs	Principals	Vice-principals
Andaman & Nicobar Islands	52.2	60.0	0.0	0.0
Andhra Pradesh	0.0	0.0	0.0	0.0
Arunachal Pradesh	38.1	22.5	6.0	26.3
Assam	23.8	22.0	29.7	29.8
Bihar	32.7	14.5	14.8	15.8
Chandigarh	84.5	59.0	77.3	86.4
Chhattisgarh	54.4	31.2	39.7	45.1
Dadra & Nagar Haveli	36.5	45.5	33.3	50.0
Daman & Diu	50.9	20.0	20.0	50.0
Delhi	0.0	78.1	66.0	58.6
Goa	78.7	55.0	50.0	77.8
Gujarat	48.7	27.6	43.0	50.7
Haryana	61.5	35.3	34.8	45.3
Himachal Pradesh	36.7	35.2	25.8	46.3
Jammu & Kashmir	42.5	31.1	23.4	48.4
Jharkhand	23.2	22.1	22.2	58.5
Karnataka	51.2	42.3	47.4	56.8
Kerala	80.9	62.1	57.2	73.8
Lakshadweep	44.4	9.1	33.3	0.0
Madhya Pradesh	39.0	33.1	34.7	52.2
Maharashtra	30.3	34.7	25.0	32.0
Manipur	34.4	22.0	25.6	8.9
Meghalaya	54.1	54.2	35.7	65.0
Mizoram	35.4	31.9	0.0	0.0
Nagaland	29.3	24.2	46.1	51.9
Odisha	26.2	26.5	26.6	48.8
Puducherry	76.7	0.0	44.4	44.7
Punjab	58.6	62.3	54.5	70.5

(Continued)

(Continued)

State/UT	A-HMs	HTs	Principals	Vice-principals
Rajasthan	26.5	19.6	19.2	22.2
Sikkim	40.6	23.0	33.3	45.2
Tamil Nadu	69.6	59.6	58.4	65.1
Telangana	0.0	0.0	0.0	0.0
Tripura	8.3	20.4	31.3	25.0
Uttar Pradesh	32.3	29.4	19.7	24.8
Uttarakhand	37.6	38.7	20.7	45.3
West Bengal	27.5	25.8	49.5	45.5
All India	33.16	32.3	33.3	50.1

Source: Author's own calculations using raw data from UDISE, NUEPA-MHRD (2016–2017).

presented in Table 3.12. Barring these states/UTs, a large proportion of states continue to show UR of women in school leadership positions in India. This calls for a greater understanding about a few other important factors which have an impact on the representation of women in school leadership positions in India.

OTHER FACTORS INFLUENCING THE REPRESENTATION OF WOMEN IN SCHOOL LEADERSHIP POSITIONS

Recruitment Policy and Representation of Women: Level Playing the Field and Compensation

As education is in the concurrent list, variations in the recruitment policies across the states are imminent. Some states have well laid out rules and procedures for selecting school heads through departmental selection having written tests and interviews, whereas a few other states/UTs promote teachers as school heads based on seniority. States/UTs also adopt direct recruitment through public service commission (PSC). The proportion between direct recruitment either through department or PSC or both and seniority-based promotion varies in terms of 25:75, 50:50 to 100:0. Though there is a 100 per cent direct

Table 3.12 *Emerging Pattern of Women in School Leadership Positions in States/UTs Having HR*

School leadership position	1 leadership position	2 leadership positions	3 leadership positions	4 leadership positions
A-HMs	Haryana, Puducherry	Andaman & Nicobar Islands, Karnataka	Meghalaya	Chandigarh, Goa, Kerala, Punjab, Tamil Nadu
HT		Andaman & Nicobar Islands	Meghalaya	Chandigarh, Goa, Kerala, Punjab, Tamil Nadu
Vice-principals	Jharkhand, Madhya Pradesh	Karnataka	Meghalaya	Chandigarh, Goa, Kerala, Punjab, Tamil Nadu
Principals				Chandigarh, Goa, Kerala, Punjab, Tamil Nadu

Source: Author's own calculations using raw data from UDISE, NUEPA-MHRD (2016–2017).

recruitment stated on records in Assam and West Bengal, it is not implemented (refer to Table 3.13 for details).

A few states/UTs, such as Gujarat, Sikkim, Jharkhand and Punjab, adopt departmental examination. Selection is made based on the proportion fixed between direct recruitment and seniority-based promotion that includes teachers from elementary, secondary and senior secondary levels. States/UTs such as Karnataka, Rajasthan, Delhi, Chandigarh, Telangana, Andhra Pradesh, Uttarakhand and Manipur conduct examinations through their PSCs to directly select Grade I education officers, which starts from the post of designated school head in most states and pursue higher in the academic stream. In Uttarakhand and Manipur, selection is exclusively for educational administration. In Karnataka, these recruits start as designated HMs, but quickly move to higher levels having a combination of academic and administration in the department having to work in DIETs, CTEs, Block education offices and district education offices. There

Table 3.13 Recruitment Criteria and Process Adopted by the Government School Heads in Indian States/UTs

States/UTs	Proportion of direct recruitment to seniority-based promotion	Level of schooling for direct recruitment to school leadership position	Process followed for recruitment
Andhra Pradesh & Telangana	25:75	Secondary to senior secondary schools (designated HM and principal)	Written test and interview for both regular government schools and residential schools for tribal children under Tribal welfare department
Assam	100:00	Senior secondary schools	Interview. But implementation is an issue
Delhi	50:50	Senior secondary schools (principal)	Written test and interview through UPSC
Gujarat	50:50	Elementary schools (designated HM) Secondary and senior secondary school heads directly	[a] Written test only (objective type questions) direct appointment for those who completed a minimum of 5 years of service as teachers Gujarat PSC Grade II
Jharkhand	50:50	Secondary Schools (designated HM)	Written test only
Karnataka	25:75	High schools (designated HM)	Written test, interview through Karnataka State Administrative Services (KAS)
Mizoram	50:50	Secondary and senior secondary schools	Written test and interview—departmental examination held through Mizoram PSC
Punjab	50:50	Secondary and senior secondary schools (designated HM and principal)	[a] Written test and interview (departmental examination)

Rajasthan	50:50	Secondary schools (designated HM)	Written exam and interview on the lines of Rajasthan State Administrative Services
Sikkim	100:00	Elementary, secondary and senior secondary schools (designated HM and principal)	[a] Written test and interview
Uttarakhand	25:75	High schools (designated HM)	PSC in Uttarakhand
West Bengal	100:00	Elementary and secondary schools (designated HM)	[a] Written test and interview. Implementation in full compliance with merit and competition alone is an issue
Meghalaya, Manipur, Madhya Pradesh, Puducherry, Goa, Kerala, Bihar, Himachal Pradesh, Chhattisgarh, Maharashtra, Haryana, Tamil Nadu, Lakshadweep, Tripura	0:100	Promotion based on seniority at all levels	There is a deeper issue of a large number of untrained teachers in Meghalaya and Tripura. So, promotion-based policy also cannot be applicable fully In Chhattisgarh, hardly there are designated school heads In Madhya Pradesh, the post of principal of secondary school is superior to that of block education officer. S/he is the signing and disbursing officer for other schools in the district Manipur conducts direct recruitment but only for administrative posts starting from block and district levels

Source: Data collected through discussions with various officials from all states. Wherever available, state Gazettes and official orders are referred additionally. Also see end notes.

Note: [a] Departmental examination is held for the selection of candidates, which is different from examination conducted by PSC.

is a separate Pre-University board in Karnataka for 11th and 12th standard for which principal's position is meant. In Andhra Pradesh and Telangana, direct recruitment is also carried out exclusively for residential schools meant for tribal children under the Tribal welfare department. In Mizoram, direct recruitment for school head's position has been introduced recently. Direct recruitment provides an opportunity for aspirants to become school heads at a young age without having to wait for promotion mostly coinciding with retirement. Principals for Navodaya Vidyalaya and Kendriya Vidyalaya schools are selected through such direct recruitments conducted at the all-India level for those completing a minimum experience of 10 years as post-graduate teachers (PGTs). Apart from these, Ministry of Human Resource Development (MHRD) separately conducted examination in 2010–2011 to select HMs for 300 model schools which were set up in different states across the country. It allowed open competition including for those working in private schools. In UTs, seniority-based promotion is adopted besides selection through Union Public Service Commission (UPSC). There is no direct recruitment of school heads for elementary, secondary and senior secondary schools in Bihar, Punjab, Haryana, Kerala, Himachal Pradesh, Maharashtra, Arunachal Pradesh, Tripura, Orissa, Uttar Pradesh, Meghalaya, Chhattisgarh and Madhya Pradesh. They are promoted as school heads on seniority basis at elementary, secondary and senior secondary schools.

The availability of opportunity for school leadership also depends upon sanctioned posts and vacancy existing in the education system. Appointment of HMs for elementary schools is mostly through seniority-based promotion accompanied with no increase in salary and other benefits in many states/UTs. Such promotions also culminated in retirement or a few months prior to retirement carrying no significance. Hence, many, especially women, may not prefer to take up this role as it comes with an unholy mix of absence of benefits and higher responsibility. In case of seniority-based promotion for secondary and senior secondary schools, the chances of further promotion into administrative posts depends mostly on state's policy and age of the employee. By contrast, direct recruitment in many states/UTs has scope for career progression in terms of promotion to block- and district-level administrative positions, increase in salary, power and authority, execution of duties and many more, in which both men and women wish to compete. In Sikkim, Manipur, Mizoram, Karnataka, Telangana and Andhra Pradesh, one can become the joint director of a district and also reach up to state cadre as administrative officer by the end of his/her service if the person joins the service at a young age.

Disaggregated results for different school categories at state/UT level indicate an encouraging trend. Women are higher represented as HTs for secondary level in seven out of 36 states/UTs in P+UP+S school categories which account for nearly 1/5th of the total states/UTs despite showing UR at the national level aggregate results. It may be possible due to the unequal distribution of opportunity that fails to address gender parity in some states/UTs resulting in UR at the aggregate for the national level. For example, in Delhi, the seniority list for promotion as head of schools (HoS) and later to principal's position is maintained separately for men and women. Delhi has a significantly HR of women teachers. Men who are lower in the overall list of seniority get quicker promotion as HoS as their number is less, whereas women who have completed equal or more years of service as PGTs wait much longer than men for their turn to become HoS and principals. Some of them may not become principals at all as they reach the age of superannuation. In Kerala, most teachers become school heads for secondary level 6 months to 1 year before retirement. This may be due to excess teaching staff present in the system. In Karnataka, the policy of promotion and recruitment of school heads also depends on whether the school has a designated post of HM as it is linked to enrolment of students. Schools which do not have more students, especially elementary level as well as some high schools, will not have a designated HM's post. A-HMs serve the role of a school head. In case of Meghalaya, more than 50 per cent of the teachers working in the system are untrained and do not fulfil the minimum qualifications of basic graduate degree in arts, science or humanities with a bachelor's degree in education.

In general, now there is a direct recruitment for the leadership position in the highest school category present in the states/UTs. For example, in Karnataka, Andhra Pradesh, Rajasthan, Uttarakhand and Telangana, direct recruitment is for secondary schools as designated

HMs in P+UP+S schools. Whereas in Delhi and Sikkim, direct recruitment is meant for vice-principal and principal's position, where P+UP+S+HS or UP+S+HS schools are predominant school categories. Women representing higher as vice-principals and principals at the national level shows that they compete to prove their merit besides seniority-based promotion. Capabilities have also contributed to HR of women principals and vice-principals. This is in contrast to their representation as designated HMs because only few states/UTs conduct direct recruitment for secondary schools.

Wherever the representation of women teachers is high and there is seniority-based promotion in states/UTs, women teachers have higher chances of becoming school heads. It is, therefore, natural to expect Kerala, Tamil Nadu, Puducherry, Delhi, Chandigarh, Karnataka, Punjab, Maharashtra, Gujarat, Daman and Diu, Goa, Dadra and Nagar Haveli, Himachal Pradesh, Nagaland, Tripura, Meghalaya and Sikkim to show an HR in at least one or all three designated leadership positions as women teachers are more than men teachers. So, promotion based on seniority has also provided opportunities for women to get into leadership positions, but direct recruitment accelerated the access to school leadership in many states/UTs.

The proportion allocated between direct recruitment through open competition and seniority-based promotion is a form of 'level playing the field' (Roemer, 1993) to recognize and promote the meritorious who are also young having potential for greater contribution. This approach provides opportunity to equalize capabilities to function in various degrees of responsibility putting their efforts and exploiting capabilities especially between the young and experienced teachers. Seniority-based promotion values the experience and service having worked in the system taking less time to adapt and understand the new role constitute the 'principle of compensation' (Fleurbaey, 1994). It depends on 'fairness' (Fleurbaey, 1995) in rules explicitly recognizing the individual responsibility despite differences in the outcomes. Equalizing the access to opportunities for school leadership positions using the principles of 'compensation' and 'level playing the field' provides scope for equalizing the opportunity for taking responsibility to access school leadership positions and taking into account the people's differential backgrounds, circumstances and capabilities, which need not necessarily be under the control of the individual all the time, thus achieving 'shared power and shared responsibility' while 'respecting the differences' (Mark, 2002). In this sense, recruitment policies and processes are mostly gender neutral providing equal opportunities for women to compete for school leadership positions except in rare few cases, such as in Delhi, promotion based on seniority is maintained separately for men and women.

When the recruitment policy in the states/UTs across all four regions were studied, there was neither any particular trend of recruitment policy within the region nor any association between direct recruitment and HR of women. It further reinforces the gender neutrality maintained in direct recruitment as well as in promotion-based policies. This indicates a higher degree of equalization of access to opportunities for school leadership positions.

Parallel Leadership Positions as Alternate Choices Available in the Education System

In some states/UTs, parallel leadership positions equivalent to that of the school head's position exist in the education system at block-, district- and state-level administration, especially in programmatic structures of SSA or Rastriya Madhyamika Shiksha Abhiyan (RMSA). These positions enjoy better decision-making powers, autonomy and control mechanisms. School heads can exercise their choice between alternative parallel leadership positions available in the same cadre within the education system choosing to be in the academic stream or to be in administrative stream alone for getting promotions.

Some states/UTs even have opportunities to move between academic and administrative posts as in Karnataka, Telangana, Andhra Pradesh, Rajasthan, Madhya Pradesh and Puducherry. For example, in Karnataka, instead of working as school head at elementary/secondary level/s, one can become a cluster resource person and/or cluster resource coordinator, block resource person or block resource coordinator. Gaining seniority, school heads can also work as junior lecturers at higher secondary level or DIET. In Andhra,

Telangana and Puducherry, secondary school heads can work as academic monitoring officers in SSA and RMSA or state project officers, etc. In Sikkim, principals are promoted to the administrative position as Joint directors. In Rajasthan, one has the choice to choose between being a principal or block education officer as both are of the same grade. In Kerala, Manipur, Uttarakhand, Mizoram, Meghalaya and Himachal Pradesh, academic and administrative positions are separate, and their progression through promotion also remains distinct without scope for crossing over from academic to administration and/or vice versa. The opportunity to move within the education system to take up different roles and responsibilities other than the school is perceived as recognition of good performance and to show case their abilities at the system level. It also facilitates them to move up in the career and profession in due course of time. In this sense, parallel leadership positions turn out to be ethically legitimate and a form of fair treatment that rewards the individual efforts based on the responsibilities chosen (Fleurbaey, 2008). Women also prefer to choose options wherever available depending on the advantage and convenience to strike a work–life balance. Parallel leadership positions are a form of 'level playing field' compensating the individual's desire to move beyond her comfort zone, try harder than her peers to excel, exercise power and exploit other opportunities available in the system by accessing them to function in various ways apart from that of HTs.

In contrast, principals and vice-principals at higher secondary level enjoy greater autonomy and decision-making powers, advantage to take greater risks or/and understand the positional advantage in parallel leadership positions. Women may wish to exercise choice to be principals or vice-principals. Here, family background and socio- cultural, educational and economic contexts of the society and educational, social and cultural capital in the family influence the choices. Ascending to these positions, especially, principal and vice-principal, is influenced by fulfilling the criteria of passing the competition, fulfilling the essential qualification and a proven record of career besides seniority. Hence, intellectual acumen also plays a predominant role especially in case of direct recruitment through open competition. Thus, becoming principals and vice-principals refer to a person's abilities to do valuable acts or reach valuable states of being to achieve what an individual reflectively considers valuable (Sen, 1992). In this sense, capabilities are also valuable opportunities to exercise choice for school leadership positions. Women vice-principals and principals might not prefer parallel leadership positions despite limited opportunity available, therefore, represented higher in the system.

Capabilities as a Form of Opportunity Influencing Representation of Women's School Leadership

Qualification, experience, age, location of work and caste can be considered as different forms of capabilities (Sen, 1993) for ascending to school leadership positions in India. While academic and professional qualifications can be called 'acquired capabilities', caste and age can be called 'ascribed capabilities'. Location of work is dependent mostly on the decisions of higher authorities and so it is also ascribed to school heads. These two capabilities impact representation of women as school heads.

Achieved Capabilities: Essential academic qualification for an HT is graduation with a professional degree in teaching such as BEd Over and above this essential qualification, a school head having acquired additional qualifications indicates their enhanced capabilities at least to a certain extent. Similarly, essential qualification for vice-principals and principals is post-graduate degree in any curricular subject with a BEd degree and should have a teaching experience of at least 10 years as a PGT. Many of the women vice-principals and principals have moved beyond the level of essential academic and professional qualifications by acquiring research degrees and other additional professional degrees.

Ascribed Capabilities: HTs, principals and vice-principals ought to be appointed against the vacancies and posts created in the schools. Direct recruitment policies in different states/UTs have encouraged more and more young teachers to occupy the position of school leadership in a significant way in the recent years. Direct recruitment system encourages young women from all social backgrounds such as General, Scheduled Castes, Scheduled Tribes, Other Backward

Classes and other groups to compete for school leadership positions. There is an active role of 'level playing field' for women aspirants to ascend to school leadership positions. Nonetheless, due to the lack of transport facilities, inadequate facilities for stay and provision of higher education facilities for their children and also other compulsions of life including the preference to live in urban areas, which are more modernized than rural areas, women leaders may be found more in urban areas than in rural areas. It may also be due to the norms for access to different levels of schooling such as within 1 km for primary, within 3 km for elementary, within 5 km for secondary and more than 5 km for senior secondary schools. Obviously, senior secondary schools are not found in greater proportion in interior rural areas. They are mostly found in semi-rural and urban areas. These are the school categories where women as vice-principals are represented higher. In contrast, primary, elementary and secondary schools are mostly found in larger proportions in rural areas.

A rich data on these parameters would have been definitely useful to throw more insights. But, U-DISE does not provide the data on men and women HTs, vice-principals and principals at state and national level. It provides data on the total number of school heads who are HTs, vice-principals and principals. Hence, this analysis regarding capabilities of women school leaders could not be taken up. An in-depth study of school leadership practices that is dealt in the subsequent chapters using qualitative data provides the necessary substitution and beyond for the lack of availability of secondary school heads with respect to their educational qualification, professional qualification, age, location and caste at state/UT and all India levels.

CONCLUSIONS

An equitable society is one that secures for all its members an equal chance to attain the outcomes they care about. Thus, opportunity rather than achievements becomes an appropriate currency of egalitarian justice (Ferreira & Peragine, 2015). In India, even though there are 10 school categories, only 40 per cent of them have designated school leadership positions. Remaining 60 per cent of school categories, which are stand-alone primary, upper primary, secondary and senior secondary schools, do not qualify for having designated school leadership positions. Thus, there is an acute shortage of opportunities for school leadership positions coupled with dysfunctional school categories severely affecting teachers (both men and women) to access school leadership positions. It is a significant achievement if women have been able to compete successfully within the acute shortage of opportunities and get represented higher as vice-principals in P+UP+S+HS schools, which constitute a mere 3.2 per cent of total schools. In all, only in 5.3 per cent of senior secondary schools (P+UP+S+HS and UP+S+HS school categories considered together), women are represented higher as vice-principals and principals. Seven states also show HR of women HTs.

Recruitment policies affect the representation of women for all three designated leadership positions. Women are represented higher as teachers and school heads wherever there are robust direct recruitment policies. Wherever women teachers are higher in proportion, women are also promoted as school heads when states have adopted seniority-based promotion that are gender neutral. Therefore, recruitment policies have been largely gender neutral, helping women to gain entry into school leadership positions. Parallel leadership positions which are also gender neutral offer opportunities for women to make choices for system-level leadership in some states like Karnataka, Andhra Pradesh, Telangana and Rajasthan. While promotion based on seniority has also provided access to opportunities, direct recruitment accelerated the accessibility of school leadership positions for women in India, especially in higher echelons of school leadership positions such as vice-principals and principals.

End Notes
Gazette notifications or government orders on recruitment of school heads for different states wherever available

- Haryana Govt. Gaz. (Extra), 11 April 2012 (p. 1451) Schooleducationharyana.gov.in/downloads_pdf/Service%20Rules/ Haryana%20State%20Education% (accessed on 18 August 2017 for Haryana).

- The Mizoram Gazette (extra ordinary) Vol NLV Aizawl, Issue No. 333, published on 9 September 2016.
- Government of Assam, Secondary Education Department, Dispur, Assam (2014). Office Memorandum: Guidelines for selection of principals in provincialized higher secondary schools. No. ASE 82/2014/Pt/6, dt. 6 June 2014.www.madhyamik.in/news/.../guideline%20for%20appt%20of%20Regular%20PL.pdf (accessed on 18 August 2017 for Assam).
- Office Order, Himachal Pradesh. No. EDN-H (19) B(2)1/2016-HM-Promotion Directorate of Higher Education, Himachal Pradesh, Shimla-171001, 19 September 2016.
- Notification: Government of Karnataka, No. ED DGO 2005. Karnataka Government Secretariat, M.S. Building, Bangalore, Dated: 30 October 2006.
- karnatakaeducation.gov.in/pdf files/Ser00005.pdf (accessed on 18 August 2017 for Karnataka).
- https://www.simpli.com/web?o=604696&l=sem&qo=serpSearchTopBox&q=Recruitment+Policy+for+principals+and+HMs++in+government+schools+in+Punjab+ (accessed on 18 August 2017 for Punjab).
- wbxpress.com/recruitment-rules-assistant-headmaster-headmistress-school-madrasah (accessed on 18 August 2017 for West Bengal).
- http://www.jharkhand.gov.in/education (accessed on 18 August 2017 for Jharkhand).

APPENDIX A

Table 3A.1 Distribution of School Categories in States/UTs and at All-India Level

S. No.	Percentage of school categories as proportion of total schools in the state	Primary only	Primary with upper primary	Primary/ upper primary/ secondary and higher secondary	Upper primary only	Upper primary with secondary and higher secondary	Primary with upper primary and secondary	Upper primary with secondary	Secondary only	Secondary with higher secondary	Higher secondary only/ junior college	National level
1	Andaman & Nicobar Islands	52.53	20.24	10.36	0.00	3.86	11.33	0.72	0.00	0.96	0.00	0.03
2	Andhra Pradesh	63.70	16.69	0.28	0.00	0.29	2.84	16.17	0.02	0.00	0.00	4.01
3	Arunachal Pradesh	56.78	30.83	1.70	1.28	1.28	6.23	0.99	0.00	0.86	0.05	0.26
4	Assam	67.96	3.03	0.37	16.08	0.96	2.52	1.82	5.57	0.46	1.21	4.65
5	Bihar	51.29	38.83	1.32	0.33	0.10	3.07	0.27	1.36	2.99	0.43	5.53
6	Chandigarh	5.97	5.97	5.97	5.97	5.97	5.97	5.97	5.97	5.97	5.97	0.01
7	Chhattisgarh	60.78	5.25	2.26	21.91	0.60	1.07	2.49	1.14	4.47	0.03	3.53
8	Dadra & Nagar Haveli	49.86	36.89	2.02	0.29	0.29	3.17	0.00	3.75	3.46	0.29	0.02

(*Continued*)

(Continued)

S. No.	Percentage of school categories as proportion of total schools in the state	Primary only	Primary with upper primary	Primary/ upper primary/ secondary and higher secondary	Upper primary only	Upper primary with secondary and higher secondary	Primary with upper primary and secondary	Upper primary with secondary	Secondary only	Secondary with higher secondary	Higher secondary only/ junior college	National level
9	Daman & Diu	40.00	4.14	5.52	26.21	2.76	4.14	0.00	8.97	6.90	1.38	0.01
10	Delhi	47.53	15.44	20.36	0.61	9.56	4.43	1.99	0.00	0.05	0.02	0.37
11	Goa	61.77	4.38	0.84	0.71	0.32	11.35	14.25	0.13	0.00	6.25	0.10
12	Gujarat	22.26	54.65	2.99	1.55	0.55	1.36	0.23	6.82	8.18	1.42	3.47
13	Haryana	43.74	11.23	10.96	10.65	8.50	8.47	6.25	0.00	0.18	0.01	1.48
14	Himachal Pradesh	62.22	4.64	3.36	11.34	9.57	3.72	5.08	0.00	0.02	0.04	1.19
15	Jammu & Kashmir	50.34	34.69	1.69	0.46	0.32	9.35	1.38	0.13	1.63	0.01	1.90
16	Jharkhand	56.40	33.15	0.97	0.18	0.97	4.74	1.25	1.10	0.68	0.56	3.11
17	Karnataka	34.94	39.77	0.93	0.61	0.09	4.15	1.00	13.25	1.22	4.02	4.95
18	Kerala	48.69	19.65	8.41	3.84	5.98	7.34	2.13	0.97	2.61	0.38	1.12
19	Lakshadweep	37.78	26.67	8.89	2.22	11.11	4.44	0.00	0.00	8.89	0.00	0.00

20	Madhya Pradesh	57.80	11.53	2.63	20.01	0.16	1.82	0.03	3.23	2.78	0.01	9.95
21	Maharashtra	48.95	27.27	4.81	0.11	1.30	8.41	5.71	1.19	0.18	2.07	7.08
22	Manipur	58.44	17.90	2.11	1.21	0.54	14.34	2.97	0.80	0.40	1.29	0.32
23	Meghalaya	64.03	1.31	0.24	23.45	0.23	0.83	1.15	7.10	0.43	1.24	0.95
24	Mizoram	39.50	11.13	0.00	28.49	0.00	0.00	0.00	16.66	0.00	4.22	0.25
25	Nagaland	45.00	27.34	3.67	1.41	1.62	13.74	6.32	0.11	0.11	0.67	0.18
26	Odisha	51.54	27.12	0.25	5.65	0.23	2.84	10.26	0.44	0.00	1.68	4.59
27	Puducherry	38.13	10.72	14.79	0.14	7.06	22.66	4.88	0.00	0.95	0.68	0.05
28	Punjab	49.17	8.84	9.24	9.27	7.17	9.49	5.96	0.02	0.22	0.61	1.89
29	Rajasthan	38.01	34.81	15.31	0.20	0.77	10.39	0.23	0.00	0.29	0.00	6.89
30	Sikkim	55.96	26.58	6.07	0.00	0.53	10.48	0.38	0.00	0.00	0.00	0.09
31	Tamil Nadu	61.02	16.51	5.09	0.22	7.27	3.24	6.58	0.01	0.03	0.03	3.78
32	Telangana	50.11	17.26	0.57	0.00	0.48	12.69	14.73	0.00	0.00	4.17	2.81
33	Tripura	52.39	26.14	7.22	0.02	1.42	12.61	0.19	0.02	0.00	0.00	0.32
34	Uttar Pradesh	60.23	5.42	1.17	24.08	3.28	0.57	1.19	1.95	2.11	0.01	17.26
35	Uttarakhand	63.58	7.29	2.16	14.20	6.68	0.71	3.77	1.03	0.49	0.07	1.57
36	West Bengal	79.80	1.60	0.69	7.86	6.63	0.43	2.98	0.00	0.00	0.01	6.28
	All India	54.72	18.71	3.16	9.61	2.19	3.88	3.32	2.21	1.47	0.74	100.00

Source: Author's own calculations using raw data from UDISE, NUEPA-MHRD (2016–2017).

Table 3A.2 Distribution of Women Teachers in different school categories at the State level (in percentage)

S. No.	State/UT	Primary only	Primary with upper primary	Primary with upper primary & Secondary higher secondary	Upper primary only	Upper primary with Secondary higher secondary	Primary with upper primary & secondary	Upper primary with secondary	Secondary only	Secondary with higher secondary	Higher secondary only/ junior college	Total % of females in the state from all school categories
1	A & N Islands	65.0	66.1	61.9	0.0	53.7	62.6	57.9	0.0	43.6	0.0	62.0
2	Andhra Pradesh	51.3	52.3	59.3	66.7	45.8	56.0	41.7	58.9	41.7	0.0	48.3
3	Arunachal Pradesh	41.6	45.7	35.4	58.5	29.4	45.9	36.8	0.0	29.2	30.0	42.8
4	Assam	37.5	43.5	54.8	25.4	36.6	54.8	35.5	27.8	28.2	39.0	35.8
5	Bihar	44.6	38.5	30.6	37.9	24.0	32.9	23.8	20.8	23.9	15.8	37.9
6	Chandigarh	83.1	76.9	81.6	0.0	75.7	74.4	0.0	0.0	0.0	0.0	79.1
7	Chhattisgarh	38.4	68.0	62.5	32.3	39.4	63.5	36.0	41.1	41.5	37.9	43.6
8	Dadra & Nagar Haveli	54.8	60.9	78.1	100.0	30.4	63.8	0.0	44.9	60.5	70.8	61.7
9	Daman & Diu	75.9	85.9	80.9	50.7	34.1	69.4	0.0	42.6	43.3	37.5	62.9
10	Delhi	72.2	86.3	78.9	57.6	48.7	84.5	52.4	0.0	53.8	50.0	72.8
11	Goa	90.8	80.4	76.5	75.0	56.4	82.7	69.8	20.0	0.0	67.9	78.7

12	Gujarat	51.4	55.8	66.0	60.0	33.4	70.2	37.7	25.9	30.7	35.6	52.2
13	Haryana	45.7	70.3	69.4	32.5	46.2	66.2	39.4	0.0	57.4	52.2	57.3
14	Himachal Pradesh	45.0	72.5	70.3	26.2	36.8	70.1	34.4	0.0	51.6	48.6	47.9
15	Jammu & Kashmir	42.2	42.3	62.5	86.7	33.0	49.4	29.1	29.4	35.1	33.3	44.5
16	Jharkhand	31.8	33.4	50.2	46.4	54.0	37.3	33.3	32.1	21.3	25.4	34.4
17	Karnataka	53.2	59.0	80.5	65.2	32.9	73.2	37.5	37.8	37.9	33.8	54.2
18	Kerala	81.0	78.4	81.6	70.2	70.3	85.4	79.2	62.5	60.2	75.9	77.1
19	Lakshadweep	48.1	43.4	50.0	41.7	46.5	42.6	0.0	0.0	44.2	0.0	46.2
20	Madhya Pradesh	33.8	56.9	61.4	30.4	38.7	58.8	40.8	33.1	34.1	37.5	42.8
21	Maharashtra	46.6	47.6	32.8	45.7	29.4	40.6	35.1	40.4	32.1	35.7	41.7
22	Manipur	48.4	50.9	50.0	45.3	44.7	50.6	52.2	33.6	53.0	48.2	49.8
23	Meghalaya	57.7	71.4	67.6	47.5	52.2	73.2	51.4	46.8	50.2	67.0	54.7
24	Mizoram	50.2	58.1	0.0	38.8	0.0	0.0	0.0	35.1	0.0	46.2	45.0
25	Nagaland	48.5	51.7	62.7	32.5	49.8	55.8	34.0	41.3	60.3	55.2	51.2
26	Odisha	46.0	48.4	58.9	34.9	33.3	45.5	29.5	26.6	0.0	29.3	43.1
27	Puducherry	76.7	69.2	75.1	72.7	54.7	77.6	59.9	0.0	63.9	24.2	71.7
28	Punjab	67.3	87.1	82.4	56.7	60.2	86.5	56.6	77.3	87.0	76.2	74.2

(*Continued*)

(Continued)

S. No.	State/UT	Primary only	Primary with upper primary	Primary with upper primary & Secondary higher secondary	Upper primary only	Upper primary with Secondary higher secondary	Primary with upper primary & secondary	Upper primary with secondary	Secondary only	Secondary with higher secondary	Higher secondary only/ junior college	Total % of females in the state from all school categories
29	Rajasthan	36.9	38.8	31.8	86.9	32.6	34.8	37.9	0.0	31.2	0.0	35.4
30	Sikkim	52.9	57.8	55.9	0.0	20.7	52.2	40.4	0.0	0.0	0.0	54.6
31	Tamil Nadu	83.9	72.2	81.0	86.3	58.5	86.6	58.7	52.4	46.4	73.4	74.2
32	Telangana	51.2	54.0	62.1	0.0	43.7	53.6	44.6	0.0	0.0	23.7	49.1
33	Tripura	27.2	25.1	37.5	58.3	28.9	27.4	52.1	0.0	0.0	0.0	29.3
34	Uttar Pradesh	45.4	43.5	44.9	37.0	21.1	37.0	24.5	31.7	27.7	34.4	40.1
35	Uttarakhand	53.9	68.9	68.2	39.2	26.9	67.8	31.0	31.5	30.6	56.6	48.1
36	West Bengal	46.9	42.5	60.5	21.9	37.2	48.7	44.1	0.0	62.5	27.4	43.0
	All India	47.7	50.5	57.4	34.7	43.2	54.0	41.5	33.8	34.1	34.5	47.7

Source: Author's own calculation using raw data from UDISE, NUEPA-MHRD (2016–2017).

Note: For the purpose of the present study, proportion of women and men teachers is calculated separately for each school category using total teachers in that school category.

Ladder of School Leadership of Women

EMERGENT PROPERTY OF SCHOOL LEADERSHIP OF WOMEN: PROCESS AND OUTCOMES

The narrative inquiry seeks to identify relationships, contradictions, complexities and challenges between different events and groups of people, which may be subtle or explicit, simple or overwhelming and inherent or influenced by circumstances across different systems, structures and agency. These different systems and structures affected the form, power, content and direction of their agency, creating differential path trajectories for leading schools successfully. In and through the leading processes, women focus on developing knowledge, skills, abilities, behaviours, etc., drawing from their experiences. They accumulate and evolve with varying pace and levels due to divergent beliefs, values and inherent capacities in women due to which the nature of agency also differs from one to another. Six themes emerged from the narrative inquiry carried out using the qualitative data collected and narratives developed. These themes are educational background of the family; familial support; balancing resilience and determination; leading school administration, management and academic functions; gender: is it a notion or experience; and zeal beyond school leadership and irrespective of gender. In addition to the six themes emerging from qualitative data, another theme is included from the previous chapter, namely, school leadership positions in the education system. In all, there are seven themes out of which six emerged from the primary source based on qualitative data and one emerged from the analysis of secondary data source.

These seven themes can be suitably positioned within the five major structures through which women school heads negotiate and navigate to evolve as leaders over a period. The five structures are family, school, community within which the school exists, education system and larger context of the society especially with reference to the diversity influencing the school's context. Women's interaction with these structures according to various roles and responsibilities gave rise to an emerging pattern of leadership journey for women school heads. It is called the 'ladder of school leadership', a path of leadership continuum traversed by the women school heads. It has five steps, namely, 'aspire', 'acquire', 'achieve', 'ascend' and 'transcend'. The ladder of school leadership refers to the 'Whole', implying that the causal power of structures refers to the emergent property for the school leadership of women in the Indian context.

Mapping these seven themes and five structures, one more step in the ladder called availability of opportunity is included. So, the steps in the ladder in ascending order are as follows: availability of opportunity, aspire, acquire, achieve, ascend and transcend. These six steps of the ladder constitute the 'wholes' or parts of the 'Whole', the ladder of school leadership of women.

The emergent property along with its parts, themes and different structures constitutes the overarching framework for this chapter as well as the remaining portion of the study (Table 4.1).

In arriving at the framework, themes or structures are also combined depending on the relevance and aptness for the rest of the study. Two emergent themes are combined against the step 'achieve' in the ladder to depict the manner in which women coped with gender notions while climbing up the ladder for school leadership. These themes are as follows: balancing resilience with determination and gender: is it a notion or an experience. Similarly, structures are also combined against these two related themes. All of this together refers to the fourth step in the ladder 'achieve'. In the same way, diversity of school contexts and/or society, school and education system are together associated with the theme zeal beyond school leadership and irrespective of gender. This refers to the step 'transcend'.

Broadly, the emergent themes have some predominant characteristic features, each of which is described in brief. The first theme on

Table 4.1 Emergent Themes, Their Characteristics, Ladder of School Leadership and Predominant Structure Associated for School Leadership of Women in the Indian Context

S. No.	Emergent themes	Characteristic features of the emergent themes	Predominant structure associated with the emergent themes	Emergent property—the ladder of school leadership
1	School leadership positions in the education system	Apply for the school leadership position, compete for direct recruitment, wait for promotion, acquire essential qualification, recruitment policy in the state, representation of women in leadership positions	Education system	Availability of opportunity
2	Social and educational background of the family	Use the inputs received through intellectual capital and maximize the capacity to compete, get necessary eligibility Family orientation and environment for women's employment	Family	Aspire
3	Familial support	Seek emotional support, get motivated and get child care support Take support of the technical expertise of father and husband to work efficiently in the workplace as HM	Family	Acquire
4	Balancing resilience with determination; Gender: is it a notion or an experience	Exploit the social challenges to one's advantage; face boldly the threats; limitations of traditional practices; resistance from the community, teachers and colleagues and higher officers	School & community	Achieve
5	Leading school administration, management and academic functions	Decision-making, ensuring teaching–learning process, managing people, acquiring proficiency in rules and administration, developing people skills and professional excellence	School	Ascend
6	Zeal beyond school leadership, irrespective of gender	Social service, love for children, projects of life, move beyond the limitations of education system and leadership roles, withering distinction between personal and professional life, ignore gender discrimination and stereotype	School, education system & diversity of school context/larger society	Transcend

school leadership positions in the education system refers to applying for the school leadership position, competing for direct recruitment or waiting for promotion where there is no opportunity for direct competition, achieved and acquired capabilities for becoming a school head, influence of the recruitment policy in the state and extent to which women are represented in different school leadership positions such as designated HM, vice-principal and principals at secondary and senior secondary levels, respectively. It refers to the step of the ladder 'availability of opportunity' for school leadership positions mainly associated with the education system.

The second emergent theme related to social and educational background of the family is characterized by women aspirants who use the intellectual capital as inputs received from the family members. It is possible to maximize their capacity to get necessary eligibility and compete in the job market for leadership positions in the schools. Their aspirations and acquisition of leadership positions in the education system are also dependent on the orientation of their family with the necessary environment for such competition to improve the chances for leadership positions. This step is in the realm of family, and the step in the ladder is called Aspire.

The third emergent theme on familial support specifically deals with seeking emotional support, getting motivation from family members and also getting child care support. Women also seek technical and professional support from fathers and husbands to work efficiently to avoid mistakes working in the position of leadership. The third step emerging from this theme is called 'acquire', referring to the structure of the education system.

Two themes are merged in case of the fourth, namely, balancing resilience with determination and gender: is it a notion or an experience. Women exploit the social challenges to their advantage; face the threats boldly; move beyond the limitations of traditional practices; and overcome resistance from the community, teachers and colleagues and higher officers. The fourth step in the ladder known as 'achieve' engages with school and community structures.

In the fifth emergent theme on leading school administration, management and academic functions, the characteristic features are decision-making, ensuring teaching–learning process, managing people, acquiring proficiency in rules and administration and developing people skills and professional excellence. The fifth step in the ladder, 'ascend', is formed when women focus their work chiefly on the school, the core of all structures in the present study.

In the sixth and final theme on zeal beyond and irrespective of gender, women refer to their work as social service, love for children and project of life. They move beyond the limitations of education system and leadership roles, withering distinction between personal and professional life, and ignoring gender discrimination and stereotype. The emergent theme arises from a deeper interaction between several structures such as education system, school, community and larger society, especially with regard to its diversity in contexts to give rise to the final step of the ladder of women's leadership—transcend.

In this way, emergent themes from narratives, their characteristic features, associated structures and different steps of the ladder of school leadership nest together to describe the ladder of school leadership of women and the path traversed to succeed as leaders. A detailed description of the form of narratives based on the steps of the ladder and themes as well as the agency of women leader follows in the subsequent sections.

NARRATIVES

Basic Profiles of Women School Leaders

The respective numbers of women school heads were as follows: Delhi—five, Telangana—four, Madhya Pradesh—three, Rajasthan, Haryana and Uttar Pradesh—two each and Sikkim and Himachal Pradesh—one each. Ten of the twenty women possessed two or more master's degrees, three were PhD holders and the remaining four had a master's degree each. All had at least a BEd degree. Six were direct recruits, selected by the UPSC/state PSC through the competitive examinations conducted for the principal's posts. Two were private school teachers earlier and others were government school teachers. The remaining women had become school heads by promotion on the basis of seniority as per the respective state government policies. When they were interviewed, the women from Sikkim and Himachal Pradesh were elementary school heads. All the others were secondary and senior secondary school heads. Aged between 32 and 53 years, the women were all married except for one. One of them is widowed. Most of them lived in nuclear families.

Husbands of these women were engaged in diverse occupations. They were doctors (two), owned a computer teaching centre (one), company secretary (one), pilot (one), engineer (one), sales agent for a life insurance company besides being an active political party worker (one) and five taught in under-graduate colleges affiliated to universities and one in high school (Table 4.2).

Table 4.2 Basic Profiles of Women School Heads

States which women school heads represented	No. of women Delhi—5; Rajasthan—2; Madhya Pradesh—3; Telangana—4; Haryana and Uttar Pradesh—2 each; Sikkim and Himachal Pradesh—1 each
Age of women school heads	Between 32 years and 53 years
Marital status	All married, except one from Madhya Pradesh
Profiles of husbands	Computer business—1 Other business—1 Company Secretary—1 Doctors—2 Pilot—1 Engineer—3 Sales agent in life insurance company—1 School teacher—1 Lecturers in undergraduate colleges—5 Not known—1 Government official—1 Not alive—2
Qualification of women school heads	Graduation with BEd—2 One Master's degree with BEd—4 Double master's degree—10 PhD—4
Direct selection to school head's position through PSC examination or UPSC	6 (2 from private schools and 4 from government schools)
Seniority-based promotion as school heads	14 (2 at elementary level and remaining at secondary and senior secondary levels)
Average experience of the women's group as school heads	6.5 years (ranges from 4 years to 20 years)

Source: Mythili (2019b)

Ladder Step 1: Availability of Opportunity (Related Theme: School Leadership Positions in the Education System)

The first step in the ladder referring to availability of opportunity is exhaustively discussed in Chapter 3 on participation of women in school leadership positions. All-India- and state-level analysis has been carried out. It is found that women are higher represented in the higher echelons of school leadership positions such as vice-principals and also as principals at senior secondary levels when compared with designated HMs at the secondary level. Achieved and ascribed capabilities were found to be generally higher than the minimum essentially required among those women who are represented higher as principals and vice-principals.

Ladder Step 2: Aspire (Related Theme: Social and Educational Background of the Family)

The emergent theme related to 'social and educational background of the family' refers extensively to the second step in the ladder, that is, aspire. Narrative referring to the same indicates diverse and distinct ways through which women were influenced by members of the family to aspire for leadership position.

Parents of many women school heads were highly qualified and pursued different professions. Most of them worked in government sectors holding high positions as well. Five mothers were professionally qualified with BEd degrees and served as teachers in government schools. Three of them had a single post-graduate degree with a BEd degree and two others possessed double post-graduate degrees besides BEd Eleven mothers were schooled but below graduation. Most of the fathers of these women school heads were also well qualified. They were graduates, post-graduates, engineers and PhD holders. Many of them worked in various departments in the government. Only one of them pursued a different field as an artist and served as director of Madhya Pradesh State Handicrafts emporium in Bhopal. Only one father, two mothers and a few mothers-in-law did not go to school.

As children growing up building their aspirations, these women school heads amply received encouragement from parents, which they considered as crucial support filled with high levels of inspiration. Their parents valued 'good' education and tried their best to provide the same to their daughters. This enabled many women to get 'government jobs'. Even in their husband's family, most fathers-in-law also possessed higher degrees and served the government as officers and professionals. Even though a few mothers and mothers-in-law were not formally schooled, their awareness about the need for schooling and importance for education was no less demonstrated. They rendered full support to their children to get university education and government jobs since the modern education provided the entire family with upward social mobility, enhanced confidence and gave independence that comes from possessing higher education.

The main source of inspiration for daughters is their educated and employed mothers who instilled the aspirations in the minds of their daughters to become professionals, seek a career, be employed and be self-reliant. With both parents pursuing professional careers, daughters learnt and developed skills to multi-task at home and outside. As they grew up, young daughters also began to navigate and negotiate through every day circumstances alongside their parents by observing and imitating them. They learnt to be resilient, stay focused, cope up with diverse demands, discovered the significance of acquiring knowledge about the works they should do as well as relevant educational qualifications. In this way, as daughters, these women prepared themselves well before entering the job market with prior knowledge and information including the choice to exercise certain other career options. Mothers complemented the efforts of their daughters by not insisting on doing the household chores varying from cooking, cleaning utensils, sibling care, washing clothes and so on. One of the respondents aptly captured these aspects reflecting the natural environment that prevailed in their homes: 'I never went to the kitchen until I got married. My mother used to say cooking is a duty that naturally comes to women after marriage'. Here, cooking refers to all activities related to maintaining the house including the kitchen's responsibility. The youngest women school head during the interview said, 'My mother is my greatest inspiration ... my maternal grandfather was a highly progressive man .... He used to always say "you should become a lecturer".

If the home environment described above prevailed for daughters whose mothers are employed, it is equally appealing to see how mothers who are housewives also supported their daughters, especially in rural areas. These mothers as well as fathers who are deeply engaged in agriculture encouraged both sons and daughters to get university education and seek employment in the formal job market. They did so despite the obligations for all family members, both male and female members, to put in physical labour in agrarian families. Teachers from Telangana and Andhra Pradesh who belong to agrarian families expressed that even though their parents did not go to school to study, they knew the importance of education and even encouraged daughters to go to school, complete university education and take up jobs. Many parents also lend their support to daughters by giving child care support.

In Himachal Pradesh, the mother of the cluster-school head did not want her daughter to face the helplessness she encountered every day—be it in post office or bank to fill the relevant forms to deposit or withdraw money, write letters to relatives or read the board of public transport bus before getting into it for travelling to other places and to be independent to earn her living, manage her alcoholic illiterate husband and so on. Her daughter who is currently the cluster-school head in Lahaul Spiti in Himachal Pradesh, which is one of the most geographically terse and challenging terrains, said:

> When I was nine years old, my mother asked me to leave the home secretly and go to maternal uncle's house in another village to continue schooling. My father was preparing to get me married to a man who was much older to me. I walked alone in the cold winter for three days before reaching my maternal uncle's home.[1]

The aspiration began to take shape among most of these women well before the marriage especially in those families where both parents

---

[1] This remote area covered with ice and snow is at more than 10,000 ft height from the sea level, and witnesses six months winter with temperature dipping to sub-zero degree Celsius.

were employed in which mother was a teacher. Parents also directly and indirectly instilled aspirations in their daughters for taking up teaching profession from childhood. In other words, vocational anticipatory socialization started much earlier for these women. Therefore, the lives are lived interdependently as women's life and experience of significant others, that is, parents, are closely connected with each other (Elder, 1999). Also, these parents, who are significant others, regulated and shaped the timings of their sibling's life informally through a network of control to take a certain trajectory (Elder, 1998). To ensure the expected trajectory to take place for their siblings, they passed on certain values and beliefs, activities, choices and aspirations by acting as role models, through sharing of information and experiences. They shaped the views of women on how to integrate work and family obligations (Eccles, 2009) as well as the perception about their self. In the context of South Asia, women enter education and teaching initially with male support and not as contenders to men (Nair, 1988).

All these refer to the second stage in the ladder of school leadership of women, 'Aspire'. It conveys the personal ambition of women to become a school leader that is deeply influenced by significant others who are parents. Thus, family plays a crucial role in building and shaping the future goals of women to take up leadership positions in the school. It is especially visible in case of younger women working as teachers in government schools. This stage is one of collective efforts put together by parents, the woman aspirant. For the younger women, aspiring to become a school head is also intertwined with negotiating multiple roles and identities. By contrast, for older women, it turned out to be a means of self-actualization, having already negotiated and settled with multiple roles, expectations and identities. So, family is a vital structure that shapes the aspiration of women to become school leaders.

Ladder Step 3: Acquire (Related Theme: Familial Support—Parents and Husband)

The emergent theme related to 'familial support from parents and husband' deals largely with the third step in the ladder—acquire.

Narratives implying to the same indicate multiple ways through which family lends its support for the women to acquire school leadership positions as head mistress or principal.

In India, many women perceive that support from husband is crucial for their career. On a number of occasions, conversations during focused interviews invariably referred to professional support, emotional support, cooperation and encouragement provided by their husbands. It also indicated the extent of husband's influence in shaping women's career as school heads. Nature of support varied significantly from person to person. It included identifying the strengths of their wives, taking personal interest to guide the wife to get the school head's job, support by lending help in the household chores and provide free time to prepare for the competitive examinations by accommodating for the demands of household work and also encourage wife to take up career after a certain level of stability is achieved in the family life as the children grow up. Some instances narrated by women reflect these aspects:

> I was always good at studies ... my husband encouraged me to take up public service commission (PSC) exam for Grade 1 officer's post. He got the application form, filled it online, bought a smart phone for me and taught me how to use the phone, etc.
>
> Having completed most of my family responsibilities, with children grown up, I am now able to focus on my career and profession. I was working in a private school near my home till recently. I got selected as HM in Arohi model schools in Haryana government. My husband always supported me.

Some women even attributed their success as leaders even to their maid servants. One of the principals from Delhi said, 'we are able to perform well because of the support from family, husband and maid servants'. A couple from Madhya Pradesh considered their profession as 'projects of their life' and considered these projects as their 'children'. The woman who is working as a principal in Bhopal explained:

> My husband said, our projects are our children—your work in the school, my computer business and supporting your three sisters in their education, marriage and employment.

Continuing she said:

> My husband gave me the mental stamina. Before marriage, I was a very serious person He taught me how to laugh and also enjoy (relax) in life.

In some cases, women may also have to support the husband rather than expecting support from husband. The school head from Rajasthan supported her unemployed husband to complete graduation, obtain a teaching degree and secure a teaching job in the government school. The support which she can get from her husband is ferrying her to district education office in the evening whenever there is work and taking care of children. The source of steady family income was from her job in case of another HM from Madhya Pradesh, as her husband was a political party worker and pursued a part-time career as an agent for a life insurance company. In an extreme case, woman cluster-school head from Himachal Pradesh had to negotiate with her husband. He resisted strongly for a prolonged period regarding her desire to study for a BA degree.

Women in Telangana felt that teaching in schools is a 'family friendly profession' that is suitable for 'ladies'. Most of them got married at a very young age of 16 or 18 years while studying in schools. So, emotional and psychological support from their husbands was crucial whom they looked upon as elderly person having the ability to guide them as they were young. So, they treated husbands as superior than themselves. For them, if their husbands are in a teaching profession, they should be a college/university level, which is socially considered higher to that of teaching in schools. As wives, they preferred to work in elementary or secondary schools. They were also content with comparatively lower or lesser aspirations than their husband's. They also felt that professions such as medicine, demanding more time outside the family, is difficult for ladies to pursue as their primary responsibility is running the family. Blackmore (1999) interprets this kind of scenario as the tension between being a 'good woman' and a 'good leader'. One of them described which also reflected the sentiments of others in the group:

> \When I got married, I was only 16 years old ... 'saar' (that is, husband) encouraged me to continue studies. I completed graduation. By then, I had

two children. Later, I completed D.Ed. (that is, D.El.Ed). I got teacher's job. Both my parents and in-laws supported me after marriage in my studies. But, mainly because of my husband, I was able to complete my study.

Challenges were multi-dimensional for younger school heads working amidst older teachers. When preparing for the examination and/or in their new posting as Grade I officers, they faced pseudo threats, unnecessary interference and even external pressure from their colleagues in the school. Being younger and with small kids, some women had to struggle more than others. Some of these quotes indicate the resistance women faced:

> The head master in the school always used to say that I cannot pass the exam. He repeatedly said that I should not join as HM because I cannot work (efficiently); my family life would be ruined; I cannot pass the examination, cannot face the stiff competition to work as headmistress, (having failed to work) ... I cannot come back to teacher's post. He also predicted that I will not get the posting in my native town despite the fact that there is a rule in the state government which states that women must be posted in the town where their husbands' work/reside. I passed the exam, I was posted in Paalan which is in Bikaner—my husband's native place. He could not do anything later.

Another woman HM said: 'I passed ten government examinations and also got selected in all of them. But I chose teaching profession and became a HM'. Women principals from Delhi proudly announced that they passed the examination conducted by UPSC to become principals. They also announced their names with a prefix I am 'Dr ...', indicating that they hold PhD degrees too.

Nonetheless, the manner in which women utilized their merits and faced challenges in acquiring the leadership position showed another facet of women leaders. Women from Delhi, Rajasthan and Haryana achieved school leadership position through direct recruitment conducted by the state PSC. Acquiring a school leadership position meant an important milestone achieved with a sense of self-worth, recognition and pride for these women. For women from Madhya Pradesh, Telangana, Uttar Pradesh, Himachal Pradesh and Sikkim, acquiring school leadership position was through seniority-based promotion. However, the fact that they are members of state resource groups for several quality improvement programmes including the present school leadership development (during which time they were interviewed) proves the fact that they made a difference to schooling processes. While some of them had an opportunity to face the open competition as they could appear for PSC's examination conducted in their states, others had to wait for the opportunity that came through promotion based on seniority as per rules. Nonetheless, they were also ready to be relocated to rural areas/towns/cities to pursue their dreams. A few others had to wait long to enter the system because they had to fulfil the family responsibilities of bringing up the children and managing the family and fulfil other expectations, roles and responsibilities of married life.

Acquiring the school leadership position, therefore, is a combination of making choices, complying with obligations and compulsions, seeking opportunities and prioritize or balancing between family roles and career responsibilities. In and through these conflicting expectations and responsibilities, women negotiated their roles diligently and navigated their way to attain leadership positions as school heads. This is the third step in the ladder—Acquire.

Ladder Step 4—Achieve (Related Theme: Balancing Resilience with Determination; Gender: Is It a Notion or an Experience)

Young school heads had to work harder amidst older teachers in their new posting as Officer Grade I HMs. The senior teachers challenge the capabilities of these younger school heads and sometimes even pose pseudo threats, interfere with the works of the women school head, attempt to overpower, exert pressure through external political connections and question the authority of the school head. Being younger in age and having to look after small kids, some women struggled more than others. Especially during this crucial juncture, parental support was crucial for them to support with child care and give emotional strength to strike a balance between work and life. While parents filled this space, husbands did not fall behind. Underneath the challenges they faced in the workplace as young women teachers preparing to take up the state's PSC examination, there was a strong ambition to grow professionally and excel as leaders.

The male predecessors may also add to the difficulties for the new women HMs. Some of them even resisted the women HM to perform even her routine duties and responsibilities. These duties especially referred to taking rounds in the school, visiting classrooms for observations, applying certain rules in the school and so on. To avoid such situations, women felt comfortable to act according to rules and adhere to rules. Women HMs developed their confidence using rules. They interpreted the use of rules as having dual role of working efficiently and use it as a safety net in the workplace. This is reflected in the experience shared by the school head from Rajasthan:

> The only male teacher (who is also blind) in the school also hails from the same village. He complained to the elected Member of Legislative Assembly (MLA). The MLA sent a word to see him. I answered (silenced) him suitably ('*maine usko dhamki de diya*'). The blind man also complained to the district education officer. I was even called to give explanation by the office. But nobody could do anything to me. I act according to rules.

By contrast, women principals from Delhi opinion that some officers in the education department do recognize merit rather than gender. They also create opportunities for those who are willing to work beyond their prescribed roles, who are willing to exploit their knowledge, skills and experience to excel and deliver results. According to them, recognition also comes quickly for those who work hard and they also soon become leaders. Women school heads considered it as an encouragement and reward. One of them even said, 'It is not about gender bias. I worked in a boys' school as principal and most of the teachers were men'.

Many a times, challenges are neither uniform for all women leaders nor specific only to women. They may be outside the control of school head situated in the social, cultural and economic contexts of the community. For example, girls dropping out of school due to child marriage in Rajasthan, poverty affecting the attendance and participation of children in the school adversely or non-cooperation of a dominant community in Madhya Pradesh. The manner in which women perceived and addressed these challenges is greatly influenced by the confidence arising from the professional competence and one's own gender notions. So, leadership of women school heads is a combination of professional competence, confidence, understanding the gender stereotypes in its perspective to suitably address and also questioning their own assumptions on gender stereotypes, which are acquired during their life course. The significance of determination is visible in the form of achieving headship in secondary or senior secondary schools. By contrast, resilience is evident, which is expressed in the form of sustaining themselves in the headship position by working hard, exercising grit and will, accommodating and adjusting to the changing needs and circumstances and not losing their core identity as leaders and heads of institutions. Women school head from Rajasthan narrated her experience indicating these nuances:

> When I joined the school as HM after passing the public service commission's officer Grade 1 examination, many said to me that it's not a good school as jat community lives there who indulge in fighting. 'Woh ladhai karte rahete hain aur kutch nahi hotaa hai'. I was the youngest of all teachers when I joined there as HM. The male teachers who hailed from the same village even suggested that I take a transfer to a different school in another village as I am too young to handle the responsibility. When I wanted to take rounds in the school, they used to say, 'you take rest'. When there is any little problem they said, 'you go home, we will take care'.

Nevertheless, the experiences of women, especially regarding gender discrimination and gender-based biases, were varied. While some women strongly experienced these, a few others did not. For example, a woman HM responded to the question related to gender discrimination as 'What is there to experience gender bias when the work is the same for both men and women? It is defined by the roles, responsibilities and job chart issued by the department. It is same for all'. Another said: 'There is no problem at all'. While listening to one of the HM's description about gender discrimination in the workplace, another HM reacted in a low voice, 'Being young she feels it more. It is also to do with age and maturity. Actually, there is not so much gender bias as she describes. It is also to do with her perception'. Principals from Delhi rejected the idea that there is any gender bias and even reiterated that education officers prefer women over men for higher responsibilities.

Some women preferred to avoid confrontation with male officers. The degree to which these tensions were experienced also varied from acute to none from person to person and across states. Some preferred to ignore as they worked their way without much expectations from their male colleagues and officers. A few others preferred to remain silent during the visit of male officers for the fear that these officers may issue notices against them. Many of them felt that the male officers are heavily influenced by the patriarchy, which is a difficult barrier to accept in the workplace. The subtle mindsets prevailing in the department was captured by one of the respondents:

> We cannot contact the DEO even in case of emergency. If it is a women HM, they want to put pressure and give more work and try to put us in a troubled situation, thinking 'What can these women do?'

Men colleague teachers in Rajasthan and SMC member in Madhya Pradesh have even filed complaints with the District Education Officer against the women school heads. A woman school head in Rajasthan expressed her anguish and helplessness about not being able to prevent child marriage in the village where she works:

> We (women) have difficulties men do not face ... Juggling between home, school, community, officers ... men have more mobility, freedom ... they can also engage in social work ... we cannot.

In addition, the parental support extended beyond getting employment as teachers in case of a few women is immense. They inspired and supported their daughters even after marriage to cope with changes in life's circumstances, which was amply recognized by younger women who passed the competitive examination to become HMs at a young age. One of them echoed what most women felt deeply from within: 'We are able to perform well because of the support of our parents, husbands and maids'.

Achieve is a stage in the life of women who strives hard to establish as a leader in the initial stages of their career as a school head. They are in the process of becoming school leaders, having to encounter resistances, gender stereotypes and patriarchy, which is somewhat different from what they faced as teachers. Responding to situations with caution and diligence, they negotiate various challenging circumstances, asserting oneself in case of tough situations, or exercise resilience wherever feasible with an explicit attitude of 'all is well'. They also refuse to recognize tensions, explicitly reiterating that there is no problem in achieving their goals. So, they mostly prefer to work silently, prove positively, neutralize sensitive situations which conflict and depoliticize complexity to defuse tensions. For this, they create a safety net of shadow neutrality. Yet, they do not shy away from problematizing a situation wherever possible to effectively negotiate to reach their goals and seek greater acceptance from colleagues and higher officials. Amidst all these, they continue to face implicit or explicit tension while trying to balance between realizing their personal goals and fulfilling the expectations and obligations on the family front. It amounts to balancing between determination and resilience in climbing the fourth step in the ladder—'Achieve'.

Ladder Step 5: Ascend (Related Theme: Leading School Administration, Management and Academic Functions)

The core functions of the school head lie in efficient school administration, resource management and academic leadership, which constitute the core functions of school leadership in any school. Decision-making is a critical component in school's administration. A popular perception generally prevailing among all school heads in general and women school heads in particular is that efficient leadership is to correctly follow rules and regulations, execute orders and follow circulars received from their officers. Nonetheless, these women also preferred to be diligent when they had to act independently by exploring alternate possibilities for making correct choices to make decisions and exercise authority. In higher primary schools, women principals had the responsibility to balance to ensure cordiality between teachers working at elementary and secondary levels. While practising transparency, they were also tactful and tacit as they emphasized their teachers to stay on in the school for full time, teach all classes as per the time table and ensure that syllabus is completed on time for all classes. Many of them also voiced that there is a critical difference in the functioning style between men and women school heads. Accordingly, they perceived that women spend more time on the in-school processes by being physically present in the school, whereas men spend more time lobbying and networking in block and district offices. All of them concurred on one aspect that is distinct to women school: women are more focused and emphasize the academic aspects of schooling such as students' achievement, punctuality of teachers and their teaching in the classroom.

Popular approaches which women respondents mentioned include relationship building with colleagues, mothering, caring and nurturing functions, especially in respect of children, role modelling, influencing and good planning. Their responses indicated the spontaneity and uniqueness in their approach to create a cordial relationship among colleagues. One of them said, 'I even 'cook-up' stories to stop the clashes between teachers in primary and high school sections'. She continued, 'when I am caught in the arguments of between two factions of teachers in the school, I cook-up stories to convince both the parties and resolve the problem. It works effectively!!!' Another teacher working in purely girls' school in rural areas emphasized the importance of women school head: 'yes, especially in girls' school, girls get influenced by us (*ladkiyan prabhavit hoti hain*), ... even if it is a co-educational school, we can influence boys too'. By contrast, the dynamics of managing people in an urban coeducation school in Delhi was aptly explained by another woman respondent who managed one such school earlier:

> If you are a principal in a co-educational school, you have to be more tactful. It is important to keep in mind the psychology of the men while working with them. They are generally more vigilant. They observe keenly than women teachers. Once convinced, they fully cooperate with women principal and respect her. They also go out of their way to help. They learnt that they cannot fool me.

Most of the women interviewed were successful in ensuring that at least 70 per cent of students score first class marks in X standard board examinations. Women school heads also perceive themselves to be more sincere and hardworking than their men counterparts. Another woman expressed the manner in which they used diligence and diplomacy: 'though we do not like to impose, we have to project ourselves in that way to get the work done'. While taking decisions, they adopted different approaches such as compromise, issue circulars or enforce order as well as exercise caution in executing administrative and management duties. It was echoed by the principal from Rajasthan as '*shant hote hein*... (peace prevails ...)'. A principal from an urban school in Bhopal said, 'I use the knowledge based on the experience that I have got'. This principal is trying to express that knowledge arising out of experience works better in the workplace than those in the books.

Parents continued to inspire and support their daughters even after marriage in coping and recasting certain lifestyles by providing guidance in family matters, on emotional issues in the family and so on. At times, it extends beyond to lend professional support in taking decisions, address challenges on how to apply rules in apt ways, etc. that range from simple advice to technical guidance. This is expressed in diverse ways, indicating the different approaches women adopt. One of the HM from Haryana expressed the support sought from family as 'I discuss with my husband to assess the issues and then take a decision'. Another women HM succinctly narrated her method of taking decision:

> I do not take decisions hurriedly. I cannot be influenced by others. I discuss with all. I will explore for correct choices before taking a decision. Knowledge makes a difference [here]. If there is knowledge, then there is no problem [whatsoever]. I consult my father before taking critical decisions in the school. He understands the government rules very well. If he does not, he will inquire with his friends, search the internet and helps me in the decision-making process with school's matters. I also talk to BEO and take him in to confidence before giving my decision to teachers.

The principal from Uttar Pradesh explained her approach to decision-making or in addressing challenges:

> The whole family is in education (teaching profession). All of us discuss freely when we take dinner together in the night. We learn how to resolve matters by discussing, suggesting and supporting each other.

Women school heads stayed in the school full time and beyond school hours to complete the task. They carried out different tasks including teaching students, observing teaching–learning processes, establishing required contacts with community, encouraging teachers for teaching effectively, improving the student learning and so on.

On the aspect of facing the gender stereotype behaviours and discrimination, some women did not choose to alter or question them directly, especially in the workplace even though they understood the apathy. Nonetheless, three approaches were largely seen to be adopted to indirectly address the helplessness they faced in the workplace. First, women school heads relied on the support from family, especially parents and husbands. Second, they did not expect support from the leadership above. Third, they also accepted the school leadership positions with its systemic constraints and had very little expectations. Fourth, they negotiated between family compulsions and workplace expectations to fulfil their duties. Fifth, they tried to avoid any kind of confrontations with male officers to circumvent the difficulties in facing strong patriarchal mind sets.

By contrast, a few others attempted to alter the gendered practices by working with a positive approach to neutralize its adverse effects. These approaches include different ways in which they increased their visibility, shifting the focus away from the impediments of gendered practices and discrimination and suitably positioning the achievements in front of higher officials and getting leadership responsibilities beyond schools at zonal levels to conduct mega events in sports, cultural and literary activities. These women did not expect or seek much support from family members. Instead, the extent of independence enjoyed in the family mattered more for them for accomplishing their personal aspirations in the profession. Here, modernity that these women cultivated, educational and social contexts of the family and such other related factors played a crucial role in developing the ability among these women to grow as independent individuals. These observations receive greater impetus through Nair's study (1998)—there is more upward mobility and egalitarian outlook as well as higher occupational role commitment among secondary school principals.

The tensions which the women school heads experienced varied significantly. For example, Rajasthan's HM defended herself against allegations made to the local MLA by a teacher working in her school. By contrast, she was silent in front of male officers for the fear of notice that may be issued against her. However, situation need not necessarily be anti-women always and everywhere. Male officers can be friendly and cooperative too according to women principals in Delhi, Sikkim and Madhya Pradesh. All these emotions can even be surface acting to maintain emotions and acting out certain emotions may lead to unexpected outcomes too (Zammuner & Galli, 2005, p. 356).

The question that comes is: Is that all about school leadership of women—the experience of gender biases, discrimination, neglect, fear, frustration, seek support from parents and husband and so on? Or is there something beyond giving a meaning to their work and enriching them as leaders? It is aptly reflected in the responses of few women HM who tried to move beyond to establish themselves as leaders. Some instances discussed earlier amply indicate the ability of women to act as leaders and work on their own to navigate challenges successfully. These include the following: the way HM faced boldly when she had to meet the local MLA due to a complaint given by her male colleague to the MLA in Rajasthan; circumventing men teachers who tried to stop from doing work in case of another HM from the same state; and facing the open confrontations with community effectively in an urban school in a religiously sensitive area of urban Bhopal. In Delhi, women school heads also exploited their knowledge, skills and experience to performer higher. Therefore, self-efficacy comes from forge together performance accomplishments, verbal persuasion, vicarious learning and psychological states (Lent, Brown, & Hackett, 2002). Women also cope with 'routine stress' more quickly and defuse conflicts by not displaying anger (Ozga, 1993). These women leaders conspicuously exercise their agency, which was echoed by principals from Delhi: 'That's the privilege we enjoy ... we don't mind working a little extra'. Nevertheless, it is not only about how women perceive their role but also the gender stereotype contexts within which they work. Men in urban areas may be less stereotyped and more egalitarian in their approach towards women colleagues than those in the traditional regions. It may also be due to goal orientation of women leaders that influence the approach of men colleagues towards their women counterparts.

All these refer to the fifth step in the ladder for women leaders—Ascend. Crossing the threshold level, women excel and achieve their personal vision as leaders to move up the ladder of leadership. As school leaders, these women cross the professional barriers and systemic constraints besides meeting the demands of multiple roles. They amply exhibit a readiness to take up greater challenges and ignore gender biases. Due to the intellectual capital in the family, core professional competencies and people-centred approach, most of these women neither encourage patriarchy nor succumb to status quo that is veiled beneath the women's employment. Leadership values of these women school leaders differ from that of the fourth stage 'achieve' wherein women are yet to cross over the threshold levels of socio-cultural barriers. So, leadership in the fifth stage, that is, ascend, is about taking a stand between opposing forces: asserting merit over gender-based choice, address covert and overt gendered practices cautiously, excel by raising the bar, exhibit confidence and maximize the different capitals that are inherited and acquired—social, cultural, financial and intellectual.

Ladder Step 6: Transcend (Themes: Zeal Beyond School Leadership, Irrespective of Gender)

Despite gender notions and challenges faced, merits reaped and social mobility enjoyed, something more than leadership was also displayed by a rare few women. They considered leadership position as a means to fulfil a greater purpose in life. It made a significant difference to their leadership practice.

For the cluster-school head from Himachal Pradesh, teaching meant to serve the children in the remote hilly areas of the Himalayas. She gradually unfolded herself from earning for a living to serving the cause of education of children. She appealed: 'If you want to do social service, don't get married'. For her, the strongest support and inspiration came from an unimaginable source at a very young age. It was from her illiterate mother who asked her nine-year-old daughter to leave the home secretly and go to her maternal uncle's home to continue schooling. Her mother avoided the child marriage which her father was secretly planning. Now, she has grown to a stage where the marriage or divorce from marriage does not matter any longer. Years ago, her husband threatened to divorce her if she continued her studies. She expressed humorously, 'I completed my graduation along with my daughter. I waited for 22 years to do BA (Bachelor of Arts).... I got my BA degree in the same year when my daughter got her graduation. Now, I stay alone and serve children by giving my best for them to learn and do well in their life'. The wish to become a graduate could not be fulfilled for the entire prime period of her life and even lost its significance. But, it did not stop her from fulfilling the wish, aiming higher and being optimistic.

When she was transferred on promotion to Lahaul Spiti as cluster-school head, she accepted it even though it is situated at a height of 12,000 ft in Himalayas and cuts off from rest of the world for 6 months during winters. She decided to go to that place where men teachers hesitated to go. She freely hosts a number of children at her home during winter vacation and gives intense training to prepare them to appear for entrance examination to get admission in Navodaya Vidyalaya Schools. Navodaya Vidyalaya schools are those which identify meritorious children from rural areas and provide higher quality education. She cooks for them, washes their clothes, gives them hot water for bath, beds to sleep, etc. Throughout the day, she ensures that children are continuously engaged in studying for the entrance examination. At least five to six children get admission every year under her guidance. She also invites anybody who has some free time to teach children. Her daughter who is studying in Shimla comes home and teaches these children during the weekends. The HM even developed a unique method of teaching alphabets to children with special needs through dance. She emerged as a successful school leader in Lahaul Spiti.

Another woman leader living on the other side of the Himalayas in Sikkim voiced similarly: 'If you love children and love teaching them, then, don't get married. You cannot give your full once you get married, so many explanations are asked by the husband, in-laws, relatives, despite knowing who you are'. She used to wake up in the morning seeing the school building and its garden. Her house is open to children all through the day and even during weekends. She spent her evening with children, nurturing the school garden and visiting the houses of the children regularly to ensure that they attend school. She adopted effective disaster management techniques in the school after the earthquake hit Nepal and India in 2011 and continued the functioning of the school quickly. She was given best teacher award later.

A different dimension to the zeal was visible from the Delhi school principal when she shared her experience leading the school for nearly 20 years.

> I went on working ... did not think about whether I am a woman or man, nor did I see my teachers as women or men. I worked mostly with men in the school management committee. I must think 'how should I talk as a woman leader? I was never conscious while working that I am a woman. The focus for me was the school, children and my teachers ... If you ask me what leadership is, I cannot tell (articulate) ... But if only you ask me how to run a school where all teachers learn, teach and students learn ... how best to do, I can tell'.

In yet another case, the HM from Madhya Pradesh works in a school located in the area declared as communally sensitive by the district administration. She referred to her struggles in trying to balance between the majority Muslim community dominated by Urdu-speaking children and minority Hindus in a Hindi medium school. Juggling with non-cooperation of community members and power politics by a few male teachers who joined with the community are part of her everyday struggle. She refuses to take a transfer from this school as she feels that it is running away without facing the challenge to manage efficiently. She also admitted that the situation was not this bad three years ago. An elderly SMC member who is a Muslim took keen interest in the school's functioning. He supported the school by keeping away the miscreants till he was alive. After his death, things were not smooth for the principal. She even avoids a particular teacher from entering the (her) principal's room for signing in the morning register because of his harsh behaviour.

In a gesture of recognizing the advantages reaped by the education system in which women work, a principal from Delhi said, 'I do not have any complaints against the education system. It has given me immensely'. She was sent to the United States on Fulbright scholarship to undergo professional development programme by the government. So, school leadership was not a mediocre option left with for these women to pursue. Rather they gradually rose from being a teacher to excel as leaders moving beyond the system's limitations.

An incident that the cluster-school head from Himachal Pradesh narrated gives a clue about how women tried to ignore gender and orthodox stereotypes:

> When I was transferred to another village some years ago, people of the village asked me if I am a Brahmin. I said, 'yes, I am a Brahmin'. Really speaking, I am a Buddhist, and we do not have these castes in our religion. I told like that for the sake of children, otherwise they will not send children to school.

The woman principal from Madhya Pradesh working in communally sensitive area captured her transit from struggling like a warrior to winner as: 'Though I face a lot of challenges every day, school located in communally sensitive area, I have now begun to relax'.

> Smiling she said: 'I feel something missing ... a vacuum on the day when there is no problem ... if there is no quarrel, tension and struggle, there is no spice ... something has to be there ... (*kuch masala to hona padega*)'.

On a closer examination, it is evident that these women moved beyond considering themselves as leaders within the school. These women also experienced gender stereotypes and discrimination but did not allow them to affect their psyche. Even though they began like any others as teachers, they realized their strengths and ambitions to set clear goals for oneself to move up the ladder with a passion to pursue their dream despite knowing that it is not easy. It is the passion to teach children, create a culture of excellence and derive a sense of satisfaction and fulfilment by giving their best with a deeper commitment and intense engagement with the schooling processes. It cumulatively enhanced their confidence and conviction over the years through small successes achieved and inhibitions dropped. Working with conviction and passion together is a unique bending factor for these women. They translated these two factors into actions paving the way for a distinctness to think, act, face challenges and redefine the profession of teaching and school leadership not only for themselves but for greater good of the society. Leadership is not manifested in their talks nor is it fully possible to capture them in words. It is best understood by being with them, experiencing the deeper insights and moments of silence, ecstatic glimpses of the moments deeply felt and expressed through non-verbal gestures. Some of these women had no two facets for life—personal and professional. It was only one—to serve, to love and to nurture these children for learning.

The sixth step in the ladder, 'Transcend', is to consider school leadership as a means for rising to a higher realm of life with an attitude of service. It is an important phase in the life of women school head who gradually reached the goal irrespective of the different forms of capitals that their family possessed and offered them to use. These women gradually transformed from the position of school heads to visualize and interpret their leadership role as one which is meant to serve the cause of children's education. Thus, school structure serves as an important means to strengthen their agency to crossover the norm-based leadership effectively to mediate the constraints and challenges. Hence, transcend is a stage achieved even while facing the challenges and overcoming barriers, limitations in the form of deriving a sense of self-worth through leadership, achieving a sense of fulfilment and confidence having worked to one's satisfaction and respecting whatever opportunities are available to them. In other words, transcend is a stage when women surpass the boundaries of structures such as education system and family even when they are in it as school heads. These women apply the transformational leadership effectively in the school.

AGENCY OF WOMEN

All women school heads working in the government schools occupy designated positions against regular vacancies that is stable characterizing defined rules and responsibilities. It allows them in 'doing' leadership on a fairly regular basis for a longer time through diverse activities such as administration, teaching students, managing people and leading academic processes in the school. A long period of engagement on a regular basis enables them to develop a deeper understanding about the scope of school leadership and its meaning. This long-term engagement to lead schools not only develops an understanding but also changes or enhances their understanding from time to time. Further, it facilitated them to exercise agency. Nonetheless, this agency differed from woman to woman due to changing abilities and competence inherent and acquired by them, dynamic situations and contexts and their own internal motivation. Women expanded their knowledge of leading, skills of addressing risks and challenges, leading practices and the like by exploiting opportunities as well as challenges. They even utilized traditional practices covertly or overtly to reap advantages in improving school quality and student learning.

As indicated in the narratives, women effectively navigated the obstacles posed by orthodoxy, stereotype, and gender discrimination. They also effectively braced through the backlash vetted out by their colleagues, community members and/or education officers. Non-cooperation, resistance to accept change and inadequate cooperation were also navigated by these women especially in schools located in the traditional communities. Such instances were predominantly seen in Rajasthan, Uttar Pradesh and Madhya Pradesh. A few among them are presented here which also include challenges converted into opportunities:

> The charge as principal of the school was not handed to woman principal by her male colleague in Uttar Pradesh for more than a year. Even the higher officers did not resolve the issue. A time came when she felt that she should assert silently and continue to work to prove herself. She prepared her students to participate in INSPIRE awards and made them participate in district level competitions. Her students won the prizes too. She continued her silent yet a positive protest by improving students' pass percentage in the school.
>
> Similarly, the principal working in the school located in urban Bhopal endured the tension on a daily basis that is communally sensitive in the

vicinity of her school. She converted this extremely challenging situation into positive pressure for achieving good results in the school. Her school performs high as nearly 60 per cent to 70 per cent of students pass with first class in X standard board examination.

The two HMs from Haryana passed the examination conducted by MHRD to appoint head master/head mistress posts to model schools. They transited from working in small private schools as teachers to school heads in model government schools. However, they reached this stage after achieving a certain stability in life. All through, they had to continuously balance between family obligations and job. As HMs, one of them sought the support from community whenever required whereas the other took the Block Education officer into confidence whenever she had to take a decision and act. In this way, both of them tried to negotiate through challenging situations.

A HM from Delhi strongly believed in demonstrating oneself as a role model. She quoted an incidence from her experience. She was appointed as principal in a boys' school where most of the teachers were men and very few women teachers. She was acutely aware of the dynamics of men teachers who observe first before getting convinced with the leadership of the principal. However, she was able to convince them effectively by building trust. The trust developed between them was so strong that even after she was transferred to another school, she took the help of these men teachers whenever required. This kind of mutual reciprocity to build trust developed more confidence in her about her own leadership abilities and she adapted them in different schools wherever she was transferred.

Women traversed their way as school leaders from seeking parental and family support to becoming self-reliant; from discovering their strengths to exploring new opportunities; and from being guided by significant others to choosing their own path to succeed as school leaders. In the process of traversing the leadership path, they also grew by changing their perspectives, knowledge, skills and abilities. Their socio-educational reality was constructed in a dynamic interaction between themselves as school leaders and members of family, education system and community.

The aspirations of women are influenced by their own internal motivation and external factors such as family, social and cultural context of the society. Also, orthodoxy, stereotype and gender biases may deeply affect them in their levels of awareness about their own stand as women and leaders in the school. They may even lack the ability to question these practices which work against them. Despite being aware, a few other women may not prefer to question these stereotypes and discrimination for maintaining harmony in the family. Some of these women also accept their role as subordinate to men in the family especially in decision-making processes regarding family. So, while they are leaders in the school, they need not necessarily be so in the family. Most of them may not be uncomfortable with regard to this dual role of leader and subordinate in different spaces leading to different identities and roles. They interpret it as a way of balancing between home and workplace and personal wishes and family obligations. In this way, even though they aspire for moving up in their professional career, they accept gender stereotypes and orthodoxy in the family.

The socio-cultural frameworks within which women seek support from husbands are also potential spaces for simultaneously perpetuating the mutually contradicting purposes such as patriarchy on one hand and women's career and professional advancement on the other. In short, the stage of 'achieve' is about balancing between determination and resilience, and examining gender stereotypes and discrimination to be notions in the mind or an experienced reality. Nevertheless, in and through the opposing forces operating socio-cultural and educational contexts, these women continued to focus on their professional development by way of enhancing their knowledge, improving the skills and introspecting the experiences gained over the years. The pace varied between these women mainly due to varying beliefs, values, inherent capacities and familial background and support which resulted in differing nature and pace of agency they exercised. The agency, thus, differed in its content, direction and power from person to person and from school to school. It gave raise to differential path trajectories for leading schools. This emerged as a 'ladder of school leadership for women' in the Indian context.

The present chapter has dealt in detail with the causal power of structures or the emergent property referring to the 'Whole'. The previous chapter on participation of women extends its analysis. Two other subsequent chapters dwell in-depth analysing the narratives presented necessary to delete as they are conceptually incoherent—determinants of school leadership of women; path traversed by women school heads to succeed as leaders; and legitimization of women as school leaders. Out of these three, determinants of school leadership and path of success constitute the key focus of discussion in the next chapter.

Determinants of School Leadership of Successful Women in India

CONCEPTUAL FRAMEWORK FOR STRUCTURE–AGENCY INTERACTION: THREEFOLD MATRICES

A detailed description of the conceptual framework that is developed for studying the interaction between structure and agency using several theoretical underpinnings is given first and then applied to the narratives presented in Chapter 4 for identifying the determinants of school leadership of successful women.

Capacity–Agency Relationship

Agency is a reflective and regulated thought, the skills at one's command and other tools of influence affecting the choice of and support to the selected course of action (Bandura, 1982 p. 1182). It refers to value-motivated actions of individuals in response to the environment that involves accommodation to existing rules and norms, but it is especially promising when it involves different forms of resistance to existing structures (Stromquist, 2015). Agency may be categorized into projective or practical evaluative agency (Emirbayer & Mische, 1998). Using projective agency, individuals reconfigure their existing understanding and action by inventing, orchestrating and pursuing a desired path for future, driving impetus from conflicts and challenges of social life instantiated through micro political dynamics to actualize their competing interests. Using practical evaluative agency, individuals make practical and normative judgements about alternatives and

Table 5.1 *Capacity–Agency Interaction to Study Structure and Agency Interaction*

Capacity ↓ Agency →	Projective agency	Practical evaluative agency
Fundamental human capacity	Fundamental human capacity with projective agency	Fundamental human capacity with practical evaluative agency
Domestic capacity	Domestic capacity with projective agency	Domestic capacity with practical evaluative agency

possible trajectories of action in response to emerging dilemmas, demands and ambiguities of evolving situations (ibid.).

Kriestiansen (2014) identifies two types of capacities for exercising agency, namely, fundamental human capacity and domain-specific capacity. The fundamental human capacity refers to self-reflectivity, initiating one's own action and consequently influencing one's own life. Domain-specific capacity refers to particular areas where the agency is operational such as profession. An agency may be a combination of fundamental human capacity with projective agency and/or practical evaluative agency. It may also be a combination of domain-specific capacity with projective and/or practical evaluative agency (Table 5.1).

Nature–Magnitude Relationship for Structure

Macro structures are fundamental structures situated farther from the school and hence considered distant to women school leader. Micro structures provide intimate support to the women school leaders. The meso structure is domestic, wherein school leadership is located situating between distant macro and micro structures (Everett & Charlton, 2014). Structures considered for study vary in the ascending order of its magnitude—micro, meso, exo, macro and chrono (Bronfenbrenner, 1994). Family is a micro structure. School is the meso structure, which is also the primary domestic structure close to the women. Community is also a domestic structure but mostly perceived as external to the school by women and hence exo

Table 5.2 *Relationship between Nature and Magnitude of Different Structures Influencing School Leadership*

Nature ↓ / Magnitude →	Chrono system	Macro system	Exo system	Meso system	Micro system
Distant fundamental structure Situated farther from school—chrono structure	Diversity in school contexts				
Distant fundamental structure Situated farther from school—macro structure		Education system			
Domestic distant structure Situated between macro and meso structures			Community		
Domestic primary structure Situated between macro and micro structures				School	
Intimate support structure Situated close to the individual—micro structures					Family

structure. Macro structure is the education structure, and diverse school contexts constitute the chrono structure, both of which are distant fundamental structures to the school. All these structures frame the experience of school leadership in which the agency of women as school leaders is exercised. Nature and magnitude of all these structures are closely related to each other and are central to the present study (Table 5.2).

Structure–Agency Interaction

The agency depends upon situational strength and opportunity for agency of the structure. Situational strength refers to explicit or implicit cues provided by external entities or structures having an impact on the agency. Opportunity for agency refers to loosely coupled options/ choices available within the structure. Situational strength explicating 'opportunity for agency' is the interaction between structure and agency (Kriestiansen, 2014). The interplay of agency and structure is of three types, namely, one of opposed to each other giving rise to structural determinism wherein structure determines the agency; dominance of agency over structure, giving rise to volunteerism wherein agency determines the structure; and structure and agency influence each other, and hence mediated (ibid.). Depending upon the nature of interaction between structure and agency, the determinants influencing the interaction can be deterministic, voluntary or mediated.

The conceptual framework to study the interaction between structure and agency is developed based on the three theoretical constructs interwoven into a single matrix incorporating the interaction process with the help of situational strength of the structure and opportunity for agency (Table 5.3). The determinants identified from the analysis are categorized into deterministic, mediated and voluntary. Table 5.3 forms the basis of analysing the fivefold interaction between different structures and agency of women for successful school leadership discussed in the section.

Procedure: Iterative

In analysing the data, each type of agency with explicit and implicit cues of a structure is juxtaposed to derive the opportunity for agency in terms of available choices or loosely coupled options leading to identifying the latent constructs or determinants. Several iterative steps described serially identify the different structures influencing the school leadership with one structure at a time vis-à-vis structure–agency interaction. Significant factors from the analytical description of qualitative data in each structure against a particular type of agency best explain the process of interaction positioned as explicit

Table 5.3 *Interaction between Structure and Agency for Identifying Determinants of School Leadership of Successful Women in the Indian Context*

Nested Structures Referring to Chrono, Macro, Exo, Meso and Micro Structures in Relation to Diversity in School Contexts, Education System, School, Community and Family, respectively

Structure-agency interaction	Situational strength of the structure		Opportunity for agency	
	Explicit cues in the structures having an impact on agency →	*Implicit cues in the structures having an impact on agency* →	*Loosely coupled options or available choices* →	*Determinants*
Fundamental human capacity with projective agency				Deterministic (D) Mediated (M) Voluntary (V)
Fundamental human capacity with practical evaluative agency				
Domain-specific projective agency				
Domain-specific practical evaluative agency				

cues to assess the situational strength of a structure for exercising the agency; from each of these explicit cues, implicit cues impacting the agency are derived to facilitate the situational strength of a structure vis-à-vis a particular type of agency of women school head and/or her family. Further, possible options or choices with respect to opportunity for agency related to the explicit and implicit cues are also derived followed by the situational strength along with its explicit and implicit factors and opportunity for agency together to logically deduce the latent constructs, which are nothing but the determinants. Depending on the comparative strengths of structure and agency factors in the interaction, the determinants are categorized as voluntary, mediated or deterministic.

STUDYING A FIVEFOLD STRUCTURE-AGENCY INTERACTION

The narratives suggest identification of five important structures within which agency of women interacts, namely, diversity in the school context, education system, family, school and community. The description of results presented here is based on the analysis carried out using Matrix 3.

Diversity in School Contexts and Agency of Women School Leaders

Schools which women lead are located in the different geographical contexts—difficult terrains of the interior ranges of the Himalayas and plain lands where there are both urban and rural areas. The communities in urban and rural areas that are economically poor in the context of schooling are considered under the present study in this book. School's social contexts are characterized predominantly by orthodoxy, gender stereotypes and communal sensitivity in Rajasthan, Madhya Pradesh and Telangana. In Himachal Pradesh and Sikkim situated in the Himalayas, extreme weather conditions and seismic zones influence schooling. Social context in Delhi, Uttar Pradesh and Haryana is characterized by a contrast of urban poverty and modernization. Accordingly, challenges also vary, influencing the school leadership behaviours.

In hilly regions, ensuring continuous availability of opportunity for schooling to all children is the primary challenge. Teachers face challenges of protecting the school's property, infrastructure and so on from natural calamities such as snowfall, heavy rains, landslides and long winters of 6 months when temperature dips to sub-zero levels. It calls for adopting disaster management techniques as a necessity besides ensuring access to communication and reaching out to support children and their families during uncertain times. This makes continuous maintenance of the schooling facilities critical. Women leaders from the Himalayan region work tirelessly to ensure that children do not miss any schooling opportunity. Being able to work under harsh weather condition assumes importance rather than competing for excellence. Notwithstanding this, schools in these regions excel in student learning outcomes when compared with many other states.

Challenges in schools located in the urban plains such as Bhopal, Haryana and Delhi differ significantly. These schools have adequate facilities, staff strength and sometimes more than adequate funds, as in Delhi. Pressure from parents to ensure that students get a higher percentage in Delhi's private schools is inevitable. Management also supports the principal to put the school on national and international maps. Tackling the communal tension within the close vicinity of the school is a perpetual challenge in one of Bhopal's urban government schools, compelling the principal to adopt a cautious approach, seeking police protection to insulate the school at times.

These diverse school contexts cause diverse challenges, which call for unique solutions; demand alertness and readiness on the part of the school head at all times; develop an ability to adapt, face challenges, exercise resilience and balance between contradicting situations; and bring determination to ensure safety for children. Changing circumstances demand school leadership of women to exercise immense confidence even when plans fall apart, provide inspiration to teachers and students and lead from the front. As a result, women develop situational leadership styles and proactive leadership behaviour that gradually pave way for maturing into a transformational leader. This was visible in case of women school heads from Himachal Pradesh, Sikkim, Madhya Pradesh and Delhi.

Efficient management of people and school administration in navigating the socio-cultural, economic and religious contexts is critical for women to succeed as leaders. The nature of interaction between contextual factors and the agency of women school head can alter the external situations, providing scope for women to change into a reflective practitioner and a meta-cognitive thinker. Reaching the stage of transformational leadership calls for transcending the limitations of the system as well as one's own psycho-social and professional barriers, shifting from being preventive to proactive as leaders. In the present study, it is found that dealing with the macro structure such as diversity of school contexts calls for capacities and skills moving beyond the specific domain of school leadership. Such skills are acquired while facing harsh climatic conditions and experiential learning. These are life skills whose scope is beyond school leadership. The abilities used to perform their roles in the schools are also not restricted to practicing school leadership alone. It requires maturity and understanding of the school context in its totality. The determinants of school leadership of successful women, therefore, are skills and abilities to practice situational leadership and gradually mature into a transformational leader, both of which are voluntary in nature (Table 5.4).

Education System and Agency of Women School Leaders

Various hierarchical leadership positions at school, cluster, block, district, state and national levels constitute the dynamic site for school leadership. Designated school leadership positions such as principal and vice-principal certainly exist in secondary and senior secondary school categories having classes from 1–10/12 standards or 6–10/12 with HM. These two together constitute only 5.3 per cent of the total schools in India. Head teacher's post exists in secondary schools having 1–10 standards or 6–10 standards, constituting 7.2 per cent of the total schools in the country. Put together in terms of school categories, their proportion is only 40 per cent. The remaining six school categories such as primary-only (1–5 standards), upper primary-only (6–8 standards), secondary-only (9–10 standards), higher secondary-only (11–12 standards), secondary and higher secondary (9–12 standards) and elementary schools (1–8 standards) account for 60 per cent of total schools. These are stand-alone school categories mostly without designated school leadership positions (refer to Chapter 3 for more details). So, the opportunity for school leadership positions is extremely limited for aspirants. Within this limited opportunity, it is a hard battle to win, especially for women. Most aspiring women encounter a lack of access to leadership positions rather than the rights to earn those (Cubillo & Brown, 2003).

In the recent times, competitive examinations conducted by the PSCs in different states select Grade I officers for the education system.

Table 5.4 *Interaction between Diversity in School Contexts (Chrono Structure) and Agency of Women School Head for Identifying Determinants of Successful School Leadership for Women*

Structure–agency interaction	Situational strength—explicit cues in diversity in school contexts ⟶	Situational strength—implicit cues in diversity in school contexts ⟶	Opportunity for agency—loosely coupled options or choices exercised ⟶	Determinants ⟶
Fundamental human capacity for projective agency				
	Ensure opportunity for schooling Ensuring school safety	Adaptability to challenging contexts and face challenges boldly	Leadership practised even when plans fall apart	Situational leadership skills and abilities (V)
Fundamental human capacity for practical evaluative agency	Navigating through social, cultural, economic and religious contexts of the community Insulate school from communal tension	Required resilience and/or exercising the determination at appropriate situations	Exercise confidence and preparedness; inspire teachers and students for achieving school quality and higher learning outcomes	Gradually mature into a transformational leader (V)
Domain-specific projective agency				
Domain-specific practical evaluative agency				

It provides an opportunity for aspirants to become school heads through direct recruitment at a younger age without waiting for a promotion that mostly coincides with the tenure of service due for retirement. The proportion of direct recruitment varies from 25 per cent to 50 per cent across different states (for more details, refer to Table 3.13 given in Chapter 3, p. 64). In Assam and West Bengal, though provision for 100 per cent direct recruitment is specified, it is difficult to practice. Sikkim adheres to interview to select school heads for all school categories. In states like Karnataka, those recruited directly for school leadership positions stay for a short time of 5 years or so, before moving on to other system-level administration and academic leadership positions.

The availability of opportunity for school leadership also depends upon sanctioned posts and vacancy existing in the education system. Women are prepared to relocate to distant places wherever the posting is made. For example, the cluster-school head in Himachal Pradesh relocated to Lahaul Spiti, a difficult terrain 12,000 ft high characterized by long snowy winters for 6 months and very short summers. To compete for school leadership position through open competition and skipping a few intermediary steps while teaching within the system without waiting for seniority is gaining popularity. Some of the women considered in this study belonging to Rajasthan, Haryana and Delhi accessed school leadership positions through the direct mode of recruitment. A school head from Rajasthan said, 'I failed when I wrote the exam first time ... I could not prepare well, I was newly married. I wrote again and passed the Grade I officer's exam'. Women from Delhi introduced themselves proudly as principals selected through UPSC's examination. In Madhya Pradesh and Himachal Pradesh, where only promotion policy for teachers is practiced, contribution and merit of teachers are supported by providing opportunities for training to become successful leaders.

Some leadership positions such as academic monitoring officers and project officers in SSA and RMSA[1] are parallel to that of school

---

[1] SSA—Sarva Shiksha Abhiyan; RMSA—Rashtriya Madhyamik Shiksha Abhiyan. These are flagship programmes for improving school education in India.

leadership positions in Andhra Pradesh and Telangana. Some prefer to work in these positions as they enjoy greater autonomy, flexibility, decision-making powers when compared with school head's position. These parallel leadership positions also give a sense of higher identity. It also depends on the aptitude and willingness to lead teaching and learning as a career choice, which is where domain-specific agency predominates along with fundamental human capacity. Women HMs directly recruited may even opt for lecturer positions in DIETs, CTEs or SCERTs[2] after a few years of service. Some of these are also parallel positions above school level in the system. After gaining experience and seniority, many of the directly recruited officers prefer to move into administrative positions having decision-making powers. Most women prefer to work in academic structures such as DIETs and SCERTs, as it provides scope for work–life balance, especially for the young directly recruited women.

The determinants of school leadership with respect to the education system structure are mostly deterministic in nature, as there is not much scope for change except to compete for the leadership position through open competition or wait for seniority-based promotion. Opting for parallel leadership positions depends on the willingness to be flexible, ability to make decisions, exercise powers—all of which depend on the availability of opportunity in these positions.

These women clearly understood that all their leadership roles are limited in nature predominantly characterized by following the rules and abiding by orders within the education system. At the same time, they do not forget the fact that the education system in which they work is an important source of identity even within their family because it empowers them. Education system serves as a means to diffuse conflicts and tensions arising from gender stereotypes, orthodoxies and gender-blind ways in one's own family. Probably this is what it implies when some women denied that there is gender bias or discrimination in the workplace. Instead, they highlighted the fact that women are preferred more as they work and deliver results. A

---

[2] DIET—District Institute of Education and Training; CTE—College of Teacher Education; SCERT—State Council for Educational Research and Training. These are prominent academic structures in India.

few others even referred to the rules that are same for all irrespective of gender. So they opined that they all have to do their duty and that there is no scope for gender bias! Thus, women would rather prefer to navigate through the deterministic nature of the system for ascending and sustaining in the leadership positions as it gives them a status to diffuse the impact of stereotype and orthodoxy.

Some women exercised their agency to circumvent the systemic limitations to the extent possible for them. They exploited the available opportunities that different structures offered to stand out as leaders and even cross the threshold levels of the leadership role to 'serve the cause' of children's education. The interaction between agency and education system structure creates a unique shift in some women leaders to develop confidence, self-awareness and the zeal to cross over the norm-based school leadership roles. These were observed in the case of women school leaders from the Himalayan regions of Himachal Pradesh and Sikkim, Delhi and principals working in the communally sensitive area of urban Bhopal in Madhya Pradesh (refer to Table 5.5).

It is obvious that interaction between the education system and agency of women requires a combination of both fundamental human capacity and/or domain-specific capacity along with projective and/or practical evaluative agency. It is a challenge to find school heads having both types of capacities and agencies, a higher order in the capacity–agency spectrum. This implies two things: one, achieving school leadership position is a huge challenge, demanding extraordinary capacities and skills on the part of the women; two, a magnitude of this kind of capacity–agency is disproportionately higher when compared with the expected role of school leadership. It disregards the capacity of women leaders by applying rigid rules, issuing circulars and orders to carry out duties. This mismatch between capacity–agency of the school head and duties to be carried out widens as the education system is dwarfed with rigidity, outdated cadre and service rules and inappropriate and under-qualified leaders at cluster and block levels just above the school. So, the very high order of capacity–agency combination which a woman brings with her when she enters the system is rendered useless, often goes unrecognized and even misrecognized sometimes. The mediated determinants obtained in this category of

Table 5.5 *Interaction between Education System (Macro Structure) and Agency of Women School Head for Identifying Determinants of Successful School Leadership for Women*

Structure–Agency Interaction	Situational strength—explicit cues in education system	Situational strength—implicit cues in education system	Opportunity for agency—coupled options or choices exercised	Opportunity for agency—loosely coupled options or choices exercised → Determinants
Fundamental human capacity for projective agency	Opportunity for school leadership	Availability of vacancy, sanctioned post	Search for information. Apply and compete for leadership position. Ready to relocate wherever leadership position is available/allocated	Provision and access to school leadership positions (D)
	Direct recruitment versus promotion for school leadership position on seniority basis	Ability to be a school leader versus duration of experience, leading to school leadership position	Compete to achieve the school leadership position rather than waiting to be pushed up by the education system after a prolonged wait	Core professional competence influencing the choice as a school leader (M)
	Parallel leadership positions in same cadre across SSA, RMSA, Department of Education	Availability of choices for a professional identity that is valued better than the position as a school head	Exercise personal autonomy in decision-making. Readiness and willingness to work to overcome challenges in the system	

Fundamental human capacity for practical evaluative agency			
Domain-specific projective agency			
Domain-specific practical evaluative agency	Choice of identity as a school head when parallel leadership positions in the same cadre available	Work allotment in the school by the education department as school head Departmental policy for transferring the school head to other parallel leadership positions	Preference for working in school or other leadership positions in the education system	Extent of willingness and aptitude to undertake academic leadership versus administrative and managerial leadership (M)

macro structure aptly indicate the efforts of the women to navigate the deterministic nature of the education system by focusing on their academic leadership skills, which are carried forward to school leadership from her earlier experience as teacher, a space where women mostly use their core competencies as leaders.

The important determinants of school leadership of successful women while interacting with education system are as follows: provision and access to school leadership positions, core professional competencies influencing the choice of school leadership and willingness and aptitude for practising academic leadership vis-à-vis administrative and managerial leadership.

Family and Agency of Women School Leaders

Family is an important structure that influences the school leadership of women through parental support that builds confidence, courage and perseverance in the women during the initial stages of her profession. Most of the women expressed their heartfelt appreciation for the support and guidance received from their parents who continue to do so even beyond the initial stages and after marriage. Some of them considered parents as role models. A-HM from Rajasthan began her conversation with a deep appreciation not only for her father but also grandfather and said that even her grandfather inspired and encouraged her to become a lecturer. Another remarked that she depends on her father, who is retired from government service, for technical guidance in the matters of school administration. A-HM from Haryana also said that her parents supported her fully and there was no compulsion for her to cook for all in the family when she was studying. In this way, parents took active interest in their daughters, getting them adequate formal education, guiding them in their profession, preparing them to achieve school leadership positions and suggesting methods to navigate gender biases and stereotypes built into the education system.

Besides parental support, the family's intellectual capital in the form of higher levels of formal education among parents and other family members served as an important source of inspiration for women. The requisite environment naturally prevails in the families for daughters to dream a career by observing their employed parents, developing skills and abilities to negotiate between different family roles, fulfilling expectations as daughters, daughters-in-law, wife, mother and professionals. Some of these women also reported that parents while searching alliance for their marriage discussed with the prospective grooms and his parents about the prospects of continuing the career even after marriage. Women also quoted instances of when parents refused to marry their daughters off into those families which were not open to accept an employed daughter-in-law. They acknowledged that husbands shared the family responsibility and actively engaged in shaping their career. In this way, women transit from being loved daughters to progressive wives, career seekers and professionals as school leaders supported actively by parents and husbands.

While these women continue to depend on parents for emotional and child care support after marriage, they also show a distinct shift in terms of increased levels of risk-taking behaviour to compete in acquiring school leadership positions and overcoming gender stereotypes related to workplace. They attribute it to their husband's support and professional guidance, especially for those who have come from semi-rural areas in Rajasthan, Telangana and Madhya Pradesh. They also learn to practice work–life balance and gain higher trust with other family members. A principal from Madhya Pradesh made an interesting observation about herself. She said that she began to relax after her marriage as her husband made her not to take tensions and feel strongly about anything in work or in life. She also said that both of them decided to support each other in their projects (meaning professions) and considered them as their own children. Delhi principals attributed their success not only to the support received from their husbands, parents and in-laws but also to their maid servants. The youngest of all school heads amongst interviewees from Rajasthan said, 'My husband even brought her the application form, personally filled it and encouraged her constantly to study and pass the exam to become a Grade I officer. After she became the head mistress, he also bought her a smartphone and taught her how to use it'. In most cases in India, husbands play a significant role in shaping the career of the women, especially in middle-class families that attach high value to government employment.

A continuous source of income, even if limited, is an accepted norm in the families of these women, parents and in-laws. Over time, there is an enhanced financial capital due to a regular source of income and savings. Women also develop their capabilities, skills and knowledge. Consequently, the agency of women school leaders also gains momentum steadily due to increased confidence. Therefore, the socio-economic context of the working middle-class orientation in the family significantly influences school leadership of women. It is powered by the family's intellectual capital, visualizing it not just limited to seeking a job or earning money but as an investment to life that facilitates one to access higher social class, acquire modernity, shape cultural climate in their homes and workplace and develop a deep sense of conviction to face life at large.

The preparation to take up the role as school professionals beginning with studying at the university level and during the initial stages of employment and career formation supported and guided by parents and husband stretching to mid-career phase as school heads is referred to as 'extended vocational anticipatory socialization' (Shenoy-Parker, 2014). In this endeavour, vocational anticipatory socialization, intellectual capital and family support provide the women with much-needed preparedness to assume leadership roles in schools by empowering them to ignore, face and overcome professional and gender-based challenges. Therefore, there is a collective aspiration in the family of the women who seek a career in school leadership. All these give rise to a unique bending factor positioned within the safety nets of the family to traverse the important trajectory in the life course of women as professionals working in school leadership positions in the Indian context.

The intellectual capital is an investment and a substratum of working middle-class orientation in the families. The support from parents and husband fructifies into vocational anticipatory socialization. These result in the emergence of determinants of family for the school leadership of women in the form of strong belief in one self, conviction to act, higher levels of preparedness for competing in job market and a career, greater access to information and knowledge and collective aspiration and collective ownership.

The agency of women leader manifests in the form of increased confidence to face the challenges, manage and lead schools, balance effectively between personal and professional life, interact and work with community, multi-task, undertake different leadership roles at zonal and district level competitions and so on. The agency also enables women to respond, negotiate and manage the demands of leadership roles and personal demands of family as a wife, mother and daughter-in-law with an increased sense of empowerment, self-awareness, adequate skills, knowledge and capabilities.

Two generalizations can be drawn with respect to interaction between family members as a structure and agency for school leadership of successful women. First, the fundamental human capacity within the family with projective agency of women and her family causes practical evaluative agency for the aspiring women and her family accompanied with fundamental human capacity for achieving school leadership positions. Second, the domain-specific projective agency of family is transformed into domain-specific practical evaluative agency for the women who receive vocational anticipatory socialization and its extension to aspire and achieve school leadership positions.

In conclusion, aspiring for the school leadership position is not solely an individual choice but a collective one involving parents and husband in India. Family members actively lend support, own up the responsibility to fulfil the women's aspirations and celebrate the success collectively as a family. This is precisely the process of interaction between family and the agency of women where aspiration is shaped, owned and achieved collectively by family members such as parents and husband rather than by the women alone in most cases. For this, intellectual capital in the family, vocational anticipatory socialization and the orientation of working middle-class act as positive catalysts to develop a strong belief in oneself, have the conviction to act, gain higher access to information and be better prepared to compete in the employment market. Women also exercise their choice of independence with diligence to sustain, strengthen and consolidate the support received from family members and strive to enhance the trust levels built with them (Table 5.6).

Table 5.6 *Interaction between Family (Micro Structure) and Agency of Women School Head for Identifying Determinants of Successful School Leadership for Women*

Structure–agency interaction	Situational strength—explicit cues in the family →	Situational strength—implicit cues in the family	Opportunity for agency—loosely coupled options or choices exercised →	→ Determinants
Fundamental human capacity for projective agency	Intellectual capital in the family as an investment for life	Ease of access to higher and professional education Provides an edge for accessing latest knowledge trends and nature of competition in the employment market	Discuss with family members Being open to information Exploring new options available in the employment market	Develops strong belief and conviction in oneself (M)
Fundamental human capacity for practical evaluative agency	Working middle-class orientation of the family	Encourage daughters to get government jobs that ensure stability in life Freedom of options for different types of professions and jobs before settling for a school leadership position	Strive to get a socially acceptable and respectful job preferably in the government sector	Higher levels of preparedness to compete in the employment market (M)
Domain-specific projective agency	Parents' support	Enable daughters to acquire the necessary qualification Prepare them gradually over time to acquire school leadership position	Create confidence and courage to face challenges and develop perseverance Act suitably to navigate through the gender biases	Collective aspiration and collective ownership of the family in shaping woman's career as a professional and a school leader (M)

		Understand the cultural and social roots regarding gender stereotypes in the education system's practices Guidance in school administration and decision-making		Depend on parents for child care support after the marriage
	Husband's support	Extended vocational anticipatory socialization Higher levels of risk taking Increased confidence Face gender biases and discrimination boldly to achieve school leadership position Succeed in accessing school leadership position		Making a late career choice Balance professional and personal roles between family and school Seek guidance on professional matters from the husband Exercise the choice of independence diligently at home for sustained support and enhance trust with all family members
Domain-specific practical evaluative agency	Vocational anticipatory socialization	Discuss formally and informally about the future course of action during and after the completion of graduation degree	Discuss openly with family members Learn to think judiciously about available possibilities Exercise measured risk and caution	Higher access to information and knowledge about employment (M) Preparedness for a life of career (M)

The determinants of school leadership of women interacting with family emerged from the analysis are as follows: developing a strong belief and conviction in oneself, higher levels of preparedness to compete in the employment market, collective aspiration and ownership of the family in shaping the women's career as a professional and a school leader, higher access to information and knowledge about employment and preparation for a career.

School and Agency of Women School Leaders

Women school leaders considered in this study are a heterogeneous group. Their heterogeneity is characterized by diverse social, cultural and economic backgrounds, ranging from first-generation learners to a history of at least two generations with an educational background in the family with obvious variations in their abilities and performance as leaders. It is reflected in their ability/struggle to manage with the male teachers and administrators, coping with resistance and limitation of personal strength, which sometimes compels them to manage alone. They also seek help from parents, husband, colleagues and higher officials, knowing and adhering to the rules while executing actions. These are some of the ways by which women lead administration and manage people and processes in the school.

As a group, these women heads also recognize that they are different in their views, abilities and approach to doing school leadership differently with a variety of ways and practices, which can be grouped into people-centred approach, improving teaching–learning environment, school administration and management, achieving excellence through good leadership and crossing the gendered barriers to move beyond education system's norm-based school leadership practice. These are discussed briefly in the following paragraphs. Also, refer to Table 5.7, which captures the interaction between school and agency of women using Table 5.3.

People-Centred Approach

Women, focusing on the nature, characteristics and potentials of the people, try to exploit their strengths and even accommodate

Table 5.7 Interaction between School (Meso Structure) and Agency of Women School Head for Identifying Determinants of Successful School Leadership for Women

Structure–agency interaction	Situational strength— explicit cues →	Situational Strength— implicit cues →	Opportunity for agency— exercising options/choice →	Determinants
Fundamental human capacity for projective agency	Balancing between professional and personal self	Derive strength from different roles for effective school leadership practice Develop a zeal to cross over norm-based leadership roles	Develop confidence Hard work	Adopt people-centred approach to leadership practice (V)
	Refuse to allow the effect of gender stereotypes, biases and discrimination on oneself	Negotiate between different family identities and school leadership Exercise flexibility to exploit the strength of agency	Develop dispassion towards gender biases and discrimination experienced	
	Develop the core professional competence as school head	Derive strength from performing different roles for effective school leadership practice The importance attached to child's education	Use the right technical knowledge for leading and decision-making in the school Negotiate between different roles and identities as a women, teacher, school head and colleague of senior teachers	Knowledge-driven decision-making in school administration and management (V) Academic leadership (V)
Fundamental human capacity for practical evaluative agency	Love for children Social service/service to society Teaching children is 'project of our life' Positive disregard for the negative notion of gender while working with teachers and staff	Conviction and passion for teaching profession	Think differently Act diligently Face challenges Rewrite the script of school leadership Develop self-awareness	Transcend the norm-based school leadership roles (V) Transformational leadership (V)

(*Continued*)

Table 5.7 *(Continued)*

Structure–agency interaction	Situational strength— explicit cues	Situational Strength— implicit cues	Opportunity for agency— exercising options/choice	Determinants
Domain-specific projective agency	Navigate between different structures	Explore the opportunities available between different structures to navigate challenges	Exercise flexibility to exploit the strength of agency	Objective assessment of the utilitarian value of conflicting roles in a given circumstance (M)
Domain-specific practical evaluative agency	Good school leadership practices	Accepting independent actions undertaken by colleagues, students and staff Rise above school leadership to leap into zonal-level leadership	Establish cooperation and trust between oneself as the school head, teachers, staff, students and SMC	Practice distributed leadership and/or shared leadership (M) Create an identity for the school (M)
	Relationship building	Ensure sustained support from colleagues Higher degree of cooperation from colleagues	Exploit the inherent abilities of caring and love for improving school climate Create harmony in the school	Integrate innate feminine qualities with professional roles to create a people-centred approach (V)
	Leading the school with right knowledge	Seek guidance from parents, higher officers and colleagues, ICT, etc.	Develop essential functional knowledge for effective school management and leadership	Knowledge driven Leadership Practice (M)

their weakness and challenge themselves to accomplish the role of school leadership, effectively. This is also extended to students. They show affection and care and listen to their problems. While they appreciate students' achievements and recognize their merit, women school heads do not forget to challenge these children to bring out their hidden talents, potentials and weaknesses. It helps the women heads to provide children with a congenial environment where all children feel safe and secure in the school. These constitute a people-centred approach to leadership practice. This was aptly captured by one of the respondents who said that children get immensely influenced by their HM. Children get influenced by what they do, how they behave as leaders and what they practice as leaders. Another said that it is easier for women to understand children more, primarily because of their motherhood. She thinks that women are better able to appreciate children, love them and show affection naturally as these come first, and they look into school-related issues later.

Improving Teaching–Learning Process

Women school heads indicate in their discussion about leadership roles carried out as spending additional time, personally engaging in classroom teaching and observing classroom teaching–learning process by navigating the resistance from colleagues who try to avoid them. Most of them said that they feel more confident in this role irrespective of getting support from colleagues and higher officials, as it is a familiar ground and also primary objective of school leadership. There is an increased sense of confidence having proved their worth as leaders by achieving results, especially in terms of students' pass percentage in 10th board examinations among them. Many of them said with satisfaction that more than 80 per cent of students pass in 10th standard board examination every year. Some of them even substitute for the lack of teachers in the school by teaching several extra classes. An apt expression by one of them that captures the essence of what they do is 'you need not know everything of what teachers are doing in each class, but, you must have the sense of how they are doing so that you are in control of the teaching–learning process of the entire school'. In this way, maximizing their core professional expertise enables women to establish their identity as school leaders.

School Management and Administration

Women emphasize acquiring right knowledge about rules, regulations, correctly interpret orders and circulars and translate the same into the schooling processes. In doing so, they exercise caution in making decisions, stay full time or even longer in the school to complete the tasks on time, gradually rise above the prescribed roles and responsibilities to exercise flexibility and gain confidence to assert their leadership as HoS. It was aptly captured by one of them as she said, 'Knowledge gives her strength that makes her not to succumb to anybody's opinion easily while making decisions'.

Achieving Excellence ... Leaping beyond the Threshold

School leadership for these women entails a process of change within as well as outside in the school that facilitates them to cross the glass-wall and glass-ceiling effects in the workplace. They have not only shared the power with SMC and teachers and convinced system functionaries, but have also attempted to change the very meaning of power and perception about women's leadership using gentle and hard powers, being passive and active, using persuasion and moral admonishment and caring and expediting the opportunity for agency. At times, agency superseded the structure, and at other times, structure superseded the agency. Some women leaders skilfully manoeuvred these shifts and demonstrated the zeal beyond the boundaries of school leadership to take up zonal-level leadership while working as principals in the schools. They operationalized agency by responding aptly and positioned themselves appropriately within the school structure as well as with other interdependent structures such as family and community. A sense of empowerment having surpassed the effect of gender bias experienced in the education system is echoed in their voice as a privilege they are enjoying and therefore they even do not mind working more, taking risks and working for a longer duration.

Crossing the Gendered Barriers

On a closer examination, these women school leaders focus on building good relationships, confidence among others, lead schools with right knowledge and increase one's own acceptance and acknowledgement of the independent actions undertaken by teachers, students and staff in the school to establish mutual trust towards strengthening their own school leadership practices. These initiatives have yielded results in gaining cooperation and steady support from colleagues in the school. Gradually these efforts have also transformed into shared and/or distributed leadership practice especially in large schools of Delhi. A principal from Delhi opined that being a role model to others as HM inspires and makes others follow her. She manages a school's strength of 2,500 children and 250 teaching and non-teaching staff. Earlier, she also served as a principal for five years in a senior secondary school for boys where there were more men teachers. Therefore, the success of leadership lies in integrating the agency of women to exploit her own inherent feminine qualities and abilities related to caring and establishing harmony with that of the professional role as school leader to create a people-centred approach and willingness to accept the challenges from colleagues, positively.

Zeal beyond Norms

The leadership in these women is not manifested in their talk nor is it fully possible to capture in words, here. It is best understood by being with them to get experiential insights to recognize the threshold levels of crossing beyond the norms-based school leadership roles and gender issues. The insight is that some women leaders had no two facets of life—professional and personal. It was only one and that is the cause of children's education. The cluster head teacher from Himachal Pradesh called it 'service to society'. The women principal from Bhopal referred to it as a 'project' of her life, a school head from Sikkim expressed it as 'love for children' and another principal did not think about gender differences at all while working amidst men while she went on working. This conviction and passion is a unique bending factor which only some women used effectively.

They translated it into actions with a distinctness to think differently, act diligently and face challenges to rewrite the script of leadership for themselves as school heads and also for the greater good. Only a rare few transcend the norm-based school leadership role solely because of the agency.

Negotiation and Navigation for School Leadership

School is the epicentre of all school leadership practices. The above analysis clearly reveals that women navigate through different structures while negotiating multiple roles and responsibilities. It is crucial in understanding the school leadership of successful women. Navigating between various structures refers to the efficiency with which the demands of the job at the workplace in the school vis-à-vis multiple roles and responsibilities as a family member are expected to be balanced to maintain an equilibrium. Negotiation implies the manner in which navigation is accomplished to effectively insulate oneself from meeting with failures as school leaders using the available support systems such as parents, family, husband and maids. These two act together, exploiting the opportunities available in different structures and meeting the demands arising from these structures to perform different roles in establishing an identity as a school leader. In so doing, they exercise choice and derive strength duly supported by the right technical knowledge on school leadership. An interlacing of negotiation and navigation efforts manifest as developing the ability for an objective assessment of different roles regarding their utilitarian values and making informed decisions to become successful school leaders.

For women to be a successful school leaders, both fundamental human capacity and domain-specific capacity are essential. Women have to be diligent in using these capacities, combining both projective and practical evaluative agencies. Striking an appropriate balance between having capacity and exercising agency for appropriate actions is the secret of successful school leadership for women. Leadership of successful women school heads interacting with school as a structure are as follows: adopting people-centred approach in practising leadership, knowledge-based decision-making in managing school, transcend norm-based school leadership roles, transformational leadership, objective assessment of utilitarian value of conflicting roles in a given situation, distributed leadership practice, integrate innate feminine qualities with professional roles to create people-centred approach, create an identity for the school and knowledge-driven leadership practice.

Community and Agency of Women School Leaders

Interaction of women school heads with the community varies from region to region depending on the educational, religious, geographic, socio-economic and cultural contexts. For example, in Rajasthan and Uttar Pradesh, communities are rich in socio-cultural moorings but weak with respect to educational, economic and political characteristics. In the National Capital Region belonging to Uttar Pradesh state from where two women school heads were considered for the study, there are adequate school facilities, and the economic and educational level of the community is also fairly higher. In the hilly regions, it is a mixed educational background, but mostly literate community with a greater exposure to modernization.

It is interesting to understand the underlying social dynamics in school–community relationships. The community in Himachal Pradesh was interested in knowing the background of the women school head, such as caste, whether married or not, religion before deciding to send their children to 'her' school: 'when I was transferred to a new village, the people wanted to know if I am a Brahmin. I said, yes, I am a Brahmin. Really speaking, I am a Buddhist, we do not have these castes.... But for the sake of the children I had to tell'. In Rajasthan, teachers consider the caste factors to understand the dynamics of the community's relationship with the school. The woman transferred to a new school was told by the teachers in the school that community is dominated by 'Jat', a caste that is perceived to be rough in nature and tough to handle by women, more so by one who belongs to the Brahmin caste.

The urban locality in old Bhopal in Madhya Pradesh is declared communally sensitive by district administration. The women principal working here is conscious of the community's religion, which is different from that of hers. While the community is predominantly Muslim, the women principal belongs to Hindu religion. She feels that after a prolonged duration of facing challenges and non-cooperation from the community on a day-to-day basis, she has also begun to relax in the recent times. She even joked about this change within herself as if there is no quarrel, there is no charm on that day (*maza nahi hai*). So, something has to be there (*kuchh masala toh hona padega*)!

The community is largely composed of poor and daily wage earners in rural Madhya Pradesh where the other woman HM works. She said there is very little to talk about community in her case as people are poor and they work in the field as labourers throughout the day. It is even difficult to expect them to be active in the school's affairs. They are passive in another urban school in Bhopal, Madhya Pradesh. In Rajasthan and Uttar Pradesh, the community lacks awareness about the importance of education for children due to illiteracy. It is a double disadvantage as a gender stereotype and orthodox practices such as child marriage is also high, resulting in girls dropping out of the school. By contrast, some male teachers even feared bold young girls who are from Rajput community in another school in Rajasthan. Sometimes, the community is also positive and supportive to school, as in the case of the school in Haryana.

These observations about community, however, are not static as women principals during the course of sharing their experiences also mentioned about the intermittent support received, inadequate facilities supplemented by the community's donations and support in repairs and maintenance of the school building. However, these mostly depend on the importance attached to education by the SMC members and trust established by the school head with the community. Sometimes, change in leadership in the community, that is, SMC, also causes changes in the nature of support to school received. The women school head working in a Muslim area acknowledged duly that things were working smoothly for her until the previous SMC president, who is also a Muslim, was alive. Troubles began only after his death. Another HM from Madhya Pradesh organized functions in the school and the entire village to participate to get closer to the community.

Largely, women school heads considered community as a distant structure unlike education system, school and family, which they considered as fundamental, primary and supportive, respectively. So, interaction between community and agency of women school head depends on mutual working relationship between school leader and community members as well as initiatives and abilities of the school head. In most cases, women in this study considered themselves stronger than the community.

Even though most women school heads attach a lot of importance to student learning, evidently they have yet not established adequate relationship with parents to ensure higher learning levels among children. Nevertheless, women did not wish to take risks, especially in sensitive situations. As a result, despite women's sincere attempt to use government schemes for all children in the school, achieving the goal of universal student learning is still a distant dream for many of them. This is because they cannot spend more time in meetings or during weekend holidays with colleagues and officials where as men gather informally to discuss matters related to the department, schools and school heads. All these have an effect on the functioning of SMCs. So, the interactive process between community and school is not a simple or a straightforward one. It is rather complex and encompasses a larger social, economic, religious, educational, political and geographical characteristics of the community as well as the ability and willingness of women school head to search for out-of-the-box solutions (Table 5.8).

By and large, most schools suffer from passive participation of the community, which has led women school heads to perceive community as a distant structure. They generally have minimum expectations from the community. The nature of determinants obtained indicate that all types of capacities and agencies of the women school head must be put to use for seeking coordination and establishing trust with the community to achieve the desired results for successful leadership. The

Table 5.8 Interaction between Community (Exo Structure) and Agency of Women School Head for Identifying Determinants of Successful School Leadership for Women

Structure–agency interaction	Situational strength— explicit cues	Situational strength— implicit cues	Opportunity for agency— exercising options/choice	Determinants
Fundamental human capacity for projective agency	Communal tension, poverty, illiteracy of the community	Create a protective mechanism and insulate the school from getting affected	Limited within the permission of the school's rules and norms for school head	Ability of and initiatives by school head to involve community in the schooling processes (M)
Fundamental human capacity for practical evaluative agency	Participation of the community members	Disinterest of the community, poverty, need-based participation or participate on invitation from the school	Organize programmes and functions and invite the entire community to participate	Understand the larger issues and needs of the community that is beyond fulfilling the needs of the school with the help of community (M)
Domain-specific Projective agency	Importance attached to child's education in the community	Utilize the available government schemes optimally to provide education to children in the school	Optimal use of schemes/ programmes for ensuring student learning by the school head	Direct all efforts towards achieving student learning outcomes (M)
Domain-specific practical evaluative agency	Weak working relationship with SMC, parents and community	Ineffective management and functioning of SMC— lack of regular meetings, non-participation of members	Interact frequently to establish working relationships with community	Building trust through good relationships (M)

capacities and agency in interacting with the community for schooling processes need to be mediated through community characteristics. The mediation required for interacting with the community is an important indicator of the fact that school is meant for the community. So, the role of a school head is crucial in bringing the community nearer to the school.

Women leaders have an advantage of using their feminine leadership qualities and yet being cognizant of the fact that gender stereotypes and orthodox practices would pose a challenge in the success of their efforts. They can overcome these challenges by being more empathetic to the community's needs and expectations rather than expecting help and support from the community at least in the initial stages. This particular shift in the attitudes is necessary to be inculcated among all schools irrespective of men or women school heads because it is often heard from school heads that there is no interest in the community for the schooling of children. It remains a perpetual challenge if school heads do not seek to understand the larger perspective of the community and restrict only to work within the school as both community and school require each other. Women leaders from Himachal Pradesh and Sikkim in this study have moved out of the comfort zone of school to interact with the community.

Determinants of school leadership of successful women interacting with community are mediated referring to the ability and initiatives to involve community in the schooling processes, understanding the larger issues and needs of the community beyond their role to involve in the schooling process, direct all efforts towards achieving student learning outcomes and building trust through good relationships.

TRACING THE PATH OF SCHOOL LEADERSHIP OF WOMEN

Using sociological theories, interaction between structure and agency is studied by applying two sets of dimensions: capacity and agency of individuals; and nature and magnitude of structures to identify the determinants of a successful leadership in the Indian context. What gets revealed through these results are not determinants per se, but the process of interaction between different structures and agency for school leadership of women that maps the path traversed for success.

Mapping of the path is now traced with the help of leadership behaviours. Leadership is about drivers of human behaviour, namely, universal and culturally congruent (Richard, Dhanaraj, Javindan, & Zhang, 2015). Universal human behaviours for leadership are charismatic, value-based and transformational. Culturally congruent behaviour is about culturally endorsed leadership wherein societal expectation strongly predicts leadership styles. Leadership behaviour can also be either promotion-focused or prevention-focused (Vial, Napier, & Brescoll, 2016). Universal and/or cultural congruency leadership behaviour may also interact with promotion and/or prevention-focused leadership behaviour giving rise to (a) universal-promotion-focused leadership behaviour, (b) universal prevention-focused leadership behaviour, (c) culturally congruent promotion-focused leadership behaviour and (d) culturally congruent prevention-focused leadership behaviour. Indian context being a site of Asian culture for the present study, I apply these two sets of leadership behaviour in four different combinations to the determinants obtained from the analysis to trace the path of success of women school leaders.

Path of Success: Leadership of Women School Heads in India

Certain school leadership practices of women depend exclusively on the fundamental human capacity, which they use in combination with projective or practical evaluative agency that inform, facilitate and reconfigure for the success of women as school leaders. Few other leadership practices utilize domain-specific capacity more than the fundamental human capacity to combine with projective and/or practical evaluative agency to influence the overall school improvement. How these combinations impact school leadership of women to succeed is discussed here.

Capacity–Agency Interaction: Trust, Restrained Neutrality and People Centeredness

A summary of results in Table 5.9 indicates that domain-specific capacity along with practical evaluative agency interacting with different structures need not necessarily ensure success for women school leaders. It has to be situated within the fundamental human capacity with projective agency to ensure success. Using fundamental human capacity with practical evaluative agency for successful school leadership of women means practical application of the core capabilities not solely restricted to domain-specific capacity and leadership capabilities, but as life-encompassing abilities, skills, maturity and acumen to lead, apply and work with others. Therefore, practical evaluative agency is about individual's capacity to make practical and normative judgements for taking actions arising from dilemmas, demands and ambiguities for which projective agency serves a basis.

Women in this study show that they use practical evaluative agency combining with both domain-specific and fundamental human capacities to succeed as school leaders. It is also indicated by the higher number of voluntary and mediated determinants. It implies that universal-promotion-focused leadership behaviour, particularly in terms of transformational leadership and values held by the women school heads, having a scope beyond school is embedded in the fundamental human capacity with projective agency. Women seek to develop 'trust' and 'people-centeredness' together with non-reactivity to provocations exhibiting 'restrained neutrality' in relationships using this combination. These three attributes can be referred to as feminine leadership qualities in the Indian context. In most cases, these are facilitated and nurtured by women's family, particularly parents and husband, for translating fundamental human capacity with projective agency into domain-specific capacity with practical evaluative agency. In other words, universal-promotion-focused leadership behaviour in terms of values and leadership styles are mediated by the family to make practical and normative decisions to address socio-cultural contexts through negotiation and navigation for a meaningful leadership that is culturally congruent to ensure success.

Table 5.9 Determinants of Successful School Leadership of Women in the Indian Context: Consolidation of Results

Nature of agency	Structures					No of determinants
	Diversity of contexts (the society)	Education system	School	Family	Community	
Fundamental human capacity for projective agency		Provision and access to school leadership positions (D) Core professional competence influencing the choice as a school leader (M)	Adopt people-centred approach to leadership practice (V)	Develops strong belief and conviction in oneself (M)	Ability and initiatives to involve the community in the schooling processes (M)	1 (D) 1 (V) 3 (M)
Fundamental human capacity for practical evaluative agency	Situational leadership skills and abilities (V) Gradually mature into a transformational leader (V)		Knowledge-driven decision-making in school management and administration (V) Academic leadership (V) Transcend the norm-based school leadership roles (V) Transformational leadership (V)	Higher levels of preparedness to compete in the employment market (M)	Understand the larger issues and needs of the community beyond their role to involve (M)	6 (V) 2 (M)

Domain-specific -projective agency	Extent of willingness and aptitude to undertake academic leadership versus administrative and managerial leadership (V)	Objective assessment of the utilitarian value of conflicting roles in a given circumstance (M)	Collective aspiration and ownership of the family in shaping woman's career as a professional and a school leader (M)	Direct all efforts towards achieving student learning outcomes (M)	1 (V) 3 (M)
Domain-specific -practical evaluative agency		Practising distributed leadership and/or shared leadership (M) Integrate innate feminine qualities with professional roles to create a people-centred approach (V) Create an identity for the school (M) Knowledge-driven leadership practice (M)	Higher access to information and knowledge about employment (M) Preparedness for a life of career (M)	Building trust through good relationships (M)	1 (V) 6 (M)
	2 (V)	1 (D) 1 (M) 1 (V)	6 (V), 4(M)	5 (M)	4 (M)	24

V—voluntary, D—deterministic, M—mediated.

Influence of Nature and Magnitude of Structures: Volunteerism

The study reveals that agency interacting with diversity in school contexts contributes to the development of unique leadership styles such as situational and transformational leadership, indicating that it requires maturity of mind, perseverance and stewardship for which determinants are essentially voluntary in nature.

The zeal to serve the cause of education for children drives a few women to exercise agency on the overwhelming structures to cross the threshold levels, paving way for volunteerism. Such women eventually mature into transformational leaders, a difficult phase indeed. It calls for a significant nurturing of fundamental human capacity with projective agency that can surpass the instrumental or utilitarian value of practical evaluative agency without underestimating its importance. Especially in this phase of leadership journey, women tend to underplay their success as leaders as they continue to deepen the trust, strengthen people-centred approach and diligently use restrained neutrality—a strategy adopted to create a safety net around them to stabilize and sustain their success as school leaders. They enact them mainly through fundamental human capacity with projective agency irrespective of family support, giving rise to volunteerism. It is a critical space in which they seek cultural congruency to endorse their universal-promotion-focused leadership behaviours combined with fundamental human capacity with projective agency to consolidate the benefits of success wherein adopting prevention-focused leadership behaviours that further strengthen the cultural congruency of universal leadership behaviour. Hence, voluntary determinants strongly influence and set the direction for successful school leadership of women in the Indian context.

Mediating the Deterministic Nature of Education System

Results indicate that the key structural determinant related to education system, that is, the provision and access to school leadership, has not exploited its own positional advantage to encourage women school leadership. It is a delayed process to achieve school leadership positions, rendering the role of family and women's agency inevitable for many aspirants. Hence, practising school leadership is not an independent activity for most women. The family enables them to develop core competencies for acquiring school leadership position by navigating through competition, aptly discharging duties as leaders, negotiating with multiple roles and identities, and handling issues with community, family and school structures. Mediated determinants are largely found in these spaces. Here, women tend to practice culturally endorsed prevention-focused leadership behaviour to achieve their goals including fulfilling the expectations from family, community, society and education system. Asian cultures are generally characterized by high levels of in-group (or family) and institutional collectivism, power distance and paternalism, sharing the leadership behaviours, its effects and outcomes (Richard et al., 2015).

Tracing the Path for Successful Women's School Leadership

The association of universal and culturally endorsed leadership behaviours together with the association of promotion- and prevention-focused leadership behaviours interact with each other to mediate the deterministic nature of the education system using fundamental and/or domain-specific capacities in combination with projective and/or practical evaluative agency for the success of women as school leaders in India. Depending on the combinations of capacity–agency leadership behaviours to negotiate the deterministic nature of education system, the path of success is shaped wherein voluntary and mediated determinants in varying combinations have a significant role. This path may have four milestones as women school heads experience success at different levels: (a) aspire and acquire school leadership position, (b) achieve goals, (c) ascend the path of success and (d) transcend the deterministic nature of the education system for excellence (Table 5.10). Availability of opportunity for leadership position does not fall into this domain, although it is a step in the ladder of school leadership for women.

In this chapter, a distinct attempt has been made to identify the determinants of successful women as school leaders having twofold intent: to develop a robust conceptual framework to study

Table 5.10 *Path of School Leadership of Women in the Indian Context: Role of Determinants*

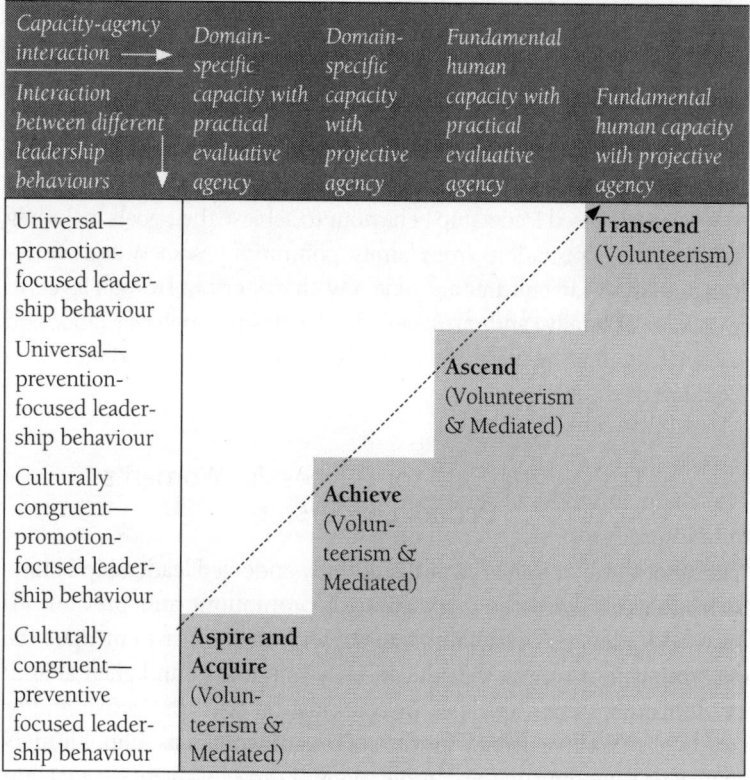

the interaction between structures and agency of women school heads; results so obtained in turn facilitate to trace the path of successful school leadership by applying leadership behaviour theories. While women negotiate and navigate between multiple roles and responsibilities, identities and issues with the deterministic nature of the education system, women's family (though not in all cases) mediates to provide support in becoming and being successful leaders who practice universal leadership behaviours endorsed by cultural congruency with its societal expectation and exercising promotion or prevention-focused leadership behaviours using capacity–agency.

Legitimization of School Leadership of Women

LEGITIMACY OF SCHOOL LEADERSHIP OF WOMEN IN INDIA: CONSTRUCTING A CONCEPTUAL MODEL

Power, Authority, Status, Degree of Acceptance and Legitimacy

The main function of legitimacy is to insulate organizations and individuals from external pressures and protect them from questions regarding their conduct (Mayer & Rowan, 1977). This utopian function of legitimacy may get weakened because of two reasons: one, if individual's action in formal positions lacks legitimacy; two, actions demanded by legitimate authority lack legitimacy (Kanter, 1977). In both these cases, legitimacy of individuals becomes questionable (Zeldich & Walker, 1984; Reskin & Ross, 1992). There is also a high chance of formal leadership losing its legitimacy as time passes if the leader in that formal leadership position does not create the required social basis for her followers to support morally and emotionally. This causes the formal leadership to lose the sight of intention, adversely affecting the legitimacy of the leader holding that position (Biswas & Biswas, 2011).

Like men, women leaders also tend to negotiate from their leadership position for two reasons: one, to seek a desirable degree of acceptance from their higher officials and subordinates and two, to grow beyond the formal leadership positions and emerge as true leaders. The first reason implies women are focused on avoiding adverse effects from their colleagues and thereby seek acceptance. The second implies to fulfil their personal aspiration for professional development. With the help of these two means, women try to gain legitimacy as school leaders.

These women tend to use two kinds of power—expert power and referent power—to overcome the adverse effects of losing legitimacy. Expert power implies the ability of the person to influence the behaviour of others through her knowledge, skills or abilities that are recognized by others also (French & Raven, 1959). By contrast, referent power is the person's ability to influence the behaviour of others due to their liking, admiration and respect for the individual (ibid.). Both these types of powers are generally affected by a combination of situational factors, gender and personality. Therefore, according to Rajan and Krishnan (2002), while studying the effects of personality on power and influence, gender is an extremely critical factor to be considered. This is because the worth of women's leadership is also high and that it cannot be ignored as they have been as successful as men in the same leadership positions (Patel, 2003).

We may say that expert power is also closely related to agentic behaviour of women leaders. Agentic behaviour indicates assertiveness, control and confidence. In the workplace, these attributes of agentic behaviour manifest predominantly among women than in men in different ways such as: assertive speech, competing with others for attention, assigning tasks, making suggestions, initiating activities and influencing others (Eagly & Schimidt, 2001).

Similarly, referent power is similar to that of communal behaviours among women leaders which are described as women predominantly exhibiting higher affection, being gentle and kind towards others. They are also seen to be more helpful to others and even nurture others. In the workplace, these attributes manifest in the form of not too keen on drawing attention to oneself and accepting others' direction. Their tone of speech is more tentative than assertive. They also support others and are soothing to others; they try to resolve relational and interpersonal problems better than men (Eagly & Schimidt, 2001).

Several leadership behaviours identified specific to women leaders by Cubillo and Brown (2003) and Trinidad and Normore (2005) also reveal these behaviours. Accordingly, women attempt to build consensus and act as role models for demonstrating good leadership behaviours to others. They are also willing to share power, work with others and interact with them. Besides these, they communicate effectively and are acutely aware of individual differences.

The above discussion also points towards the fact that power can not only be individual but also organizational. Organizational power can be rewarding, coercive and legitimate and individual power can be expert and referent (French & Raven, 1959). Individual power has been discussed extensively above. It is essential, now, to discuss organizational power.

Within the purview of organizational power comes legitimate power. Hence, in the context of the present study, organizational power is discussed specifically in terms of legitimate power. Legitimate power is the ability to exert power that is derived from the position of authority one holds. Legitimacy to the power comes because of the position of authority. Legitimacy of leadership essentially refers to the willingness of subordinates to accept both individual and organizational powers exercised by the leader holding a legitimate position with an authority. If subordinates do not totally accept the authority of the leader holding a leadership position, then there arises a perception of power differentials between the leader and subordinate. This leads to two important outcomes. The leader enjoys: (a) different degrees of acceptance by the subordinates and (b) different levels of status attribution by the subordinates. These two factors play a crucial role in establishing the legitimacy of leadership especially in case of women. Vial et al. (2016) discuss these two attributes extensively while referring to illegitimacy effects of women's leadership. In addition, incongruity between typical leader roles and female gender roles (Eagly & Schimidt, 2001) can also cause perception of power differentials causing a prejudice against women leaders in various forms, such as (a) less favourable evaluation of her potential as a leader as well as her current leadership behaviour; (b) agentic behaviour being considered less desirable for women leaders; and (c) negative evaluation of communal behaviour of women leaders.

Leadership-Focus Behaviours and Women's School Leadership

Legitimacy of woman's school leadership is also influenced by her leadership-focus behaviour and gender perspective besides the perceptual differences in power and status attribution. The leadership-focus behaviour can be either promotion-focused leadership behaviour or prevention-focused leadership behaviour (Crowe & Higgins, 1997). When a woman attempts to balance her leadership through a number of positive behavioural attributes to emerge as a powerful leader, then it is called promotion-focused leadership behaviour. Promotion-focused leadership behaviours may be in the form of generating support from higher officials and peers, developing trust in others about oneself as a leader, creating positive emotions among subordinates (Keynes et al., 2000) and so on. This is aptly captured by Crowe and Higgins (1997) as an inclination to insure hits and to insure against errors related to omissions. By contrast, if a woman leader attempts to balance her leadership behaviour through a series of behaviours indicating her hesitation and avoiding challenges and problems, then it is prevention-focused leadership behaviour. Moss-Racusin and Rudman (2010) describe this type of leadership as characterized being over-cautious, conscious about one's safety and security, evading conflicts and ignoring divergent views from others, unwilling to accept losses and avoid acknowledging one's own mistakes and so on. This type of women leaders are also not willing to showcase their performance most of the time and hence lose out on visibility despite being goal-oriented. So, prevention-focused leadership behaviour can be associated with acts of women leaders who seek to insure correct rejections and insure against errors of commission (Crowe & Higgins, 1997).

Gender Perspective and Women's Leadership Behaviour

For the purpose of this study, the gender perspectives of women leaders have been conceptualized based on Weber's conception of authority. Accordingly, the gender perspective of a women leader who is in a position of authority can be either traditional and/or rational in nature. By traditional gender perspective, it means that a woman leader is largely dependent on significant others in the family such as her parents/husband. She is also influenced more by the local traditions, family norms and culture passed on from elders, does not question the patriarchy, accepts the distinct role definitions for men and women in the family and school, etc. By contrast, rational perspective of a woman leader is influenced significantly by modernity of views and practices in the family and school such as appreciating progressiveness, questioning the relevance of unchanging traditional belief systems and their consequences creeping into the workplace, does not like to accept orthodoxy, gender stereotypes and resists gender discrimination. She exercises resilience and is willing to negotiate role conflicts and follow organizational rules.

Constructing the Model of Legitimization of School Leadership of Women in the Indian Context

The model of legitimacy of school leadership of women in the Indian context is constructed here in this study based on the discussions presented above that are related to power, status, acceptance, leadership-focus behaviour and gender perspective of women leaders.

Promotion-focused leadership behaviour and prevention-focused leadership behaviour are the two ends of the continuum of the diverse ways in which leadership behaviour can be observed in any school leader including women leaders. A school leader may exhibit both these leadership behaviours depending on the context, compulsions that a situation demands, one's own state of mind, rules and regulations that govern the school administration, power and authority exercised and so on. In the same way, the gender perspective of any school leader including that of women school leaders can lie between the two ends of the continuum of gender perspective, namely, rational gender perspective and traditional gender perspective. A school leader may exhibit both the gender perspectives depending on the circumstances, one's own gender orientation inherited and developed later on, influence of the society, significant others in the family and the school community.

In establishing legitimacy of leadership, the woman leader's leadership-focus behaviour and gender perspective continuously interact with each other. While these two interact with each other especially in the context of working with teachers, higher officials, parents of children and community members, a woman leader engages in a continuous negotiation between status attribution which these members bestow on her, perception of power differentials of the woman leader arising from the status attribution and her own negotiation to seek an optimum degree of acceptance to establish her legitimacy. Conversely, depending on the intensity with which the woman leader exercises the gender perspective and leadership-focus behaviours in the workplace, the status attribution by others, perception of power differentials by the women school leader and her negotiation also vary significantly.

In and through this two-way process of dynamic interaction between gender perspective and leadership-focus behaviour, a woman seeks to obtain acceptance from officials, colleagues and stakeholders to establish her legitimacy. Within this dynamic interaction between the two leadership-focus behaviours and two gender perspectives, there is also intra-factor interaction between status attribution and perception of power differentials resulting in different levels of negotiation to gain acceptance (see Figure 6.1).

The different ways in which the interactions between status attributions, perception of power differentials, negotiations and acceptance of leadership take place are explained in detail herewith. Four possible ways in which women may tend to interact between leadership-focus behaviour and gender perspective that give rise to variations in the intra-factor interactions are as follows:

1. Traditional gender perspective and prevention-focused leadership behaviour
2. Traditional gender perspective and promotion-focused leadership behaviour
3. Rational gender perspective and prevention-focused leadership behaviour
4. Rational gender perspective and promotion-focused leadership behaviour

Complementing the four major types of interactions mentioned earlier, the legitimacy of school leadership of women assumes different levels

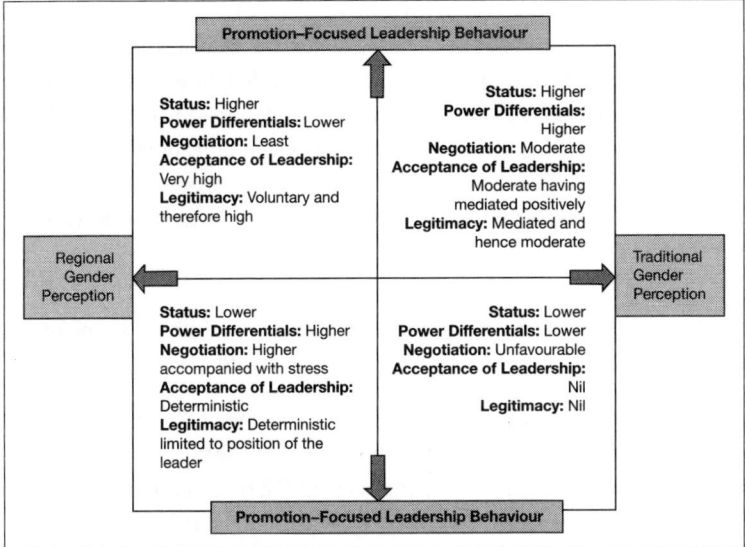

Figure 6.1 *Legitimizations Process of Woman School Leaders in Indian Context*

Source: Mythili (2019a)

depending on the interaction between the intra-factors. There may be many more ways and combinations in which these interactions might take place. However, intra-factor interactions within each of the four major interactions are explained in the following.

When There Is Interaction between Traditional Gender Perspective and Prevention-Focused Leadership Behaviour

In this case, preventive leadership behaviour and traditional gender perspective complement each other. When these two interact with each other, the following pattern can be observed. The status attribution by subordinates is lower and perception of perceptual differences by the women school head is also lower. Even though status attribution is low, due to low perception of perceptual differences, the woman school head do not show inclination for negotiation or feel that there is no need for any negotiation or may be are not even aware that a negotiation is required to rise higher as a school leader. In short, the woman school head may find that there is no need for negotiations to get at least a minimum degree of acceptance by the subordinates. If at all a woman attempts or decides to negotiate seeking acceptance, it is going to be extremely stressful. It implies that acceptance of leadership of a woman school head does not really exist despite holding a school leadership position. In other words, legitimacy of school leadership of women who practice prevention-focused leadership along with traditional gender perspective is prone to be highly questionable or even non-existent or nil.

When There Is an Interaction between Traditional Gender Perspective and Promotion-Focused Leadership Behaviour

In this case, promotion-focused leadership behaviour and traditional gender perspective do not complement each other. Rather they are at variance with each other while interacting. There is a kind of a tension and discrepancy affecting the level of legitimacy of leadership in such interactions. Though the status attribution by subordinates is higher, the perception of perceptual differences by the woman school head need not necessarily be lower. On the contrary, this perception about power differential is higher. Due to this seemingly and favourably positioned relationship between higher status attribution by subordinates and higher perception of power differentials, a moderate level of negotiations are required to accompany mediations and stress will be at minimum levels at least. As a result, degree of acceptance of leadership is moderately positive with mediations yielding favourable outcomes. Nonetheless, due to the aspect of traditional gender perspective that need not necessarily allow for flexibility at crucial times, the legitimacy of women's school leadership also tends to be mediated and hence remains at moderate levels. In these situations, women may also tend to experience and treat themselves as 'outsiders on the inside' (Glass & Cook, 2016), which is a glass-cliff effect.

When There Is an Interaction between Rational Gender Perspective and Prevention-Focused Leadership Behaviour

When there is interaction between prevention-focused leadership behaviour and rational gender perspective, there is incongruity between them leading to a certain level of stress affecting their interactive effects that yields lower than the optimum results. Accordingly, in this case, the status attribution by subordinates is lower because leadership behaviour is mostly prevention-focused. Consequently, even though the leader has a rational gender perspective, perception of power differentials will continue to be higher. It leads to higher levels of negotiations with others including subordinates. These negotiations are invariably accompanied with stress predominantly due to prevention-focused leadership behaviours. Hence, rational gender perspective is of little use in practising effective leadership in the schools. Due to these variations, the degree of acceptance of leadership of a woman is mostly deterministic in nature that is limited to her positional leadership as a school head. The legitimacy of school leadership of a woman is also deterministic limited to her positional leadership as a school head which is mostly bound by rules and regulations and not beyond.

When There Is an Interaction between Rational Gender Perspective and Promotion-Focused Leadership Behaviour

When interacting with each other, there is no incongruity between rational gender perspective and promotion-focused leadership behaviour. There is a higher status attribution by subordinates, stakeholders as well as higher officials. It is obviously accompanied with lower perception of power differentials by the school head with them. Hence, the negotiation for seeking legitimacy by the woman school head is the least. As a result of these, the degree of acceptance of her leadership is high and legitimacy accorded is highest. Such legitimacy is mostly voluntary in nature.

In the process of establishing legitimacy of her leadership, a woman school head may undergo all these four types of interactions and hence even her legitimacy is not same for all time. Rather, this model indicates the continuum of process of legitimization of school leadership through which a woman may traverse at her own pace depending on the circumstances in her life.

The following section elucidates these interactions resulting in varying levels of legitimacy of school leadership using different instances narrated by women school heads. In these examples, the nil legitimacy discussed above arises occasionally as women school heads interviewed have proved themselves by achieving at least a certain degree of success as leaders. Hence, the interaction between traditional gender perspective and prevention-focused leadership behaviour is discussed using examples from other school heads as well to understand the legitimization of school leadership of women in the Indian context.

LEGITIMIZATION PROCESS OF WOMEN SCHOOL LEADERS

It is interesting to focus on why prevention-focused leadership behaviour occurs irrespective of traditional or rational gender perspective especially because it is faced by young women who have passed the direct examination to become school heads quickly rather than those senior teachers who are still waiting to become Heads of Schools. Even senior school heads face this but the intensity might not be that high for them. It results in backlash, glass-cliff and illegitimacy effects that alter the status attribution, perception of power differentials, negotiation and legitimacy of school leadership for the woman. These are studied in detail in the subsequent parts of this section.

Women Leaders with High Legitimacy: Promotion-Focused Leadership Behaviour and Rational Gender Perspective

Some instances when women showed higher legitimacy in the study exercising promotion-focused leadership behaviour along with rational gender perspective are discussed here. A few women leaders could harness core capabilities and exploit opportunities, utilizing the advantages of power and authority that positional leadership offered them.

In case of principals from Delhi, it is working at zonal and district levels as leaders in leading mega-events and conducting inter-school zonal and district level competitions in sports, literary and cultural activities. Few women choose to exploit the opportunities that are routinely available for all in the education system and excel as leaders beyond the principal's position offered at schools. A principal chose to excel in teaching English and was sent to the United States for professional development under the Fulbright fellowship.

It is a distinct type of promotion-focused leadership behaviour in case of women cluster-school head from Lahaul Spiti, located at a height of 12,000 ft in Himachal Pradesh. She focuses on ensuring that each year at least five to six children get admission in Jawahar Navodaya Vidyalaya (JNV) by passing the entrance examination. She utilizes every single opportunity available, be it inviting a teacher from the far-flung district of Chikkaballapur in Karnataka in South India or calling her daughter who is studying in Shimla to come home on weekends to teach children or inviting any other educated person available in the vicinity. She herself engages throughout the day in preparing them for the entrance examination. She does all of this free of cost, which she interprets as 'social service'. Children stay in her house, eat the food she cooks for them and prepare for the entrance examination. She is good at pedagogy of children with disabilities by addressing the individual needs of the children.

Despite not knowing the place before taking up the cluster-school head's role, she decided to go to Lahaul, Spiti even when men teachers refused to go when they were promoted as cluster-school heads. She even ignored their warnings that it is a very cold region that is cut off from the rest of the world due to snow fall for six months in a year. Her agentic leadership behaviours in the form of taking risks, being assertive and making timely decisions led her to this unknown place. Here she emerged as a leader navigating the passivity and deterministic nature of education system by improving students' learning. Not only this but her personal ambition of studying for BA degree was also fulfilled after 20 long years of waiting due to her husband's opposition for her studying. She made up her mind to stay alone without her husband after coming to Lahaul Spiti and transformed herself as a leader. Therefore, be it a remote area in hills of very high altitudes or planes of metro cities, women are capable of developing themselves as promotion-focused leaders with rational gender perspective.

Similarly, in the high altitudes of north Sikkim Himalayan region, a woman school head working in a primary school proved her grit and will in ensuring that the school functions despite the severe cold and acute scarcity of resources commonly found in high altitude regions of hilly areas and also effectively navigated the earthquake that took place with its epicentre in Nepal in 2009. The north eastern region of India was also affected by it. Sikkim state was one of the worst affected regions. She adopted effective disaster management measures and quickly brought back the functioning of the school. All of this she puts as 'love for children'. This attitude of her made the passive community change its attitude to extend cooperation. One of the visible signs of trust that got built through her efforts was that children used to be with her from morning till evening well before the school hours and extending the same after school hours. Children and the teacher worked in the school garden after school hours. Her zeal to work as a school head—'If you want to be a teacher, you must love children'. So, one of the ways in which promotion-focused leadership behaviour with positive gender perspective manifests is through trust building that has an enlarged perspective 'to love' children beyond school's routine duties. So, women treat themselves as 'outsiders on the inside' (Glass & Cook, 2016) by their actions as leaders that neutralize challenges, contesting gender notions and positively responding to situations.

A woman school head works in a village called Poochampally in Telangana where the world famous Poochampally sarees are weaved. The entire village including elders and young children are engaged in weaving the sarees which is their traditional occupation that has now turned into a mega business due to increasing demand for sarees in these times of fashion. Very few families are not engaged in this business directly. In such a context, school education assumes secondary importance though its necessity is not ruled out. The woman HM who is working in the school has secondary education up to 10th standard and is exceptionally talented and academically very sound. She is also bold, assertive and amenable to others, which considerably reflects her agentic behaviours. She has been able to convince the community about the importance of schooling and education of children to the elders in the village. Students now attend school regularly and participate in all co-curricular and extra-curricular activities besides curricular studies. A variety of events are conducted in the school regularly and they tap students' talents and engage all teachers in the school.

Community and SMC also lend support to the school. The school head has tried to build a culture of achieving excellence in any work that is undertaken in the school. During the academic year 2017–2018, she even came out with the first newsletter of the school containing information about nearly 24 or more events conducted during that year. The Department of Education in Telangana has uploaded this newsletter on its state level ShaGun web portal. This principal has mainly exploited her academic strengths and relied on her core abilities which refer to fundamental human capacity with projective agency. Her agentic behaviours also complement her capacity–agency qualities to excel as a leader. It was also observed during a series of interactions that she is more inclined towards using her intellectual conviction based on knowledge and reasoning. So, she hardly cares for gender or gendered notions so much so that a few men school heads look up to her as their 'guru', considering her as a role model. Her expertise in subject knowledge on various areas has made her the state's key resource person for many training programmes conducted under SSA and RMSA. System level officials also recognize and respect her immensely. Therefore, legitimacy of school leadership for women comes also from the core fundamental competencies through which they influence colleagues, subordinates, community, parents and students as well as ignore gender differences and barriers in their work and life most of the time.

In a different community in an urban school of Bhopal city in Madhya Pradesh, the woman principal excelled. It is quite different than the weaver's community of Poochampally in Telangana. It is dominated by Muslim minority community and the area has been declared communally sensitive by the government. The principal is a Hindu, which is a majority religion in the country. There is hardly anybody else in the school who is a Hindu including teachers and students. So, the alienation felt by the principal seems to be higher as indicated in her conversations. It is also coupled with the non-cooperation of the community and there is little use of applying rules and regulations in the school many times. In short, adapting and accommodating to regional and local community contexts is a major expectation which the principal faces, and therefore, it is challenging. Because, the slightest disturbance in the locality, it takes the twist as communal violence for which the first casualty is the school. Principal's duty is to inform and call the police first and close the school. Given this situation, her excelling as a leader comes from the fact that despite the violence and facing rough weather from some teachers, she is able to carry on the normal school routines. Her problems surmount as HMs in charge of elementary and primary sections do not work with her in coordination. She has control over secondary and senior secondary classes only. Despite this, she is able to maintain peace and ensure that school functions almost regularly. All her efforts are reflected in more than 60 per cent of students passing the 10th standard state board's examination with first class since seven years. Her ability to manage and ensure school's success has surprised even the district education officers who want to know where her strength come from to face these challenges on a daily basis. She responds jokingly to these surprises as a kind of a different excitement as it holds surprises enlivening her every day. To take lightly her struggles and make fun of it comes from the confidence of having established herself as a leader as well as enjoying higher legitimacy despite adverse circumstances. She is able to take higher risks without fear or compromising school's rules and regulations. She is also careful all the time not to make grave mistakes. Nonetheless, she even refused to take a transfer and go to a safer and trouble free school challenging her own capacities to excel more. Besides achieving success, this principal is also facing the pressure of glass-cliff effect which she has to constantly encounter with. More will be discussed on glass-cliff effect in the next sub-section.

Another striking feature common to these women who contested gendered notions adopting diverse styles is an overt disregard for these notions. It is explained in brief in case of the school leader from Telangana earlier. Other women also are equally courageous who refused to accept that there is any problem in their schools or the education system, interpreted as a privilege they enjoyed for getting the due recognition or even extra for which they also do not mind working more than what is expected.

Nonetheless, there is also recognition and rewards given to these women leaders which is a form of support from system level leadership. Some of them have received best teacher awards. These have also consolidated the legitimacy of school leadership.

From the instances discussed above, characteristic features of women who practice promotion-focused leadership behaviour and rational gender perspective can be identified:

1. Legitimacy of school leadership for women comes also from the core fundamental competencies through which they influence colleagues, subordinates, community, parents and students.
2. Women ignore gender differences, gender discriminations and barriers in their work and life most of the time.
3. Women try to neutralize challenges, contest gender notions and respond positively to situations.
4. Women can excel in any/all regions irrespective of remote area in hills of very high altitudes, planes of metro cities, urban slums, communally sensitive areas, semi-rural areas, rural areas with inadequate school facilities where orthodoxy stereotypes are prevalent, unique context of specialized occupation yielding higher economic benefits irrespective of being literate or not, that is, where education is not necessarily an acutely felt need for parents or children.
5. Women with promotion-focused leadership behaviour and rational gender perspective are sensitive and responsive to the sentiments of colleagues, students, parents and community.
6. They accomplish their goals without compromising on their roles and responsibilities as leaders.

Higher capabilities lead to capturing and identifying diverse opportunities and advantages within the education system's structure, exercise agency more deeply while facing challenges and also to push or change that structure (Everett & Charlton, 2014). 'Confidence' and 'ability' (Bandura, 1982, 1997) reflect the strength of core leadership competencies in moderating gender biases and stereotypes. These enhance status attribution and justify the power of women's leadership (Vial et al., 2016), reduce the perception of power differentials and decrease stressful negotiations with others. These are also characteristics of promotion-focused leadership behaviour along with rational gender perspective that have provided high legitimacy to women leaders.

Women Leaders with Moderate Legitimacy: Promotion-Focused Leadership Behaviour and Traditional Gender Perspective

Women having promotion-focused leadership behaviour with traditional gender perspective experience glass-cliff effect. Hence, they experience a moderate level of legitimacy. In this section, the characteristic features of such women leaders are explored by analysing the narratives.

Due to the bias in the status quo, glass-cliff effect occurs. Women are obligated to achieve more to rise to higher levels in their jobs than men who are also striving to move to the same higher levels. That is, women have to work harder than men to reach the same position. Also, it is more likely that women are chosen to such positions as a promotion in their jobs levels in times of crisis as in contrast to men who are chosen in times of prosperity in an organization (Ryan & Haslam, 2005; Haslam & Ryan, 2008). In case of school leadership, while women are transferred to schools with lower performance and high risks, men may be transferred to schools which are performing higher and have lower risks. Hence, while perceiving women as a leader, there is an operational double standard (Eagly & Schmidt, 2001). This is referred to as the glass-cliff effect. In a glass-cliff effect, there is a perceived need to bring in a woman as leader when the organization faces crisis to turn around the circumstances and their outcomes, that is, 'think crisis, think women' (Bruckmuller & Branscombe, 2010, p. 235). Women are also likely to experience excessive work load, high risk tasks and fear of punishment. Not to mention that these are accompanied with scrutiny, bare minimum support and non-cooperation.

A few instances of glass-cliff effects which women school heads have faced are discussed below.

In Rajasthan, as two women principals said, higher officials—especially district and block education officers—put more and more pressure on women with little support and cooperation than that for men. There is also a fear of punishment in the form of issuing notices, fault finding practices and giving excessive work that forces them to work beyond office hours to complete it. These tasks are also risky. It compels the women to be extra careful in what they are doing and how they deal with the officers. In such cases women also feel the need to take the support of the family especially if that includes the husband ferrying them to district offices when meeting these officials.

The women HM narrated her trial of conducting the public examination as the in-charge for the entire district. The district education officer did not provide any support staff or other form of assistance to her. She had to do all the work by herself. Situation turned tense when a candidate writing the examination fell ill. Even then, she did not get any assistance despite requesting several times and making telephone calls to at least provide assistance to take the sick candidate to the hospital. Finally, she had to call the student's parents to the school and ask them to take their daughter to the hospital.

In Delhi where the principal worked in a boys' school said that as a woman principal she had to be more careful and also tactful with men teachers who are majority in number. These men observe their woman boss keenly to catch her weak points. Also, they are hard to be convinced about the abilities of the women as a leader. Hence, as a woman leader she had to be a role model and demonstrate before she tells them to do something or follow her. These men teachers cooperate with woman principal who is their boss only when they are convinced fully.

In Bhopal's communally sensitive school, the principal had to be careful all the time without giving room for any small clash at any time. She even had to withstand the ill-mannered behaviour of a male teacher silently to ensure that her work as a leader is not hampered. Complaints were filed against her in the district education office.

So, chief characteristics of glass-cliff effects for women school leaders in the Indian context are:

1. Leading the school comes under excessive vigilance from male colleagues, higher officers and community.

2. As a leader, women school heads suffer from continuous pressure to maintain a flawless working style that does not disturb the peace and order of the school.
3. Women school heads had to struggle hard to be free from the unnecessary interference of the community.

Jain (2015) referred to such instances of narrating the glass cliff in case of woman panchayat leaders as 'rockets with fire in their tails'. Where there is higher gender discrimination and stereotypes coupled with numerical minority of women, their performance comes under continuous scrutiny (Glass & Cook, 2016). So, women are forced to face challenges continuously demanding higher efforts and take higher risks despite proving themselves as leaders (Eagly & Karau, 2002). It is a critical threshold point for women to gain higher legitimacy moving from enjoying moderate legitimacy despite working hard.

Women Leaders with Deterministic Legitimacy: Prevention-Focused Leadership Behaviour and Rational Gender Perspective

Women practising prevention-focused leadership behaviour with rational gender perspective are likely to experience more of illegitimacy and backlash effects in their workplace. This makes them experience legitimacy that is more deterministic in nature and which is rigid. This makes it difficult for them to cross the threshold to practice promotion-focused leadership behaviour in the workplace. Hence, challenges faced continue for a long time before actual positive leadership can be practised and gender perspectives start yielding results. In this section, characteristic features of deterministic legitimacy are explored by studying narratives.

Backlash Effect

When a woman leader does not willingly comply with the prevailing gender stereotyping practices and reactions by individuals and also does not accept discrimination based on gender by covertly or overtly opposing them, she is most likely to face non-cooperation, hindrances to her work, conveniently avoiding or refusing her directions and orders by her subordinates, complain to higher authorities, emanate negative reactions and abstain from attending to duty and other such activities are indications of backlash effects. As a consequence, even when the woman occupies leadership position, she is not looked upon as a leader and hence lacks adequate legitimacy levels. In other words, occupying the formal leadership position does not automatically ensure leadership legitimacy in that position even though it is important (Kanter, 1977; Read, 1974; Reskin & Ross, 1992).

According to the Peabody study, there are nine types of negative reactions exhibited by subordinates questioning the authority/leadership which is not desirable to them. These are as follows: consciously question the order but accept it as binding; inform the administrator of their views and seek to be converted to administrator's point of view while complying the order; discuss the situation with the administrator and try to work for change while complying with the order; attempt to gain support for their contrary views by appealing to co-workers; go to superiors to gain support; discuss the order, but ignore, evade; try to modify it while seeming to comply; ignore, evade, modify the order without discussing it; openly reject the order; transfer or resign (as cited in Gorton & Alston, 2012, pp. 78–79).

Instances of 'backlash effects' for women school leaders in the Indian context are discussed here:

Out of her enthusiasm and deep interest in leadership development, a woman leader (state not mentioned to maintain confidentiality), requested for a deputation to SSA to work as coordinator for SLDP launched by MHRD in the state. It came to an abrupt end when her office was ransacked. She was not allowed to work by refusing to give her a place to sit in the office. Even the SLDP programmes suffered for two years as they could not be conducted in the state. Finally, she ended her deputation at SSA and went back to the school as principal. However, she continues her interest in the programme and acts as a resource person even now.

In the communally sensitive area of urban Bhopal, the principal had to brace the RTIs filed and complaints lodged with higher officials continuously. Non-cooperation was common from colleagues and community for her. It was possible for her to continue in that school since higher officials knew her well as a high performing principal and supported her despite the RTIs and complaints lodged against her; nevertheless she was utmost cautious. It was reflected in her question during the interview as a respondent in this study too, 'Should I be formal and just be official with you? Or should I talk openly with you?'

In Rajasthan, the woman HM seemed very bold. So as a researcher, I asked her whether she behaves the same with the higher officials. To this question she responded *'Mein bilkul chupke raheti hoon'* (I am completely silent). On asking the reason for her silence with higher officials she said that these officials when they return to their headquarters, they might even issue a notice against her. She did not want to face that situation.

In Uttar Pradesh, the principal narrated the story of a principal (man) who did not hand over the official charge to her for a year when she was transferred to that school on promotion. Even when he left the school, without officially handing over the charge to her, she found that he had not maintained and updated any of the school records. Even higher officials did not take any action against him or even warn him when she brought it to their notice. The matter remains unresolved and she works as principal without the official charge handed over to her. Due to this experience she said, 'it is better to be silent while working'.

To avoid backlash, a woman even denies that there is gender bias, as in the case of an HM working in semi-rural area. She not only ignored gender discrimination in the workplace but also denied that there is any such thing in the education system.

Key characteristic features of backlash effect on women school leaders are as follows:

1. Fear of punishment.
2. Create a safety zone to avoid interference from others and escape backlash.

3. May do the extra work assigned to satisfy officials even if it amounts to taking the risks of facing the backlash.
4. Overtly deny the occurrence of any gender discrimination happening in the workplace.

So, prevention-focused leadership behaviour might be partly due to the fear of experiencing backlash in some women leaders who try to avoid, ignore or deny that there is any gender bias or discriminatory practices even though they possess a rational gender perspective. It may also be due to social and economic penalty incurred by those engaged in gender stereotype-incongruent roles (Rudman, 1998) that is predominantly seen in the workplace conversations (Brescoll, 2011).

As a researcher, I sincerely acknowledge the willingness of women who shared their experiences about backlash, which many would not dare to do so. It was also observed that non-verbal expressions and gestures of woman leaders who were silent as though they are spectators, while intensely listening to others' conversations, seemed to have much more to say which could not be captured in words.

To avoid backlash, women are forced to work harder than men. By doing so, they supersede the expectations of higher officers that set higher standards for them. To maintain the new standards set, they work harder than before to keep up the momentum of work. It leads to formation of a cyclical effect between glass-cliff and backlash effects and therefore, the two are intertwined with each other in the Indian context.

Illegitimacy Effect

Illegitimacy effect refers to the under evaluation of a woman's leadership than what she is actually worth. Even though the members of the group expect the woman leader to make valuable contribution, they may not expect her to be successful, even though she is legitimately appointed. These members consider it as lower to their status if they acknowledge the success of the woman leader as one who has risen to the position of influence (Lucas, 2003, pp. 465–467). In the process, woman is evaluated as less effective. This is called illegitimacy effect. The popular perception aptly captures the illegitimacy effect—men manage, women teach.

Few instances capturing such illegitimacy effects are presented here:

Rajasthan woman school heads faced more illegitimacy effect than those who were interviewed. They were young with small children and were striving hard balancing home and work. As school heads following rules, they were trying to come up in their profession. Being directly recruited, achieved this leadership position mainly through their efforts, proving their merit in the PSC examination, they faced more resistance in gaining acceptance of men teachers who were senior in age and experience in the system. Some of them opposed the youngest woman HM respondent directly as well as indirectly including preventing her from performing her routine duties such as taking rounds in the school, observe classrooms, inspect toilets, etc. In one such adventure, she noticed that girls were going outside to the fields instead of using the toilets. To her surprise she found that they were kept locked. On enquiring she found that there was no water connection given to these toilets all these years. The apathy was largely evident and realized why senior men teachers used to tell her indirectly not to do her duties in such expressions as 'Do not strain yourself', 'take rest', 'we will do it, why do you worry', etc. She had faced this resistance from her own HM when working in previous school as a teacher. When she appeared for the PSC examination his opposition was highly intense. It was reflected in his threats to her saying that it will ruin her family life and threatening that he will not allow her to pass the exam and so on. This kind of resistance, threats and non-acceptance arises mainly due to insecurity feeling among the senior teachers when the young women occupy leadership positions superseding the older and senior colleagues under whom they were working before.

On the day of taking charge in her first appointment as a new HM, another woman teacher in Rajasthan faced a different kind of illegitimacy threat. A senior male teacher did not even come to the school. Even on the later days when he came to the school, he did not care to introduce himself nor took notice of the new woman HM. The orderliness in the school was also low. Teachers were relaxed about their work. During recess time, they did not see who is going home and did not return to the school. When persuasions did not give desired results, she had to issue orders to teachers to do certain functions regularly. The male teacher even complained to the local MLA about her. She was called by the MLA to talk, but did not concede to his accusations. She even replied back assertively. She concluded the conversations saying with a pun in her expression as he was physically blind and also behaved blindly towards her '... and this male teacher is blind'. The women school head from Uttar Pradesh captures this behaviour as '*I am the boss* feeling is very high among male teachers'. She experienced the non-recognition of her principal-ship by her predecessor.

In order to counter this illegitimacy and backlash effects, most of the women leaders focused on ensuring that students appearing for 10 standard examination pass with first class and more than 60 to 70 per cent students pass the examination in the school. In this way they tried to counter the low status attribution given to them by subordinates.

Characteristics of Illegitimacy Effects

Subordinates showed and expressed their apprehensions about a woman's leadership, leading to illegitimacy effect in a number of ways. Some of these are as follows:

1. Overt and covert opposition to a woman's leadership, resistance to work to meet the expectations of the woman HM, trying to stop a woman HM from doing her work.
2. Threaten the woman leader by bringing political pressure.
3. A strong sense of insecurity feeling among the subordinates, especially among the men.
4. A perception that a woman easily concedes to threats, which are issued when they see a woman can also perform.
5. Non-acceptance by senior colleagues of a young woman occupying leadership position.

Eagly and Karau (2002) capture the women countering the illegitimacy effects as women principals had to resort to a combination of methods asserting their behaviour of 'stereotype violations'. These may also be due to those circumstances which force the woman leader to take a tough stand, apply rules despite her unwillingness to act in that manner and so on. Woman leaders resort to these stereotype violations when they are forced to control the subordinates for their unruly behaviours.

Women Leaders with no Legitimacy: Prevention-Focused Leadership Behaviour and Traditional Gender Perspective

A woman practising prevention-focused leadership behaviour with traditional gender perspective is likely to experience no legitimacy in her workplace despite holding the leadership position. Such a situation renders her to listen to her subordinates more often and leave the decisions into their hands. Being in the leadership position, she may not be able to take control of situations and even tend to rely on a select few subordinates excluding others to carry out her work. She may not be able to control the informal power hubs generated within the power dynamics operating between her subordinates. Rather, she may be prone to be influenced by those power dynamics of subordinates and incline towards believing the power used by her select few subordinates. This results in lack of understanding of her subordinates and their abilities and capacities, misunderstanding the situations and subordinates and misrecognition of the talents and competence of her subordinates. In extreme cases, some subordinates may be excluded from the entire group under these influences.

In this section, characteristic features of no legitimacy are explored considering the instances discussed by school heads in Telangana. Even though these school heads from Telangana were considered successful, some instances indicated their vulnerability of losing legitimacy as leaders. Later, the lack of legitimacy in general is also discussed considering school heads from other states visited on different occasions.

A woman school head in Telangana opined that teaching is a women friendly profession most suited to ladies. She reasoned that there are more holidays and less work in teaching profession which help ladies to do their family responsibilities well. She also felt that other professions do not allow women to take up responsibility of the family after marriage as much as teaching profession does. Some women also felt that husbands have to be in higher posts than wives if both are working in the same profession. For example, woman can be in schools as HM whereas men have to be working in university or college as lecturers and professors. Such women preferred to be subordinates at home even though they were school heads. These women accepted gender stereotypes as though it is given to them which cannot be changed or altered. Hence, the status quo was not questioned either. They altered their ways to accept, accommodate and adjust with patriarchy. By so doing, due to the acceptance of the men in the family, they also felt a sense of safety and could maintain harmony in the family. They accepted the support and guidance coming from men as that which is received from above.

In the workplace they were donning the role of 'accommodating mother' to younger men and women teachers in the school and depended on them more for their work than on other senior teachers in the school. For example, in Pondicherry, celebrating religious festivals like Pongal is common with a HM to gain acceptance. Though such practices may not receive acceptance from her subordinates, especially senior teachers who are not in her circle of influence, disagreeing openly also does not usually occur. These spaces give her some opportunity to try to project as the head of the school. Sometimes they also end up being highly vulnerable to men who question her legitimacy as a head of the school and even overpower her, especially in SMC meetings. Heavily influenced by the patriarchy, stereotypes and orthodoxy, these types of women seem to be practising culturally congruent practices but lacking domain-specific practical evaluative agency to position themselves as pedagogic and academic leaders in the school.

In the near absence of universal leadership behaviour, practical evaluative agency, instructional leadership and domain-specific content knowledge of school subjects, efforts of these school heads do not necessarily accord a decent status attribution from their subordinates.

They may not feel the power differentials as other women leaders do. These women may also prefer to practice prevention-focused leadership behaviour to avoid risks in the workplace, taking decisions or face colleagues who try to question such un-leader-like behaviours. So, question of negotiation to seek a degree of acceptance for establishing legitimacy may be none or very low.

The key characteristic features of women school heads having no legitimacy despite holding leadership position can be stated as follows:

1. Accepts patriarchy, orthodoxy and stereotypes in the education system.
2. Avoids facing the troublesome situations and challenges; does not take decisions.
3. Subordinates may overpower the leader especially in decision-making.
4. Excessive dependence on the subordinates for her official work.
5. Very thin distinction between personal views as working in leadership position and subordinates' views.
6. Listens to a few subordinates who are mostly new to the job, are young, with whom she feels safe and comfortable, and tries to avoid others whose competence is higher.
7. Weak in instructional leadership essential for a school head.
8. Highly compromises having dependent on less competent subordinates that is deterrent to school's quality and interprets this as managing and balancing different compulsions.

Those women who practice traditional gender perspective with prevention-focused leadership behaviour are likely to receive very less or no legitimacy especially from their subordinates and higher officials.

A CONTINUUM OF INTERACTION FOR LEGITIMACY BETWEEN LEADERSHIP-FOCUS BEHAVIOUR AND GENDER PERSPECTIVE

In this section, the continuum of interaction for legitimacy between leadership-focus behaviour and gender perspective from nil to high is discussed based on the four types of legitimization processes studied and discussed above in this section. A continuum for legitimization is proposed as no legitimacy is constant spatially and time-wise. It does not remain the same for an individual on all occasions and at all times. Also, it differs from individual to individual across space and time.

The present sub-section, therefore, begins with a discussion on the continuum between preventive and promotion-focused leadership behaviour. It moves on to discuss and explore the continuum between traditional and rational gender perspective. Lastly, the interaction continuum between leadership-focus behaviour and gender perspective is attempted to be explained.

Promotion and Prevention-Focused Leadership Behaviour as a Continuum

When women are young and also married, as in case of Rajasthan's women leaders considered in this study, their compulsions to negotiate multiple roles and identities within the family as well as in the workplace are higher. During this time, to maintain their focus on their profession, attend to the family responsibilities and child care duties and at the same time fulfil their personal aspiration of becoming a school leader, they interact continuously with others among the host of many other obligations, expectations and responsibilities. During this juncture, when they are amidst intense negotiations between family and work pressures, they prefer to practice prevention-focused behaviour exercising caution despite having a rational gender perspective.

By contrast, middle-aged women who have been able to complete most of their family responsibilities now that their children have grown to become independent enough to carry on their own as well as have fulfilled their aspiration of becoming school heads, it can be said that they have negotiated their roles and multiple identities and are fairly settled in their life. Such women school heads practice more of promotion-focused leadership behaviour. They also draw their strength from the experience of having led their life, facing challenges and taking risks on various occasions during their earlier stages. In this study, most of the women were middle-aged—in the 50-year age range. However, the age of women leaders from Haryana and Madhya Pradesh ranged from the early forties to the late forties. Nonetheless, even these women were able to balance their work and life responsibilities, roles and compulsions.

Women are likely to face higher stressful negotiations for the legitimacy if they hail from predominantly agrarian, traditional communities and first generation learner families. Their transition to white-collar jobs does involve intense negotiation for legitimization of school leadership as status attribution is low and power differentials are high. These women are mostly from Telangana and Rajasthan. In order to overcome this, legitimization of school leadership depends increasingly upon the core capabilities, agency and disregarding gender notions. Women from urban backgrounds are likely to have less stressful negotiations due to their orientation to urban lifestyle and exposure to competition as in case of women from Delhi, Madhya Pradesh and the National Capital Region parts of Uttar Pradesh. In both these cases, it is more likely that women predominantly practice promotion-focused leadership behaviour.

Nonetheless, these women who were observed to be having promotion-focused leadership behaviour were seen to adhere to traditional gender perspective as well as rational gender perspective in the work place. It may be due to the stressful negotiations with colleagues arising from inherent contradiction between differing perspectives, expectations, status attribution and perception of power differentials. Hence, though recognized for their success, these women might engage in practising both promotion-focused and prevention-focused leadership behaviours depending upon the situations and persons.

Irrespective of young or old, these women leaders hesitated to show case their achievements at times, accept visibility and recognition openly to avoid backlash, illegitimacy and/or glass-cliff effects. So, they were careful in continuing their normal routine works, completed the tasks on time and maintained the records and so on in the school. They continued to work as efficiently as before despite working over and above their expected roles and responsibilities in the school.

Many women also maintained a delicate balance in practising both types of leadership behaviours that would enhance their status attribution and reduce the perception of power differentials so that negotiations are moderate and minimum to achieve legitimacy for their leadership. These were reflected in their actions that narrowed the gap between what is expected of a leader and what is expected of a woman. These actions mainly pertained to exercising optimism, taking higher risks, using opportunities and not willing to be bogged down by setbacks. Thus, the women leaders considered in this study sought a continuum in the leadership focus between prevention and promotion depending on the demands of the situation and time.

Women also change the interpretation about school leadership from achieving the set goals to excellence. As they traverse from preventive to promotion-focused leadership behaviour, women engage others in more and more activities in the school. They also create opportunities for other teachers and facilitate them to enhance their core capabilities. Exploiting the advantages of different structures becomes natural for them. In this way, women leaders transit from prevention-focused to promotion-focused leadership behaviour.

Traditional and Rational Gender Perspective as a Continuum

In the Indian context, traditional gender perspective is mainly reflected in terms of a high degree of acceptance of gender discrimination, stereotypes and orthodoxy as 'givens' despite coming in the way of a woman's professional growth or career advancement. There is a perception of safety and comfort in this acceptance that does not disturb the status quo and does not question the patriarchy as it offends none in the school or family. Women do not deny receiving guidance and support from men assuming a higher position. By doing so, they may experience lesser perception of power differentials and lesser negotiations than those with a rational gender perspective. In this way, they come to even avoid risks, backlash and glass-cliff effects. A gender perspective does not depend on age of the woman or her place of work or family background completely. It is what she nurtures within herself by taking a stand in her life and profession.

Rational gender perspective of a woman gets indicated through a variety of behaviours such as ignoring gender stereotypes, garnering support from higher officials, diligently discussing with colleagues, maximizing the vocational anticipatory socialization, leading activities in the school and beyond at the system level, ignoring constraints and the like. They even effectively avoid, negotiate or navigate through gender discrimination, orthodoxy and patriarchy to emerge as leaders and create situations so that their efforts and achievements are recognized by officers. They work in their own ways according to their pace under different circumstances. They subtly question the notions about a woman's ability as a leader and gendered notions like women cannot act tough, cannot take decisions, etc., through their actions.

In the narratives we see that older women school heads not agreeing with the younger school heads who were narrating their tales of gender discrimination. So, as experiences are accumulated over time from young adults to matured professionals, a shift in the perception about gendered notions also takes place in women. Accordingly, the perception of power differentials also changes without much expectation about status attribution from subordinates. Hence, the stress of negotiating for acceptance loses its gravity to an extent. The woman with rational gender perspective is able to negotiate her legitimacy with much ease than the woman with traditional gender perspective. In this way, not only subordinates, community and higher officials interpret and decide the legitimacy of a woman's leadership but also the woman leader herself interprets her own legitimacy.

Continuum of Interaction between Leadership Behaviour and Gender Perspective

Traditional style of leadership strengthens the rigidity, gendered notions and orthodox practices in the hierarchical nature of education system especially referring to excessive control, lack of understanding about the contextual factors especially with reference to women as a distinct category, bind application of rules, unnecessary importance to hierarchy and so on. So, variations in the hierarchical education system, traditional leadership styles or gendered notions lead to changes in the perception of power differentials by the leader and status attribution by the subordinates. It results in variations in the degree of acceptance of leadership and hence legitimacy of the woman leader. Here, there is a continuous and dynamic interaction between leadership focus and gender perspective of women school leaders causing different levels of legitimization of women leaders in the Indian context. It refers to the continuum of interaction on which women school heads traverse to establish legitimacy as successful leaders. In this way, legitimization of women school leaders is a complex process involving dynamic interaction between leadership-focus behaviours and gender perspectives to create varying levels of status attribution, power differentials and negotiations to create a certain degree of acceptance.

Theorizing School Leadership of Women in the Indian Context

LOOKING THROUGH THE LENS OF SOCIAL ONTOLOGY

The principles of social ontology are applied to theorize school leadership of women by considering the Indian context through the means of answering the research question raised in a comprehensive manner. The method used so far to address the four objectives involves developing distinct conceptual frameworks for analysing different themes in the previous chapters. It adopted a process-based approach of analysis to arrive at a set of distinct results for each objective. As a next step in this chapter, a nested matrix will be created using these conceptual frameworks, process of analysis and their respective results from the preceding chapters by consolidating, aligning and establishing synchronous relationship between them.

The emergent properties referring to 'Whole' and 'wholes' discussed in Chapter 2 under the theoretical framework are elaborated and applied here for theorizing school leadership of women in the Indian context. Elder-Vass (2010) articulates in detail the process of identifying the emergent properties having causal power creating the 'wholes' of the parts and the 'Whole' as well as the relationship between them. According to him, the causal power of social structures is understood through 'emergent properties' referring to the 'Whole' or 'entity' that explains how the entities can have a causal impact on the world in their own right, which is not equal to what the sum of their parts would have if they were not organized into one particular kind of 'Whole'. The capability of having such an impact is the causal power of the entity or the 'Whole' concerned. Therefore, causal power or emergent property refers to some intrinsic aspect of an entity that can have a causal impact on the world of social phenomenon (ibid.). Emergent property or causal power/property arises because of the particular relationships that hold between the parts in a particular kind of whole. A full understanding of any given case of emergence depends on morphogenic and morphostatic processes that create and sustain its existence (ibid.).

For an entity or the 'Whole' to continue for more than an instant, there must be some set of factors causing from behind, those that maintain stability of the entity and those that change the phenomenon. The process by which a set of factors tend to 'elaborate or change' a system's given form, structure or state is called 'morphogenesis'. Those set of factors or processes that tend to 'preserve or maintain' a system's given form or state is called 'morphostasis' (Buckley, 1967, pp. 57–58). Nonetheless, it is impossible to explain the causation of events except as the outcome of a causal interaction between the 'wholes' that are viewed in laminated terms (Bhaskar, 1975).

Elder-Vass (2010, p. 59) provides a framework for constructing the social ontology composed of identifying the following:

- Particular entities or 'wholes' constituting the objects of the disciplines.
- Parts of each entity and sets of relationships between them.
- Mechanism through which their parts and characteristic relationships between them produce emergent properties of the 'whole'.
- Morphogenic and morphostatic factors cause the continuity of existence of the entity.
- The ways in which these entities or 'wholes' interact to cause events for the 'Whole', the discipline that we seek to explain.

The first three steps are exhaustively dealt with in Chapters 3 to 6. The ladder of school leadership is the 'Whole' and six paths, which are noting but the steps of the ladder are the 'wholes' that constitute the objects of the ladder of school leadership. The parts of each of these steps, relationships between them and mechanism through which they produce the 'whole' and characteristic relationship between them have also been identified through an exhaustive analysis in the preceding chapters. These particular entities or 'wholes' constituting the objects of the discipline, the school leadership of women, are: availability of opportunity for school leadership, path of school leadership of women, determinants of successful school leadership of women and legitimacy of school leadership of women.

Different parts of each entity are the factors identified and used in the analysis. These can be either morphostatic or morphogenic. The process by which 'wholes' are formed and interact with each other to cause the 'Whole' is explained in this chapter—the ladder of school leadership of women, including answering the question on how women succeed. This entire exercise through this book marks a beginning for the discourse on women leadership as a distinct category in the Indian context.

AN OVERVIEW OF THE PROCESS OF THEORIZATION OF SCHOOL LEADERSHIP OF WOMEN IN THE INDIAN CONTEXT

The causal power or emergent properties of each type of entity are briefly mentioned here as an overview of the entire exercise. It would be elaborated subsequently in the following sections. Seven themes emerged from the narratives of women school leaders, which led to 'wholes' referring to different steps in the ladder of school leadership of women. To this, one more step is included from the secondary data analysis on the representation of women in different school leadership positions. In all, there are six steps constituting six 'wholes' for the causal power of structures of the emergent property, the 'Whole'— called the ladder of school leadership of women.

The conceptual framework and the process of analysis adopted for examining the availability of opportunities for school leadership positions for women led to unveiling the pattern of representation of women in different school leadership positions in all states and UTs as well as at the national level. This discourse on availability of opportunity for school leadership also led to the understanding of the system's constraints and limitations in providing opportunities for school leadership positions. This is the first step in the ladder of school leadership of women in the Indian context.

From the seven themes that emerged from the narratives, five more steps for the ladder of school leadership of women emerged. It emerged due to the interaction between the agency of women school head with five different structures. The conceptual framework consists of emergent themes, its characteristics, related structure/s and the path of school leadership. Narratives inquiry was used to identify the ladder of school leadership, the Whole, from the narratives.

The conceptual framework and process of analysis to identify the determinants of successful school leadership of women led to positioning the ladder of school leadership of women between different coordinates of capacity–agency on the x-axis and leadership behaviour on the y-axis to create a special characteristic feature for the path traversed that is within the leadership discourse (Figure 7.1). It happens within the system's context of availability of opportunity for school leadership. In the figure, numbers 1 to 4 that are given for the leadership behaviour and capacity–agency interaction represent the following:

Explanation for Leadership behaviours from 1 to 4:

1. Culturally congruent with prevention-focused leadership behaviour.
2. Culturally congruent with promotion-focused leadership behaviour
3. Universal prevention-focused leadership behaviour.
4. Universal promotion-focused leadership behaviour.

Similarly, The explanation for capacity–agency interactions from 1 to 4 is as follows:

1. Domain-specific capacity with practical evaluative agency.
2. Domain-specific capacity with projective agency.
3. Fundamental human capacity with practical evaluative agency.
4. Fundamental human capacity with projective agency.

The conceptual framework for the legitimacy of school leadership of women revealed the process by which different legitimacy levels are

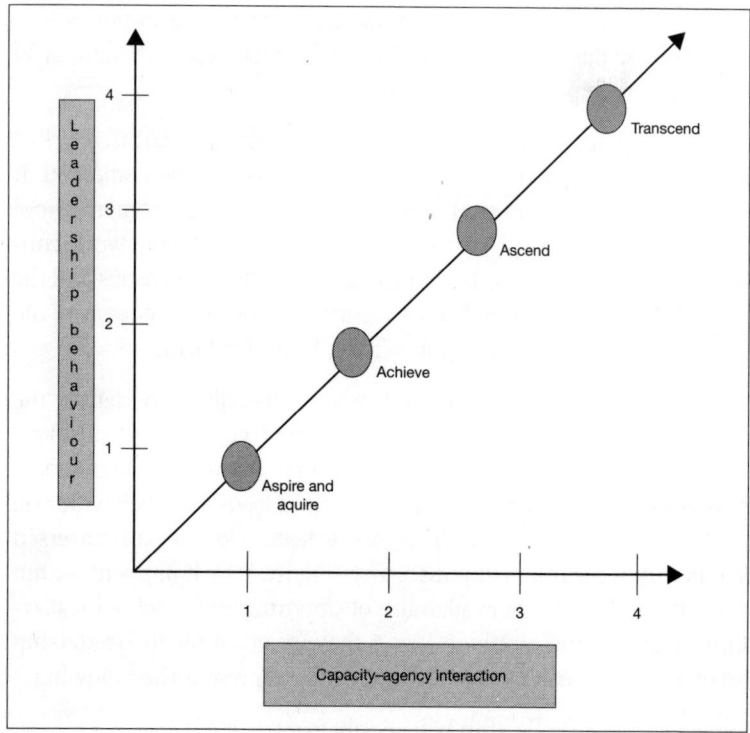

Figure 7.1 *Path of School Leadership Traversed by Women School Heads in the Indian Context*

created, varying from nil to high depending on how women school heads use negotiation, status attribution and perception of power differentials and degree of acceptance. The varying levels of legitimacy are also aligned with the different steps in the ladder of school leadership of women.

The mechanism through which different parts and characteristic relationships between them produce emergent property or the 'Whole', that is, the ladder of school leadership of women, is studied mainly through its parts—the 'wholes'. These 'wholes' are interactions between different structures and agency, interaction between leadership behaviour and gender perspective, emergent

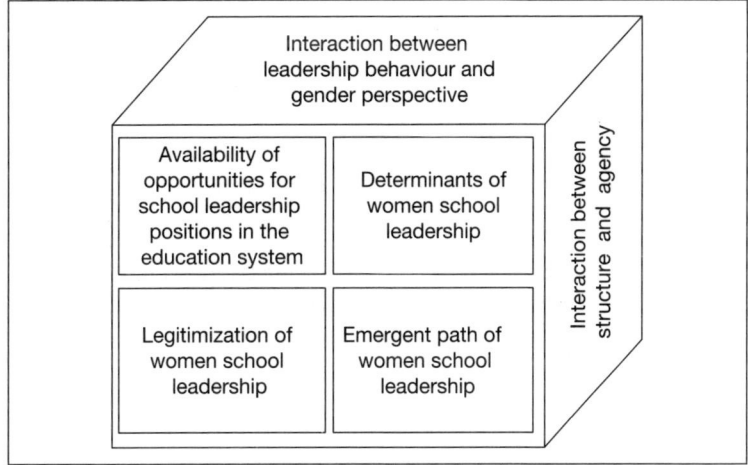

Figure 7.2 *Theorizing School Leadership of Women in India*

themes and path of women's school leadership and opportunities available and representation of women in school leadership positions (see Figure 7.2). These emergent properties are also causally associated with at least one relevant structure predominantly, while simultaneously interacting with other structures. Morphogenic and morphostatic causing the existence of the entity are identified and used throughout the process of analysis. However, it was observed that what is a morphostatic factor in one event may turn out to be a morphogenic factor in the other event. For example, gendered notions may seem to be morphostatic factor in the school when women are trying to acquire school leadership positions, whereas the same is a morphogenic factor when women are on the path to ascend and transcend on the ladder of school leadership.

Different 'wholes' are nested into a matrix for constructing inter- and intra-relationships between the 'wholes' and between different elements within the 'wholes'. Iteration between all six 'wholes' is carried out which are interdependent to describe the 'Whole'. Each step in the ladder constituting a whole is held together with the next step in the ladder due to the interaction between different actors and their social relationships with other structures and actors, causal inter-connections between other actors and their social relationships, interdependence among different agents, their actions and the positions these agents occupy with reference to the education system, which is the primary structure where school leadership exists and functions. A detailed step-wise exposition in theorizing the school leadership of women is attempted for which a matrix is also created (Table 7.1).

PATH-WISE EXPOSITION TO THEORIZATION OF SCHOOL LEADERSHIP OF WOMEN IN THE INDIAN CONTEXT

Path 1 ('whole' 1): Availability of Opportunities for School Leadership Positions

Parts of the 'whole': The primary factors influencing the representation of women in school leadership positions are school categories, schooling pattern and school leadership positions. Other influencing factors are recruitment policy in the state, parallel leadership positions as alternate choices available in the state and capabilities of women who are in the school leadership positions.

Morphogenic and Morphostatic Factors: Representation of women in school leadership positions depends on few morphostatic factors which do not change significantly and are considered comparatively stable. These are school categories and its related school leadership positions, schooling pattern in the state and recruitment policies in the state. Morphogenic factors that change in time and space are alternate choices available as parallel leadership positions in the state and capabilities of women school heads.

Process/Mechanism through Which Different Parts of the 'whole' Are Related to Each Other: Women apply for school leadership positions wherever there is direct recruitment policy. Thereby, they try to reduce the long waiting period arising from promotion based on seniority. They exercise domain-specific capacity with practical evaluative agency to interact with the provision and access to school

Table 7.1 Leadership Attributes, Processes and Functions Determining the Success of Women School Leaders in the Indian Context

Path of school leadership of women	Emergent theme	Characteristics	Structure	Capacity–agency interaction	Structure–capacity–agency interaction: determinants of school leadership of women	Leadership behaviour	Gender perspective	Legitimization process: interaction between leadership behaviour and gender perspective	Legitimacy level accorded by subordinates
Availability of opportunity	Opportunity for school leadership position in the education system	Apply for the school leadership position, compete for direct recruitment, wait for promotion, acquire essential qualification, recruitment policy in the state, representation of women in leadership positions	Education system	Domain-specific capacity with practical evaluative agency	School category and schooling pattern in the states; provision and access to school leadership positions	Not applicable	Not applicable	Not applicable	Legitimacy is not applicable for women aspirants. Legitimacy here applies to institutions where school leadership positions exist, i.e., schools.
Aspire	Social and educational background of the family	Use the inputs received through intellectual capital within the family for maximizing the capacity to compete to get necessary eligibility	Family	Domain-specific capacity with practical evaluative agency	Parents' educational qualification; collective aspiration of women and her parents and husband; develops a strong belief and conviction in the aspirant	Prevention-focused and culturally congruent leadership behaviour	Traditional gender perspective	Not applicable	Education system makes recruitment policies and creates opportunities. So, legitimacy for both of them is the highest

(*Continued*)

Table 7.1 (Continued)

Path of school leadership of women	Emergent theme	Characteristics	Structure	Capacity–agency interaction	Structure–capacity–agency interaction: determinants of school leadership of women	Leadership behaviour	Gender perspective	Legitimation process: interaction between leadership behaviour and gender perspective	Legitimacy level accorded by subordinates
		Family orientation- and environment for women's employment; vocational anticipatory socialization							
Acquire	Familial support	Parental support, husband's support, seek emotional support from parents and husband, get motivated and get child care support. Take support of the technical expertise of father and husband to work efficiently in the workplace as HM	Family	Domain-specific capacity with practical evaluative agency	Higher level of preparedness to compete in the employment market; higher access to information and knowledge about employment; preparedness for a life of career	Prevention focused; culturally congruent leadership behaviour (but unclear distinction and hazy in clarity of explicit behaviour.	Traditional gender perspective	Status attribution: low and uncertain; perception of power differentials: high; negotiation: not clear as she has only acquired the	Legitimacy is deterministic: it is of the nature of necessary and essential level

Achieve	Balancing resilience with determination	Knows the limitations of traditional practices; resistance from the teachers and higher officers	School	Domain-specific capacity with projective agency	Practice distributed leadership/shared leadership; create identity for the school, knowledge-driven leadership practice	She is trying to understand the norm-based leadership practices) Promotion-focused and culturally congruent leadership behaviour (There is a higher degree of clarity in leadership behaviour which is in the stage of establishing a norm-based leadership practices)	Rational gender perspective	Status attribution: lower; perception of power differentials: higher; negotiation: high accompanied with stress	Legitimacy is deterministic but above the level of necessary and essential leadership position now
	Gender: is it a notion or an experience?	Exploit the social challenges to one's advantage; face the threats boldly; resistance from the community	Community (diversity of school contexts)		Objective assessment of utilitarian value of conflicting roles in a given circumstance; build trust by establishing good relationships. School head's abilities and initiatives to involve the community in schooling processes				

(*Continued*)

Table 7.1 (Continued)

Path of school leadership of women	Emergent theme	Characteristics	Structure	Capacity–agency interaction	Structure–capacity–agency interaction: determinants of school leadership of women	Leadership behaviour	Gender perspective	Legitimization process: interaction between leadership behaviour and gender perspective	Legitimacy level accorded by subordinates
Ascend	Leading school administration, management and academic functions	Decision-making, ensuring TLP, develop people management skills, manage people effectively and efficiently	School, community (diversity of school contexts)	Fundamental human capacity with practical evaluative agency	Direct all efforts to achieve student learning, understand the larger issues and needs of the community beyond fulfilling the needs of the school; knowledge-driven decision-making in school management and administration; academic leadership	Prevention-focused and universal leadership behaviour (Women HM trying to move beyond the norm-based leadership practices)	Traditional gender perspective	Status attribution: higher; perception of power differentials: higher; negotiation: mediated and hence moderate	Mediated and hence moderate legitimacy
		Acquire proficiency in rules and administration as well as professional excellence	Education system		Core professional competence influencing the choice as a school leader				

| Transcend | Zeal beyond school leadership, irrespective of gender | Social service. Love for children, projects of life, move beyond the limitations of education system and leadership roles, withering distinction between personal and professional life, ignore gender discrimination and stereotypes | Education system; society—diversity in school contexts | Fundamental human capacity with projective agency | Situational leadership skills and abilities, gradually mature into a transformational leader, extent of willingness and aptitude to lead instead of spending time on routine school administration and/or management, adopt people-centred approach, transcend the norm-based school leadership, practice transformational leadership, integrate innate feminine qualities with professional roles as a leader | Promotion-focused and universal leadership behaviour (She has moved beyond the norm-based leadership behaviour) | Rational gender perspective | Status attribution: higher; perception of power differentials: lower; negotiation: least negotiation | Legitimacy is voluntary and therefore high |

leadership positions in the education system. However, the process culminating in the representation of women in school leadership position is a complex phenomenon indeed. Foremost is the availability of school leadership positions in the education system. Results show that there is an acute shortage of designated leadership positions as 60 per cent of school categories are stand-alone schools which constitute only 28.65 per cent of the total schools. Recruitment is largely gender neutral wherever there is direct recruitment. Promotion of teachers for different school leadership positions is largely based on seniority, which is also gender neutral in all the states. Parallel leadership positions influence the choice of school leadership, especially at elementary and secondary levels. However, at the senior secondary level, women prefer to be vice-principals and principals as they have comparatively more power and autonomy for decision-making. Women who are in these leadership positions are also qualified higher than the minimum essential required, younger in age, ready to be relocated to rural areas and moderately experienced. Achieved capabilities have acted as positive catalysts for women to become vice-principals and principals. Thus, the representation of women is a function of provision or availability of opportunities for school leadership positions, especially in terms of school categories, schooling pattern and school leadership positions, and the capabilities of women in terms of educational and professional qualification as well as a minimum number of years of experience as teachers within the state's context of recruitment policy. In addition, the parallel leadership positions in the education system and in the family background they acquired influence the choices of holding a particular leadership.

Path 2 ('whole' 2): Aspire for School Leadership Positions

Parts of the 'whole': Different aspects of path 2 referring to Aspire are as follows: social and educational background of the family referring to educational qualification of the parents, in-laws and husband, their occupation and location of living such as rural or urban; vocational anticipatory socialization received in the family during the formative years, especially while studying university education; and conviction and strong belief as an aspiring teacher to occupy school leadership position.

Morphogenic and Morphostatic Factors: Morphostatic factors are social and educational background of the family whose primary members include parents, husband and in-laws; occupation of different members of the family; and location where the family lived—rural and urban areas which are also closely linked to the occupational pattern. These two sets of factors influence the vocational anticipatory socialization, which is a morphogenic factor, during the formative years of education, especially at the senior secondary and university education.

Process/Mechanism through Which Different Parts of the 'whole' Are Related to Each Other: Women aspirants exploit the intellectual capital available in the family in terms of educational qualification of parents, husbands and in-laws. The debates and discussions about the dilemmas, apprehensions as well as the resolution to achieve provide the required space for getting clarity about their goals, aspirations and various means and ways to possess leadership positions irrespective of seniority-based promotion or direct recruitment. It means to say that chances of rejecting the promotions are far lesser when the opportunity knocks the door, and the probability of passing the examination and facing the competition is high for direct recruitment. This is also dependent on the orientation of the family and its members towards women's aspirations. Hence, family as a structure plays an important role in determining the extent and quality of vocational anticipatory socialization that the woman receives. Higher the educational qualification with greater exposure to the employment market and its competitiveness, the middle-class orientation, considering education as the intellectual capital and an investment for life in the family, provides a wider scope for the women to explore, discuss and try out a variety of opportunities to seek a profession including school leadership. Hence, there is a collective aspiration for school leadership of women in the family. These impact the convictions and beliefs in the woman to strengthen her aspirations and set clear goals to grow professionally and carve a career for her.

Being cautious, treading the road to school leadership assiduously, she will exercise a prevention-focused leadership behaviour that is culturally congruent to ensure that family members facilitate her without much resistance. Hence, it is more likely that she exhibits a traditional gender perspective as a means to protect, nurture and cherish her aspiration to become a school leader. Therefore, during this phase, she has a mix of uncertainty and determination to become a school leader, especially in her explicit behaviour. At this stage, she is also trying to understand norm-based leadership so as to best fit for the role in the future.

The question of legitimacy does not arise for the women as she is an aspirant as yet. However, the aspiration finds its strong roots in the high levels of legitimacy attached to the school leadership position in the education system. This is also same as above for availability of opportunities for school leadership positions.

Path 3 ('whole' 3): Acquire the School Leadership Position

Parts of the 'whole': Different parts constituting the path involve familial support in the form of higher levels of preparedness to compete in the job market, increased access to information and knowledge about employment and preparedness for a life of career.

Morphogenic and Morphostatic Factors: Higher levels of preparedness to compete in the job market, higher/greater access to information and knowledge about employment and preparedness for a career are morphogenic factors. There are no morphostatic factors in the path on 'Acquire' school leadership position. All are morphogenic factors as they are ever evolving due to the changing policies, vacancies and needs of the education system. According to the changes in the education system, parents' and aspirant's responses also undergo changes to rise up to the expectations of the required qualifications and criteria to compete in the job market. It requires updating of information and knowledge from time to time. All these impact the nature, level and characteristics of preparedness for a life of career in the woman aspirant.

Process/Mechanism through Which Different Parts of the 'whole' Are Related to Each Other: Harnessing on the intellectual capital prevailing in the family, aspirants' struggle is a bit lesser to access higher education and professional education to qualify with requisite university degrees. Parents wish and also enable the daughters to educate to a level higher than their own, especially in working middle-class families. They also provide the required edge to access latest knowledge and information, trends in the job market and extent of competition visible for preparing and successfully passing through competition. Mostly these families, which have an orientation to middle class, do not hesitate to encourage their daughters to seek employment, specifically the government jobs, that ensure a comparatively higher financial stability for the future family life. Parents discuss with their daughters about the career options after they complete their university degrees. Women as aspirants, to get a higher status in the society, also try for other jobs besides teaching and school leadership.

Husbands also enable their aspiring wives to get essential qualification. They support and prepare them gradually to acquire a school leadership position. Young women, if not all, were also handheld to navigate through cultural and social practices of the society that influence the education system in the form of gender stereotype practices, discrimination against women teachers and school heads when they acquired school leadership positions. This is especially true for young teachers who compete to become school leaders in their early 30s. Husbands provide extended vocational anticipatory socialization, encourage them to take higher risks in their workplace, enhance their confidence and strive hard to ensure that their wives acquire school leadership positions. They are ready to walk alongside their wives by way of filling application forms, giving adequate time to prepare for examinations and participating in household chores and responsibilities. They instil courage in their wives to face gender discrimination, help remove hesitations, make them feel relaxed and make them laugh!

Women in turn respond to the familial support in a number of ways. They discuss their aspirations with their parents and husbands, seek guidance, explore all possible new options available in the job market and are abreast with information. Being aware of gender discrimination, demands and responsibilities of family life, most of the women also prefer socially acceptable jobs and preferably in the government sector. They prepare themselves to acquire confidence and courage to brace gendered notions and learn to navigate stereotypes and discrimination. They also seek the support of parents for child care. Some of them also make choices late in their life for a career in school leadership positions if opportunities are available. In these and many other ways, women engage with domain-specific capacity, exercising their practical evaluative agency to acquire school leadership positions.

Most of the women attempt to balance professional and personal life by balancing their roles and responsibilities in the family and school. They try to exercise choice of independence diligently at home for sustained support. They also learn to think judiciously about the possible and available options and cautiously exercise measured risk. In this way, women acquire school leadership positions.

Women who acquired school leadership positions practice prevention-focused, culturally congruent leadership behaviour in the initial years. They try to understand the norm-based leadership practices that give them quick acceptability to gain legitimacy from their subordinates. In the process, they may also opt to exhibit traditional gender perspective irrespective of the fact that they believe in it or not only to use it as a shield to navigate through gendered notions, stereotypes and discriminatory practices, influencing the education system. Despite the fact that they get a lower status attribution due to traditional gender practice and prevention-focused leadership behaviour, which is also coupled with higher levels of perception of power differentials and highly stressful negotiations. As a consequence, they get the initial legitimacy that is essential to begin the career as school heads. No doubt, the legitimacy is deterministic or rigid in nature, yet they quickly receive essential levels of legitimacy required for carrying out functions of leading the school efficiently and looking ahead into the future to excel.

Path 4 ('whole' 4): Achieve the Status of School Leader in the School

Parts of the 'whole': Different parts constituting the path on 'Achieve' are the processes by which women achieve the status of a leader wherein they balance between resilience and determination. It requires knowing the limitations of the traditional practices in the school to transit from the positional leadership to evolve as a leader. Women practice distributed leadership, share leadership, undertake knowledge-driven processes and strive to create a distinct identity for the school.

Morphogenic and Morphostatic Factors: To face the threats boldly and act diligently to tackle the resistance from the community demands the ability to question whether gender is a mere notion or an experience. It calls for an objective assessment of utilitarian values of conflicting roles in a given circumstance, to build trust by establishing good relationships and to undertake initiatives to involve community in schooling processes.

All these factors are morphogenesis in nature as practising leadership expects that the leader should know the limitations of in-school traditional practices influenced by the society, face the threats boldly and tackle resistance from the community. Besides, practising distributed leadership, sharing leadership, undertaking knowledge-driven processes and striving to create a distinct identity for the school are different aspects of continuous improvement in the school.

Process/Mechanism through Which Different Parts of the 'whole' Are Related to Each Other: To leap into the realm beyond positional leadership, it is essential to understand why people behave in a certain way and its implications for leadership and school quality. These are ever evolving and depend on the mutual interactions between community, teachers and parents in the school. Understanding the limitations of traditional practices comes from the manifested actions of the individuals in the school. These also change according to situations and circumstances. Hence, objective assessment of utilitarian value of conflicting roles in a given circumstance, building trust by establishing good relationships and undertaking initiatives to involve community in schooling processes are necessary for the women to evolve into leaders.

The family cannot enter into the in-school role of the woman school head, which begins once the woman enters the school. School is the space where the woman has to fight her battle all by herself as the head of the institution. Since nobody else can take that role, she has to prove herself and transit from holding a leadership position to exhibiting leadership in action. It demands ever-dynamic processes, practices and novel approaches to effectively function as a leader. She has to amply exhibit school leadership qualities, styles, processes and behaviours to cater to diverse demands from education functionaries working at higher levels, teachers in the school, stakeholders and children. She also has to attend to various challenges simultaneously at one and the same time. This is also the time when she has to establish herself as an efficient leader. It means that she must learn to understand the limitations of traditional practices of being a school head. For example, one cannot remain as a mere administrator in the school carrying out routine administration. Nor can women function as managers as the needs and demands of the school in today's changing world go beyond managing events, people and problems to look ahead, lead the change for school transformation, improve teaching–learning processes, lead the learning, ensure child focus, provide opportunities for teachers' development, etc. It means that only one leader cannot do the job but several leaders and teams have to be created and leadership must be shared and distributed. So, a woman reaches the step 'Achieve' if she practices distributed and shared leadership, believing in others' capabilities and leadership qualities. It also implies that the school can no more remain the same as before but has to create an identity of its own.

All these require robust leadership practices beyond skills and abilities to processes driven by knowledge that assure quality. School heads have to acquire a strong domain-specific capacity along with projective agency. The inherent nature of abilities has to be nurtured and protected. She has to direct all activities and efforts to ensure that all students learn and understand the larger issues and needs of the community without confining to the school.

Leadership behaviour for such a highly demanding transition on the part of the women school head cannot but be promotion focused, that is, culturally congruent and a rational gender perspective. She will have to begin with a learning curve regarding her own leadership function, role and processes. However, what she is trying through the step Achieve is establishing a norm-based leadership for herself that is in accordance with the government's directions on roles and responsibilities for a school head and gain acceptance of the school's community. Therefore, the status attribution is moderate, there is a higher perception of power differentials and negotiation is accompanied with stress, which is high. It means that a woman school head enjoys a legitimacy that is deterministic in nature but above the level of necessary and essential.

Path 5 ('whole' 5): Ascend the Path of Success as a School Leader

Parts of the 'whole': The path on 'Ascend' consists of different aspects such as develop and strengthen the core professional competencies influencing the choice as a school leader; direct all efforts to assure and achieve student learning; understand the larger issues and needs of the community instead of expecting the community to fulfil the needs of the school; undertake knowledge-driven decision-making in school administration and management; and build academic leadership. Primary structures with which women school leaders interact and engage are school, community and education system

Morphogenic and Morphostatic Factors: The school head, in an attempt to develop professionally, chooses to focus on fewer but specific factors. These factors, which are different parts of the whole, by default have to be morphogenic as the intent is to ascend the ladder of success, crossing the threshold from the level of positional leadership achieved. So, all those factors mentioned above in describing the parts of the whole constitute morphogenic factors.

Process/Mechanism through Which Different Parts of the 'whole' Are Related to Each Other: In this step of the ladder, women's primary focus is on leading school administration, management and academic functions. They engage in decision-making processes, ensure that teaching–learning processes are well conducted, give attention to develop people management skills and manage people effectively and efficiently. To achieve a significant shift in the quality of school leadership, neither mere domain-specific capacity nor projective evaluative agency suffices because these are specific only to school and its leadership. Leading must now move beyond the boundaries of the school to address people's needs and their emotions and establish connections with a humanistic approach. This calls for using fundamental human capacity that is aptly blended with practical evaluative agency. Inherent potentials exploited aptly, acquired values from the larger life applied suitably according to circumstances by adapting to school's situations and needs. They acquire proficiency in rules, regulations and administration of the school and even achieve excellence as an educational professional. Nonetheless, domain-specific capacity is a necessary and essential condition which has to be continued by the women in leading every day school's administration and management.

As a woman tries to ascend to the next level of excellence, her focus shifts away from giving attention to gendered notions, stereotypes and gender discriminatory practices in the system. She begins to ignore them and tries to concentrate more on developing a professional approach to her work and with the people around her.

In this phase of her career, a woman leader practices prevention-focused leadership behaviour, unlike in the earlier phase when she was in the stage of 'achieve'. In the former step, she practised promotion-focused leadership behaviour. This is because while she is trying to make a conscious shift in her leap to the next level, she has to encase herself to nurture the perspective shift that is taking shape within her, protect it from digressing and concentrate her attention to expand herself to work with others in the community, parents and system level officials. For doing this, she also needs to move beyond culturally congruent leadership behaviour to practice universal leadership behaviour. Hence, the combination of prevention focus with that of universal leadership behaviour aptly suits the women leaders who are trying to move beyond the norm-based leadership practices. In other words, women leaders are moving beyond their comfort zones of operations to newer arenas. However, they continues to maintain a traditional gender perspective predominantly as they cannot ignore the local contexts and have to work within the education system's limitations about gendered notions, stereotypes and discriminations. So, despite an enhanced status attribution, perception of power differentials continues to be higher but with moderate levels of negotiations as they are mediated effectively with a unique combination of a traditional perspective with universal leadership behaviour. Therefore, there is a moderate level of legitimacy gained which is greater than the essential and necessary levels unlike in case of path 'Ascend'.

Path 6 ('whole' 6): Transcend the School Leadership and Limitations of the Education System

Parts of the 'whole': Various components of the step 'transcend' are as follows: situational leadership skills and abilities, mature into a transformational leader over a period of time while working as a leader with the extent of willingness and aptitude to lead instead of spending time on routine school administration and/or management, adopt people-centred approach, transcend the norm-based school leadership, practice transformational leadership and integrate innate feminine qualities with professional roles as a leader.

Morphogenic and Morphostatic Factors: Since the stage of leadership journey is at its pinnacle of success, woman leaders are continuously expanding and growing both professionally and internally as a person. They cannot afford to consider any aspect of their practice to stagnate. They are ever evolving, characterized by a continuous process of learning and practice, which is imminent. Hence, all factors identified under parts of the whole are morphogenic in nature.

Process/Mechanism through Which Different Parts of the 'whole' Are Related to Each Other: This phase of leadership journey is accompanied with zeal that is beyond school leadership position and leadership practice. Women are mostly able to ignore gendered notions, discrimination and stereotypes to move beyond limitations of the education system and its leadership roles and responsibilities. They wither away the distinction between professional and personal life. Primary structures with which these women engage and interact are school, education system and community. This is a phase when they exploit their fundamental human capacity along with projective agency, moving beyond school leadership and gender discrimination. They refer to their work drawing from the larger goals of life and society such as social service, love for children and projects of life to do. They are ready to serve, work extra, enjoy the privilege, take advantage of the space that education system provides them, give back to the system multi-fold, accept recognition if it comes to them, be grateful to the education system and attribute their success to the support provided by the education system despite its limitations, expect from the system but carry on their work if it does not give support, provide more attention and care for children and community, etc.

Women practice promotion-focused leadership behaviour along with universal leadership practice. They no longer try to balance between traditional and rational gender perspective. Now, they practice rational gender perspective openly and willingly with a conviction. They expect status attribution from their colleagues, officials and community to a very less extent. Rather, others give a higher status to such leaders. Perception of power differentials is the lowest as these women enjoy what they do without the need for anybody's recognition and approval. The necessity to negotiate is minimal as they carry out their work irrespective of people, yet taking people along with them be it parents, colleagues, system level officials or community. The need for negotiations reduces to a great extent. Instead, a higher degree of trust building between them and others develops. The independence enjoyed having reached a level of satisfaction and fulfilment culminates in self-actualization. It may be accomplished while working as a leader in the school or later in their life after retirement since they continue to develop internally. Hence, a high level of legitimacy is given to such women voluntarily by their subordinates, colleagues, community and higher officials.

QUEST FOR SUCCESS

The Zeal

Each step in the ladder can be considered as a milestone which an aspiring woman wants to reach in the quest for success as a leader in the school. Women are said to have reached a milestone depending on the level of legitimacy earned or received by the subordinates. They traversed through different steps of the ladder of school leadership at their own pace, negotiating different responsibilities. They traverse the path by balancing between family, work and larger society and by navigating different roles, expectations and challenges. Influenced by the family, garnering support from them and being resilient yet determined to move ahead, they tread through the impediments of gendered notions and yet ignore them wherever and whenever possible. They efficiently carry out school administration without losing academic focus for ensuring student learning.

As some of these women took up school leadership with zeal, they ignored the limitations of the education system and community. Emphasizing on trust building, knowledge-driven processes and people-centred approach, they focused on school improvement. They prioritized understanding the needs of the community without expecting more from them to support school. They crossed the threshold to leap beyond leadership, facing challenges, disregarding those challenges sometimes and tackling gender discrimination in their own ways while staying put aiming at self-actualization by seeking a purpose for life, treating school leadership as an important means. They engaged with their duties and responsibilities as though it is social service for the love for children and undertook work in a project mode, and also showed indebtedness to the system for getting opportunities to excel or go abroad for professional development and recognition of some kind or the other received in the education system. Women also recognize that structures are neither static nor stable, and hence, they can be navigated effectively to succeed as per their definition of success by exercising their agency.

Leadership, Gender, Legitimacy of Women School Leaders

When exercising different leadership styles such as academic, transformational, situational, distributed and/or shared leadership, these women also adopted different leadership behaviours appropriate for the situations to be resilient and determined in their pursuit. They opted for promotion-focused behaviour and/or prevention-focused behaviour in leading the school processes. They also combined these leadership behaviours with another set of leadership behaviours, namely, universal and/or culturally congruent leadership behaviours to work with community, teachers and larger education system while dealing with gendered notions as well as worked for their professional growth.

These women not only juxtaposed different leadership behaviours according to the demands of the situations but also intercepted them with traditional and rational gender perspectives while interacting with subordinates, colleagues, community members and system-level officials. It created varying degrees of legitimacy through a process of status attribution, negotiation, perception of power differentials and degree of acceptance. These different levels of legitimacy indicate different milestones reached, which in turn indicate different levels of successes achieved in accordance with one's own pace and capacity. The extent to which legitimacy is earned by the women as head of the school indicates the degree of her success too.

Characteristic Features of Structures and Agency of Women Leaders

The different themes emerged from the narratives broadly fall across five structures. These are family, school, school context, education system and larger society. Women school heads interacted with these structures. The path emerged from the analysis of the narratives aligns with five structures. It follows, therefore, that the path of school leadership of successful women is formed from an intersectionality of determinants of structure–agency interaction, availability of opportunities, as well as varying levels of legitimacy of school leadership. It means that leadership processes, behaviours and styles of women school heads interacted with different actors influenced by their gender perspectives across different structures.

Interactions between different structures and agency of women school heads resulted in identifying the key determinants of school leadership of successful women, which are of three types, namely, deterministic, mediated and voluntary, depending on the characteristics of the structure. Depending on the fundamental or domain-specific capacities used and the extent of projective or practical evaluative agency exercised, women duly navigated and negotiated through these structures. Therefore, exercising agency, which may be either projective or practical evaluative, depends on the fundamental and/ or domain-specific capacities of women leaders.

The linear path of school leadership of women clearly indicates that the selection to school leadership positions, especially through seniority-based promotion, is due to the deterministic and hierarchical nature of the education system in which school leadership position exists. It maintains the status quo of teachers who are at the lowest level in the hierarchy. This has resulted in under-representation of women as designated HMs and principals at secondary and senior secondary levels.

Despite being predominantly determined by the hierarchical structure of the education system, women have demonstrated that it can be mediated through their agency and also with the help of their family in some cases. Women are able to practice leadership truly only when they reach the stage of ascend and transcend. Precisely due to this reason, women who are in the last step of the school leadership ladder, that is, transcend, have moved beyond the boundaries of the education system to interpret their work into a social cause or a service that is worth doing for self-actualization. Because of this reason, though the leadership positions are defined by the hierarchy of the education system, it can neither confine women leaders nor dominate their aspirations always. It is particularly in this space that agency has played a significant role in exercising leadership that is not limited to school leadership but leadership values drawn from larger life. Therefore, treating education system as static and rigid would render dependency on the positional leadership to understand women leaders, which indeed is a narrow approach.

A predominant practice prevailing in the education system is that teachers promoted to leadership positions based on seniority as per the number of years of experience accumulated. This is equated to having gained leadership qualities, which is a grossly misinterpreted criterion to develop true school leadership for both men and women. This diminutive notion of school leadership for women further suffers from the intersectionality of orthodox stereotypes, gender-blind ways and traditional leadership styles characterized by control, delegation, authority and hierarchy in the education system. As a result, earning legitimacy of school leadership is also a long-drawn process for women. Therefore, developing the school leadership in general and women in particular in India so far has been a stunted one. It implies that practising true school leadership is predominantly an individual's choice in the Indian education system. It is indeed a decisive factor influencing the predominant role of agency over education system structure.

As evident from the qualitative data, many women exercise their agency with the help of family rather than through the education system wherein the leadership position is situated—the macro system. The deterministic nature of education system structure being similar though not uniform across all states, familial background being positive and supportive for many, it is the agency of women that determines the positional holding in the ladder of school leadership in the Indian context. It means women are able to navigate the rigidity of the education system. However, the study shows that efforts by the education system to develop school leadership among women are only modest in India.

Notwithstanding, the support received from the respective families is also not the same for all women. The social, economic, intellectual and cultural contexts being unique to each family, some families facilitated these women to traverse the ladder more than other families could. It is dependent on the family's knowledge about the education system, socio-economic background, career choices and educational background of the family that could support these women. Intellectual capital in the family has an important role to play to support women to acquire, achieve and ascend school leadership in India. For example, the parent's family of the woman leader from Himachal Pradesh lacked the exposure to formal employment market due to hilly terrain, illiteracy of father and poverty. By contrast, the families of principals in Delhi, Uttar Pradesh and Madhya Pradesh were privileged as they possessed higher levels of formal education and were also aware of the competition in employment. The lifestyle of families in Telangana is largely influenced by agriculture, which is their main occupation even though they transited to an urban lifestyle. So, family's orientation to formal employment significantly influences the nature of family support in shaping the career of women.

For women from Himachal Pradesh, heading a cluster of small schools itself provided the necessary platform to transcend the rigidity of the education system. The two women heads in Delhi led themselves to zonal- and district-level leadership steadily through various opportunities that is routinely available to all school heads in the system. Women in Rajasthan and Madhya Pradesh did not fear facing the adversities in the community, school or education system. Out of many women teachers, only a few aspire to be school leaders. Out of the few aspirants, those who acquire the leadership position are still fewer. From amongst the few who acquired, women who achieve and ascend to excel as leaders are rare. Even fewer are those who transcend overcoming the structural constraints. Thus, it is crucial to recognize the importance of agency of women mediating the structures, attempting to rewrite the gender script for school leadership in India as they reach each milestone of success. Against this backdrop, the meaning of school leadership for women in the Indian context is going to be defined.

DEFINING SCHOOL LEADERSHIP FOR WOMEN IN THE INDIAN CONTEXT

The women considered in the study of school leadership in India are those who are well aware of the social norm, customs and traditions of the family. Under the routine normal circumstances, she expects support from her parents and husband. Leadership for women in school education is a stage of professional life aspired and achieved for many as self-actualization. However, a few transcend mediating between different structures, sometimes influencing changes in varying degrees in these structures through their agency, resulting in a meaningful interaction between agency and structures. They try to negotiate between the socially constructed meaning of school leadership for women in the system and society and their own interpretation and understanding arising from the experience of performing in a school leadership role. Hence, for a few women, it is also a means of self-unfoldment, which is beyond self-actualization.

In the present study, therefore, school leadership for women in the Indian context is conceptualized using the phrase 'not only ... but also' juxtaposing the contrasts, contradictions and varying manifestations of leadership roles by women school heads as lived realities. The phrase 'not only ... but also' is used with an intent to effectively represent the paradoxes, understand them and attempt to peep beyond the binaries to dive deep into defining the meaning of school leadership for women in the Indian context:

School leadership for women is not only about 'doing' leadership but also about the 'knowledge' which propels the very doing; not only about the 'will' to do but also the willingness to 'give up'; not only about achievement under 'favourable' conditions but also to accomplish 'in spite of'; not only about ownership but also the readiness to 'let go'; not only about 'problematizing' a situation but also looking 'afresh' with a hope into the future; not only about reward, recognition and merit but also about accepting limitations, under-recognition, misrecognition, non-recognition and extra recognition; not only about 'vertical growth' creating followers but also about 'horizontal expansion' working amidst people; it is not only about exercising the 'power' but also about 'understanding' the POWER of power; not only about 'celebrating' success but also about 'smiling' at failures; not only about 'experiencing' encouragement but also about developing 'dispassion' towards denial of opportunities.

Meaning of school leadership for women in the Indian context, thus, refers to deriving a meaning for oneself by seeking an answer to what is worth doing as a school leader, exploiting the opportunities, understanding the existing structures and their boundaries, translating them to lead schools by maximizing agency to leap into higher realms of self-awareness through actions, practice, review, reflection and meta-cognition. It is an outward–inward movement of raising consciousness beyond the role of school leadership to embrace the greater good traversing from aspiring to transcending the norm-based leadership using the very education system structure as a means with a moral purpose powered by agency.

Gender in school leadership of women in India is about acting independently, being fearless and self-confident, yet exercising restrained neutrality to build trust and ensure mutual interactions in a harmonious way. There is a peculiar admix of binaries in leading schools—exercising caution over fearlessness, practising masculinity and femininity, silently resisting covert compulsions arising from patriarchy yet verbalizing it occasionally, using intuition over logic and making no distinction between personal and professional life at times depending on the situation and time.

POLICY IMPLICATIONS

The present study has attempted to treat women school heads as a distinct category that is different from that of women teachers. An attempt of this nature has the potential to position women as leaders and teachers in the wider discourse of WID and GAD, since they have an immense responsibility of shaping the lives of future generations through schooling. Having treaded the path of success as leaders in the school, they have rewritten the gender script to negate the notion that women have to be empowered up to the level of men or those in other professions or by other external agencies and institutions. They have been successful in building trust, exploiting their own inherent potential to face adversities and reap advantages of the positive environment. Being aware of the ill effects of gender discrimination and stereotypes, they exercise restrained neutrality. They also establish varying degrees of legitimacy as they traverse through the path to success. Some of them even enhance legitimacy incrementally over time to reach the desired goals of their life and self-actualize their dreams and visions. In and through these processes, familial support and its educational background have played a major role for most of the women.

Since the study shows that women mainly depend on their own inherent capabilities and leadership values drawn from larger life not limited to school leadership alone, it is necessary to suggest how policies can influence the participation of women in significant ways. It is also equally important to use this study as a strong case to argue that merit of women in school leadership positions is currently independent of affirmative policies and actions to support them in the Indian context.

Increasing the Provision and Access to School Leadership Positions

School leadership is one of the popular choices which women prefer due to the exposure to higher levels of education, modernity, changing demands of lifestyle and their world view of life. They have begun to believe in themselves more than ever before and are ready to take risks to disprove the popular perceptions about the efficiency of the women, particularly as school leaders.

Fifty-five per cent of P-only schools mostly with A-HMs and an additional nearly 15 per cent of stand-alone school categories with

A-HMs in UP-only, S-only, HS-only and S-HS-only school categories presents a scenario of negligible opportunity for designated school head's position for both men and women. Altogether, a mere 40 per cent of the total school categories comprising P+UP+S, UP+S, P+UP+S+HS and UP+S+HS out of the total 10 school categories in which 306,588 schools exist definitely have designated school leadership positions as head teachers, vice-principal and principals. The schools in these four school categories comprise 19.96 per cent of the total schools in India. Hence, opportunities for school leadership positions are acutely low. Women vice-principals are represented higher only within this abysmally low availability of opportunity constituting only 3.16 per cent of the total schools for P+UP+S+HS school category. It implies that there is an acute shortage of opportunities for both men and women for becoming school heads. This is one of the critical reasons in the education system for under-representation of women in school leadership positions in India with the exception of vice-principals.

An important policy implication is that the number of school categories must be kept at a minimum of four or five so as to be able to manage as a well-defined system. These must be large-sized school categories that are economically and educationally viable for productive teaching and learning to take place. It is feasible to retain P+UP+S+HS, UP+S+HS and P+UP+S along with the feeder school categories of P-only and P+UP. P-only school category is important because children are too young to travel long distances, which also fulfils the norms of the Right of Children to Free and Compulsory Education Act, 2009 (RTE Act, 2009). Other stand-alone school categories are not viable except P+UP. But, P+UP schools are mostly schools with less than 150 students due to which there is no designated HM appointed as per the rules in most of the states, as of now. The RTE Act, 2009 also says that only those elementary schools with 150 students or more designated HMs can be appointed. For all these five school categories, designated leadership positions must be sanctioned and all vacancies filled. This is crucial in the hierarchical nature of the education system because only those who are in the position of power and authority alone have decision-making powers.

Right of Opportunity for Career Progression through School Leadership

It is also important to address the right of teachers and school heads to function in an educationally favourable environment that facilitates professional growth and career progression. There must be adequate opportunities to become leaders as part of their career progression. Availability and access to leadership positions are important criteria that depend on the distribution of school categories with designated leadership positions, recruitment policies of the state and parallel leadership positions. It provides opportunities for women in parallel structures of SSA and RMSA or department of education. Recruitment policies are mostly gender neutral in India across all states. So, opportunities available for women is the same as that of men. However, who opts for school leadership positions depends on state's policy of incentives and perks and increments in the salary for additional responsibilities as school head. At the elementary level, incentives and additional increments in the salary are not well defined or do not exist in many states. It is natural that women may not prefer to take up leadership positions as they have to balance between family's and school's responsibilities. In positions such as vice-principal and principals, roles and responsibilities are well defined and salary structure is competitive and matches with the expectations of the aspirant. Women are represented higher in these positions in several states as well as at all-India level. It means that women measure the options before making choices to take up school leadership positions. So, as a policy, it is suggested that all leadership positions must have well-defined roles and responsibilities along with decision-making powers and competitive salary structures. As elementary-level school category is important to retain, a separate cadre of school leadership position for elementary school must be created in all states and positions filled. Women may be given preference as they can use feminine leadership qualities to the fullest for ensuring higher levels of physical and emotional safety for young kids and children.

Research all over the world has shown that school leadership is essential for overall school improvement and student learning. Equitable environment, favourable conditions for working devoid of gender discrimination and stereotype practices are essential in the education system to ensure dignity to the leadership position that women hold with requisite autonomy and decision-making powers. There is a need to look beyond the education system's rigidity and deterministic nature to address the development of women's school leadership. Hence, policies have to undergo a transformation for aspiring teachers in the education system. It is in terms of the right to opportunity for school leadership positions as part of career progression, right of school leadership for autonomy and decision-making powers, right of women school heads for equality of opportunity and gender equity in school leadership positions and right of school heads to work with dignity and self-esteem.

If these rights are secured by aspiring school heads and practising school heads, a transformation from practising as a positional leadership to competency-based leadership begins, which will bring in institutional change at the school level and education reform at the system level. A policy of this nature is capable of addressing structural inequalities in the education system. Women whose family background and support system are not as favourable as that of some others to acquire school leadership positions, suitable affirmative actions can be taken up to provide necessary exercises within the system to enable them to compete and succeed. Some of the components of such preparatory exercise are building confidence, skill-based training, facing the competition in the system, ways and methods of addressing gender discrimination, training them in applying rules and regulations in the school efficiently and the like. In short, a women-specific SLDP as a special category can be considered. Providing an inclusive environment for women to take up leadership positions is a pathway to argue the case for women teachers to be consciously included in the discourses on WID and GAD.

Bridging the Gap between Women School Leaders and Community

The nature of community as a structure is that it is less/non-hierarchical when compared to schools and education system is hierarchically structured. The opposing nature of these two structures weakens the ownership of the community participation in the schooling of children. While school heads and teachers largely tend to function and operate from the mind-set reflecting the hierarchical nature with the community, the community expects the school to perceive its needs, aspirations and compulsions, interact more closely, respond to its needs and aspirations and meet its expectations. If the school head and teachers do not respond satisfactorily, the community becomes a distant structure for the school and its leadership. It is one of the reasons why women school leaders feel disconnected and attach less importance to the community. It is mainly due to the popularly accepted fact that women leaders are not networked professionally. In other words, there is professional isolation of women.

It is important to make women leaders aware of these distinctions between hierarchical and less/non-hierarchical structures and also spaces of inter-phase between them. This ensures active participation of the community and opens opportunities to shed inhibitions for a greater mutual understanding about each other. Increased interactions though informal ways pave way for greater acceptance of women school leaders blended with democratic leadership style to involve the community. In the present study also, few school heads have demonstrated it. By doing so, they moved up the ladder from ascend to transcend the limitations of the deterministic nature of the education system. The aspiring teachers and practising school heads may be provided sufficient inputs on how to deal with the community to move beyond the rigidity of the hierarchical education system through cluster-level workshops in which even the community members participate. Engaging in an open dialogue with families of school heads is crucial to learn tips to ensure more women access and acquire school leadership positions from diverse socio-economic and cultural backgrounds.

Enhancing Legitimacy of Women's School Leadership

Given the advantages of the feminine leadership qualities, women aspirants and practising school heads must be encouraged to recognize their strengths, nurture them and utilize them by applying strengths in their school contexts. Its positive implications may facilitate to redefine the role of school leadership for both men and women to leverage upon to address unique and challenging circumstances of schools trying to come off their low-base. It will provide opportunities to appropriately address the glass-wall, glass-ceiling and glass-cliff effects that would gather momentum to reduce gender discrimination in school leadership in the Indian context. It might even pave way for reducing illegitimacy effect, backlash, mis-recognition, non-recognition and under-recognition and enhance the legitimacy of women as school leaders. As an aspiring teacher to occupy the school leadership position, a woman may prepare on these lines to be equipped with sufficient skills and techniques to face the real-life situations when she gets appointed as school head.

Leveraging the Familial Support for an Inclusive Approach to Women's School Leadership

As family is playing a predominant role in preparing the women to acquire school leadership positions, it is critical for the education system to be more sensitive and proactive to recognize the contributions made by the family members. The education officers at the higher levels must gear up to learn the methods and means by which women are supported and prepared to acquire the leadership positions and succeed. These may be adapted in a suitable manner to support all women aspirants as a part of an affirmative action to encourage women's school leadership. How to build on the family's support and participate from the rear to creating a social glue between education system and family is another potential area of exploration for redefining the interaction between education system, family, school and community. Key learnings/tips from such families must be captured by inviting them to participate in discussions with education officials and interactions in various workshops on building capacities of women for preparing for a greater role as school leaders. However, such an involvement calls for treading a cautious and diligent path to be cognizant of issues related to cultural reproduction that is not congenial but has the potential to seep into the education system.

Lastly, on the agency of successful women, it is essential to recognize the leadership functions and behaviours of such women who succeeded. Collecting case studies of successful women school leaders and identifying India-specific women's leadership factors, functions and behaviours for ensuring school quality, especially enhancing student learning, provides another window for innovative practices and leadership practices in the times when the country is facing learning crisis among students.

REFERENCES

Abu-Tineh, A. (2012). Leadership effectiveness in Jordanian Educational Institution: A comparison of Female and Male Leaders. *Educational Management Administration and Leadership, 41*, 79–94.

Addi-Raccah, A. (2002). Feminisation of teaching and principalship in the Israeli education system: A comparative study. *Sociology of Education, 75*(3), 231–248.

Addi-Raccah, A., & Ayalon, H. (2002). Gender inequality in leadership positions of teachers. *British Journal of Sociology of Education, 23*(2), 157–177.

Agarwal, S. P., & Aggarwal, J. P. (1995). *Women's education in India: A historical review present status and perspective plan with statistical indicators.* New Delhi: Concept Publishing Company.

Arar, K. (2010). 'I made it': Israeli–Palestinian Women principals as leaders. *Education Business and Society: Contemporary Middle Eastern Issues, 3*, 315–330.

———. (2017). Emotional expression at different managerial career stages: Female principals in Arab schools in Israel. *Educational Management Administration and Leadership, 45*, 929–943.

Ashraf, D. (2008). Schools are like our homes: Women in teaching and school leadership in Northern Pakistan. In J. Kirk (Ed.), *Women teaching in South Asia.* New Delhi: SAGE Publications.

Bandura, A. (1982). Self-efficacy mechanisms in human agency. *American Psychologist, 37*, 122–147.

———. (1997). *Self-efficacy: The exercise of control.* New York, NY: Freeman.

Banerjee, N. (2002). Between devil and the deep sea: Shrinking options for women in India. In K. Kapadia (Ed.), *The violence of development: The politics of identity, gender and social inequalities in India* (pp. 43–68). London: Zed Books.

Batra, P. (2009). Teacher empowerment: The education of entitlement-social transformation traverse. *Contemporary Education Dialogue, 6*, 121–156.

Belliyappa, J. L., & De Souza, S. (2017). Exercising agency within professional and social constraints: The career narration of Anglo-Indian woman employed as school teachers in Bangalore. *International Journal of Anglo Indian Studies, 17*, 30–61.

Bhaskar, R. (1975). Forms of realism. *Philosophica*, 15(1). As quoted in Roy, Bhaskar (2008). *A realist theory of science* (with a new introduction). London: Routledge.

Bista, M. B. (2008). Policies and realities for women teachers in Nepal. In J. Kirk (Ed.), *Women teaching in South Asia*. New Delhi: SAGE Publications.

Biswas, S. N., & Biswas, U. N. (2001). Legitimizing leadership: A framework for institutional leadership. *Vision: The Journal of Business Perspective*, 5, 33–42.

Blackmore, J. (1999), *Troubling women*. Buckingham: Open University Press.

Booz & Co (2012). Empowering the third billion: Women and the world of work in 2012.
Retrieved from https://www.strategyand.pwc.com/media/file/Strategyand_Empowering-the-Third-Billion_Full-Report.pdf

Brescoll, V. L. (2011). Who takes the floor and why: Gender, power, and volubility in organizations. *Administrative Science Quarterly*, 56, 622–641. doi:10.1177/0001839212439994

Brinia, V. (2012). Men versus women, educational leadership in primary schools in Greece: An empirical study. *International Journal of Educational Management*, 26, 175–191.

Bronfenbrenner, U. (1994). Ecological models of human development. In *International encyclopedia of education* (Vol. 3). End Edition Oxford: Elsevier. Reprinted in M. Gauvain & M. Cole (Eds), *Readings on the development of children* (2nd ed.) (1993, pp. 37–43). New York, NY: Freeman. Retrieved from www.psy.cmu.edu/~siegler/35bronfebrenner94.pdf

Bronfenbrenner, U., & Morris, P. A. (n.d.). *The bioecological model of human development* (Chapter 14). Retrieved from https://pdfs.semanticscholar.org/d470/f7b5abc2c5b338ee88b15a38b07ef214ce57.pdf

Bruckmuller, S., & Branscombe, N. R. (2010). The glass cliff: When and why women are selected as leaders in crisis contexts. *British Journal of Social Psychology*, 49, 433–451. doi:10.1348/014466609X466794

Buckley, W. (1967). *Sociology and modern systems theory*. Englewood Cliffs, NJ: Prentice-Hall.

Chabaya, O., Rembe, S., & Wadesango, N. (2009). The persistence of gender inequality in Zimbabwe: Factors that impede the advancement of women into leadership positions in primary schools. *South African Journal of Education*, 29, 235–251.

Cohen, G. A. (1993). Equality of what? On welfare, goods, and capabilities. In M. C. Nussbaum & A. K. Sen (Eds.), *The quality of life*. Oxford: Clarendon Press.

Coleman, M. (2003). Gender and the orthodoxies of leadership. *School Leadership and Management*, 23, 325–339.

Crowe, E., & Higgins, E. T. (1997). Regulatory focus and strategic inclinations: Promotion and prevention in decision-making. *Organizational Behavior and Human Decision Processes*, 69, 117–132. doi:10.1006/obhd.1996.2675

Cubillo, L., & Brown, M. (2003). Women in educational leadership and management: International differences? *Journal of Educational Administration, 41*, 278–291.

Dasgupta, S., & Singh Verick, S. (Eds.) (2016). *Transformation of women at work in Asia: An unfinished agenda* (Chapter 1). New Delhi: SAGE Publications.

Department for Education (DfE) (2011). *National statistics: Schools, pupils and their characteristics*. London: DfE.

Dorsey, B. J. (1989). Academic women at the university of Zimbabwe: Career prospects, aspirations and family role constraints. *Zimbabwe Journal of Educational Research, 3*, 342–376.

Eagly, A. H., & Schmidt, C. J. (2001). The leadership styles of women and men. *Journal of Social Issues, 57*, 781–797.

Eagly, H. A., & Karau, S. J. (2002). Role congruity theory of prejudice toward female leaders *Psychological Review, 109*, 573–598. Retrieved from http://www.rci.rutgers.edu/~search1/pdf/Eagley_Role_Conguity_Theory.pdf

Eccles, J. S. (2009). Who am I and What am I going to do with my life? Personal and collective identities as motivators of action. *Educational Psychologist, 44*, 78–89.

———. (2014). Introduction: Conceptualising gender differences in aspiring and attainment—A life course perspective. In S. Ingrid & J. S. Eccles (Eds), *In gender differences in aspirations and attainment: A life course perspective*. New York, NY: Cambridge University Press.

Elder, G. H. (1998). The life course as developmental theory. *Child Development, 69*, 1–2. doi:10.2307/1132065

———. (1999). *Children of the great depression: Social Change in life experiences* (25th anniversary print). Boulder, CO: Westview Press.

Elder, G. H., Johnson, K. M., & Crosnoe, R. (2004). The emergence and development of life course theory. In J. T. Martimore & M. J. Shanahan (Eds.), *Handbook of the life course* (pp. 3–19). New York, NY: Springer.

Elder-Vass, D. (2010). *The causal power of social structures: Emergence, structure and agency*. Cambridge, UK: Cambridge University Press.

Emirbayer, M., & Mische, A. (1998). What is agency? *American Journal of Sociology, 103*, 962–1023.

European Union, Save the Children and NUEPA. (2013). *School management for quality inclusive education and decentralised school governance*. New Delhi: New Concept Information Systems Pvt. Ltd.

Everett, J., & Charlton, S. E. M. (2014). *Women navigating globalisation: Feminist approach to development*. New York, NY: Rowman & Littlefield.

Ferreira, F. H. G., & Peragine, V. (2015). *Equality of opportunity: Theory and evidence*. Society for the study of economic inequality (Working Paper, March 2015-359). ECINEQ. Retrieved from http://www.ecineq.org/milano/WP/ECINEQ2015-359.pdf

Fleurbaey, M. (1994). On fair compensation. *Theory and Decision, 36*, 277–307.

———. (1995). The requisites of equal opportunity. In W. A. Barnett, H. Moulin, & N. J. Schoelds (Eds.), *Social choice, welfare and ethics* (pp. 37–53). Cambridge: Cambridge University Press.

———. (2008). *Fairness, responsibility and welfare*. Oxford: Oxford University Press. doi:10.1093/acprof:osobl/9780199215911.001.0001.

Franzosi, R. (2012). On quantitative narrative analysis. In J. A. Holstein & J. F. Gubriu (Eds), *Varieties of narrative analysis* (Chapter 4, pp. 75–98). Thousand Oaks, CA: SAGE Publications.

French, J. R. P., & Raven, B. (1959). The bases of social power. In D. Cartwright (Ed.), *Studies of social power* (pp. 155–164). Ann Arbor, MI: University of Michigan Press.

Fitzgerald, T. (2003). Interrogating orthodox voices: Gender, ethnicity, and educational leadership. *School Leadership and Management, 23,* 431–444.

Fuller, K. (2013). *Gender, identity and educational leadership*. London, UK: Bloomsbury.

Garton, R. A., & Alston, J. A. (2012). *School leadership and administration*. New York, NY: McGraw-Hill.

Gaus, N. (2011). Women and school leaderships: Factors deterring female teachers from holding principal positions at elementary schools in Makassar. *Advancing Women in Leadership, 31,* 175–188. Retrieved from http://advancingwomen.com/awl/awl_wordpress/

Gerzema, J. (2013). *The Athena doctrine*. San Francisco, CA: Jossey-Bass.

Glass, C., & Cook, A. (2016). Leading at the top: Understanding women's challenges above the glass ceiling. *The Leadership Quarterly, 27,* 51–63.

Government of India (GOI). (1959). *Report of the national committee on education of women*. New Delhi: Ministry of Education.

———. (1986). *National policy on education*. New Delhi: Ministry of Human Resource Education Department.

———. (1992). *Programme of Action*. New Delhi: Ministry of Human Resource Education department.

———. (2009). *National curriculum framework for teacher education (NCFTE)*. New Delhi: Ministry of Human Resource Education Department.

Government of India (GOI) - Planning Commission (2013). *Twelfth Five-Year Plan (2012–2017), Vol. 3: Social sectors*. New Delhi: SAGE Publications.

Govinda, R. (2002). *Role of head teachers in school management: Case study of six states*. Asian Network of Training and research Institutions in Educational Planning (ANTRIEP) in Collaboration with European Union. New Delhi: NIEPA.

Grogan, M., & Shakeshaft, C. (2011). *Women and educational leadership,* San Francisco, CA: Josey-Bass.

Gupta, D. (Eds.). (1991). *Social stratification*. New Delhi: Oxford University Press.

Halsey, A. H., Heath, A. F., & Ridge, J. M. (1980). *Origins and destinations: Family, class and education in modern Britain*. Oxford: Clarendon Press.

Haslam, S. A., & Ryan, M. K. (2008). The road to the glass cliff: Differences in the perceived suitability of men and women for leadership positions in succeeding and failing organizations. *Leadership Quarterly, 19*, 530–546.

Holland, J. H. (1998). *Emergence: From chaos to order*. New York, NY: Oxford University Press.

Jablin, F. M. (1985). An exploratory study of vocational organizational communication socialisation. *The Southern Speech Communication Journal, 50*, 261–282. (printed in) Anderson, A. J. (Ed.). (2012) *Communication year book 13*. New York, NY: Routledge.

Jain, D. (2015). Understanding leadership: Lessons from women's movement. In O. Goyal (Ed.), *Interrogating women's leadership and empowerment* (Chapter 1, pp. 1–12). New Delhi: SAGE Publications.

Jandhyala, K., Mehrotra, N., & Ramachandran, V. (2014). *A study of women teachers and achievement of gender and equity goals in secondary education*. New Delhi: ERU Consultants Pvt Ltd.

Jandhyala, K., & Ramachandran, V. (2015). Why women teachers matter in secondary education. *Economic and Political Weekly, 50*, 48–54.

Jane, S., Akao, S., Kilavanwa, B., & Warsal, D. (2010). You have been a servant to all: Melanesian women's educational leadership experiences. *School Leadership and Management, 30*, 65–76.

Kandiyoti, D. (1997). Bargaining with patriarchy. In N. Visanathan, L. Duggan, L. Nisonoff, & N. Wiegersma (Eds.), *Women, gender, and development reader* (pp. 86–92). London: Zed Books.

Kanter, R. M. (1977). *Men and women of the corporation*. New York, NY: Basic Books.

Keynes, M. L., Hysom, S. J., & Lupo, K. L. (2000). The positive organization: Leadership legitimacy, employee well-being and the bottom line. *The Psychologist Manager Journal, 4*, 143–153.

Khetrapal, I. (2003). Organizational climate and job satisfaction of teachers as a function of interpersonal skills of school principals. In N. Sood (Ed.), *Management of school education in India*. New Delhi: NIEPA.

Kirk, J. (2008). Introduction and conceptual understanding. In J. Kirk (Ed.), *Women teaching in South Asia*. New Delhi: SAGE Publications.

Kirk, J., & Winthrop, R. (2008). Women teachers in community–based Schools in Afghanistan. In J. Kirk (Ed.), *Women teaching in South Asia*. New Delhi: SAGE Publications.

Klasen, S. (1999). Gender inequality reduce growth and development? Evidence from cross country regressions. In *Engendering development*. Washington, DC: World Bank.

Kriestiansen, M. H. (2014). *Agency as an empirical concept: An assessment of theory and operalisationalization* (Working Paper 9 (July). Hague: Netherlands Interdisciplinary Demographic Institute.

Kruger, M. L. (1996). Gender issues in school headship: Quality versus power? *European Journal of Education, 31*, 447–461.

Kumar, R. (2011). Policies and programmes for changing employment opportunities for women in school education—A case of Andhra Pradesh. In P. Rao (Ed.), *Status of women in education, employment and social exclusion*. New Delhi: Serial Publications.

Kurshid, A., & Saba, A. (2017). Contested womanhood: Women's education and (re)production of gendered norms in rural Pakistan Muslim communities. *Discourse: Studies in the Cultural Politics of Education, 39*, 550–563. doi:10.10 80/01596306.2017.1282425.

Kyriakoussis, A., & Saiti, A. (n.d.). *Underrepresentation of women in public primary school administration: The experience of Greece*. Retrieved from http://iejll.synergiesprairies.ca/iejll/index.php/ijll/article/viewFile/605/267

Lantolf, J. P., & Poehner, M. E. (Eds.) (2008). *Socio-cultural theory and the teaching of second languages*, London: Equinox. Retrieved from http://www.dilit.it/allegati/LeoVanLierScrittaParte.pdf

Lent, R. W., Brown, S. D., & Hackett, G. (1994). Toward a unifying social cognitive theory of career and academic interest, choice, and performance. *Journal of Vocational Behavior, 45*, 79–122.

———. (2002). Social cognitive career theory. In D. Brown (Ed.), *Career, choice and development* (4th ed., pp. 255–311). San Francisco, CA: Jossey-Bass.

Limerick, B., & Lingard, B. (Eds.). (1995). *Gender and changing educational management*. Sidney: Hodder & Stoughton.

Lucas, W. J (2003). Status processes and the institutionalization of women leaders. *American Sociological Review, 68*, 464–480. Retrieved from www.jstor.org/stable/1519733

Lugg, C. A., & Tooms, A. K. (2010). A shadow of ourselves: Identity erasure and the politics of queer leadership. *School Leadership and Management, 30*, 77–91.

Lunenburg, F. C. (2012). Power and leadership: An influence process. *International Journal of Management, Business and Administration, 15*, 1–9.

Makura, A. H. (nd). *The challenges faced by women school heads: The Zimbabwean Experience*. Retrieved from http://www.emasa.co.za/files/emasa2009/13_EMASA2009_Makura.pdf

Manjrekar, N. (2013). Women school teachers in new times: Some preliminary reflections. *Indian Journal of Gender Studies, 20*, 335–356.

Mark, E. (2002). *Equal opportunities work: Theory about practice*. Goteborg University. Retrieved from www.gu.se/digitalAssets/.../1312214_equal-opportunities-work---eva-mark-2002.pdf

Marshall, C. (1985). The stigmatized woman: The professional woman in a male sex-typed career. *The Journal of Educational Administration, 23*, 131–152.

Martin, J. L. (Ed.). (2011). *Women as leaders in education* (Vol. 1). New York, NY: Praeger.

Mayer, J. W., & Rowan, B. (1977). Institutionalised organisations: Formal structures as myth and ceremony. *American Journal of Sociology, 83*, 340–363.

McGinn, K. L., & Bowles, H. R. (2003). *Negotiating challenges for women leaders* (M. Lagace Interviewer). Harvard Business School Working Knowledge. Retrieved from http://hbswk.hbs.edu/item/negotiating-challenges-for-women-leaders

Mckinsey & Company (2009). *Women leaders: A competitive edge in and after the crisis.* Retrieved from https://www.mckinsey.de/files/women_matter_3_brochure.pdf

McLay, M., & Brown, M. (1999). *Perceptions of preparation and training for headship in independent secondary schools in England: Eight case studies of female head teachers.* Paper presented at the BMAS Conference, Manchester, UK, September 1999. Retrieved from http://www.leeds.ac.uk/educol/documents/00001217.htm

Metz, N. T., & McNeely, S. R. (1998). Women on the job: A study of female high school principals. *Educational Administration Quarterly, 34,* 196–222.

Miller, P. (Ed.). (2013). *School leadership in the Caribbean: Perceptions, practices and Paradigms.* Didcot, UK: Symposium Books Ltd.

Moss-Racusin, C. A., & Rudman, L. A. (2010). Disruptions in women's self-promotion: The backlash avoidance model. *Psychology of Women Quarterly, 34,* 186–202. doi:10.1111/j.1471-6402.2010.01561

Mutopa, S., Maphosa, C., & Shumba, A. (2006). School management and teaching: The dilemma of teaching school heads in Zimbabwean secondary schools. *Journal of Educational Studies, 5,* 146–164.

Mwebi, B. M. (2008). An international perspective on underrepresentation of female leaders in Kenya's primary schools. *Canadian and International Education, 37.* Retrieved from http://ir.lib.uwo.ca/cgi/viewcontent.cgi?article=1091&context=cie-eci

Mythili, N. (2019a). Legitimisation of women school leaders in India. *Contemporary Education Dialogue, 16(1),* 54–83.

———. (2019b). Quest for success: The ladder of school leadership of women in India. *Social Change, 49(1),* 114–131. doi:10.1177/0049085718821748.

Nair, U. (1988). *Women teachers in South Asia.* New Delhi: Chanakya Publications.

———. (1998). *Comparative education in non-western societies.* New Delhi: Chanakya Publications.

———. (2001). *Fifty years of women's education in India.* New Delhi: National Council for Educational Research and Training.

National College of School Leadership (NCSL), UK. (n.d.). *Gender and headship in the 21st century.* Retrieved from www.ncsl.org.uk

National University for Educational Planning and Administration [NUEPA]. (2010). *Report of the committee on school leadership in India.* Unpublished, manuscript, NIEPA, New Delhi.

Ogawa, R. T., & Bossert, S. T. (1995). Leadership as an organizational quality. *Education Administration Quarterly, 31,* 224–243.

Ostrom, E. (1986). An agenda for the study of institutions. *Public Choice, 48,* 3–25.

Ozga, J. (1993). *Women in educational management.* Buckingham Palace: Open University Press.

Pande, R., & Ford, D. (2011). *Gender quotas and female leadership: A review. Background paper for the world development report on gender.* Retrieved from https://openknowledge.worldbank.org/bitstream/handle/10986/9120/WDR2012-0008.pdf

Panigrahi, M. R. (2013). Perceptions of secondary school stakeholders towards women representation in educational leadership in Harari Region if Ethiopia. *International Women Online Journal of Distance Education, 2,* Article 03.

Patel, G. (2013). *Gender differences in leadership styles and the impact within corporate boards.* Commonwealth Secretariat: Transformation Programme Division.

Popescu, A.-C., & Gunter, H. M. (2011). Romanian women head teachers and the ethics of care. *School Leadership and Management, 31,* 261–279.

Preciumantuntu, M., & Bolt, L. L. (2012). Does the gender of school personnel influence perceptions of leadership? *School Leadership and Management, 32,* 261–277.

Principal Regional Office for Asia and the Pacific UNESCO (PROAP). (2000). *Increasing the number of women teachers in Rural Schools.* Bangkok: UNESCO PROAP.

Rajan, S. R., & Krishnan, V. R. (2002). Impact of gender on influence, power, and authoritarianism. *Women in Management Review, 17,* 197–206.

Ramachandran, V. (2008). *Health and girls' education in South Asia: An essential synergy.* The United Nations Children's Fund (UNICEF) Regional office for South Asia, Kathmandu, Nepal; and United Nations Girls' Education Initiative (UNGEI).

Read, P. B. (1974). Source of authority and the legitimation of leadership in small groups. *Sociometry, 37,* 189–204.

Reskin, B., & Ross, C. E. (1992). Jobs, authority, and earnings among managers: The continuing significance of sex. *Work and Occupations, 19,* 342–365.

Richard, A., Dhanaraj, C., Javindan, M., & Zhang, Z.-X. (2015). Are there unique leadership models in Asia? Exploring uncharted territory. *The Leadership Quarterly, 26,* 1–6.

Ridgeway, C. L., & Correll, S. J. (2004). Unpacking the gender system: A theoretical perspective on gender beliefs and social relations. *Gender and Society, 18,* 510–531.

Roemer, J. (1993). A pragmatic theory of responsibility for the egalitarian planner. *Philosophy & Public Affairs, 10,* 146–166.

Rudman, L. A. (1998). Self promotion as a risk factor for women: The costs and benefits of counter stereotypical impression management. *Journal of Personality and Social Psychology, 74,* 629. doi:10.1037/0022-3514.74.3.629

Ryan, M. K., & Haslam, S. A. (2005). The glass cliff: Evidence that women are over-represented in precarious leadership positions. *British Journal of Management, 16,* 81–90.

Ryle, R. (2015). *Questioning gender: A sociological exploration* (Chapter 9: How does gender affect the type of work we do). Los Angeles, CA: SAGE Publications.

Saldana, J. (2015). *Thinking qualitatively: Methods of mind* (Chapter 6: Thinking multi disciplinarily, pp. 93–118). Thousand Oaks, CA: SAGE Publications.

Sawyer, K. (2005). *Social emergence*. Cambridge: Cambridge University Press.

Schoon, I., & Eccles, J. S. (Eds.). (2014). Introduction: Conceptualising gender differences in aspirations and attainment—a life course perspective. In *Gender differences in aspirations and attainment: A life course perspective* (Chapter 1, pp. 1–3). Cambridge, UK: Cambridge University Press.

Sen, A. (1993). *Inequality reexamined*. Oxford: Clarendon Press.

Sewell, W. H., Jr. (1992). A theory of structure: Duality, agency and transformation. *American Journal of Sociology, 98,* 1–29.

Shakeshaft, C. (1987). *Women in educational administration*. Newbury Park, CA: SAGE Publications.

Shapira, J., Arar, C., & Azaiza, F. (2011). They didn't consider me and no one even took me into account: Female school principals in the Arab education system in Israel. *Educational Management Administration and Leadership, 39,* 25–43.

Shenoy-Parker, S. (2014). *India's working women and career discourses*. New York, NY: Lexington Books.

Smith, J. M. (2011). Aspirations to and perceptions of secondary headship: Contrasting female teachers and head teachers' perspectives. *Educational Management Administration and Leadership, 39,* 516–535.

Sperandio, J. (2011). *Creating and supporting women's leadership in education: Charting the effects of international, national and organizational cultures*. Presented at the Gender Equality in Education: Looking Beyond Parity an IIEP Evidence-Based Policy Forum, 3–4 October. Paris: UNESCO-IIEP.

Sperandio, J., & Kagoda, A. M. (2011). Advancing women into educational leadership in developing countries: The case of Uganda. Retrieved from https://www.questia.com/library/journal/1P3-1512631501/advancing-women-into-educational-leadership-in-developing

Srivastava, G. (2008). *Women who created History: Exemplar materials for text book writers and teachers*. New Delhi: National Council for Educational Research and Training.

Stromquist, P. N. (2015). Women in higher education today—Structure and agency from gender perspective. *Journal of Educational Planning and Administration, 29,* 287–306.

Sujatha, K. (2011). *Improving school management—Learning from successful schools*. New Delhi: Asian Network of Training and Research Institutions in Educational Planning (ANTRIEP) - National Institute for Educational Planning and Administration (NIEPA).

Symonds, E. J., Maurice, G., & Linda, H. (2014). Emerging gender differences in times of multiple transitions. In S. Ingrid & J. S. Eccles (Ed.), *Gender differences in aspirations and attainment: A life course perspective*. Cambridge, UK: Cambridge University Press.

Trinidad, C., & Normore, A. H. (2005). Leadership and gender: A dangerous liaison? *Leadership & Organization Development Journal, 26,* 574–590. Retrieved from http://www.emeraldinsight.com/journals.htm?articleid=1523647&show=abstract

U-DISE (Unified District Information on School Education). (2016–2017). *School education in India: UDISE flash statistics 2016–17*. New Delhi: NUEPA-MHRD. Retrieved from udise.in/report modules/information on teachers

UNESCO. (1990). *World declaration on education for all*. Paris: UNESCO.

———. (2000). *World education forum — Dakar framework for action*. Paris: UNESCO.

UNESCO-MHRD. (2001). *Women teachers in India*. New Delhi: UNESCO and Indian National Commission for Cooperation with UNESCO.

UNESCO-Principal Regional Office for Asia and the Pacific (PROAP). (2000). *Increasing the number of women teachers in rural schools*. Bangkok: UNESCO PROAP.

UNESCO — World Education Forum. (2000). *Dakar framework for action*. Paris: UNESCO.

Vial, C. A., Napier, J. L., & Brescoll, V. L. (2016). A bed of thorns: Female leaders and self-reinforcing cycle of illegitimacy. *The Leadership Quarterly, 27*, 400–414.

Walby, S. (1990). *Theorising patriarchy*. Oxford, UK: Basil Blackwell.

Walker, H. A., & Zelditch, M., Jr. (1993). Power, legitimacy, and the stability of authority: A theoretical research program. In J. Berger & M. Zelditch, Jr. (Eds.), *Theoretical research programs: Studies in the growth of theory* (pp. 364–381). Palo Alto, CA: Stanford University Press.

Walkerdine, V. (1990). *Schoolgirl fictions*. New York, NY: Verso.

Watt, H. M. G., & Eccles, J. S. (Eds.). (2008). *Gender and occupational outcomes: Longitudinal assessment of individual, social and cultural influences*. Washington, DC: American Psychological Association.

Weber, M. (1968). *Economy & society* (Vol. 1, G. Roth & C. Wittch, Trans.). Berkeley, CA: University of California.

Wood, R. (1987). *Assessment and equal opportunities* [Public lecture], University of London, Institute of Education, 11 November. As quoted in EURYDICE (2009), *Gender differences in educational outcomes: Study on the measures taken and current situation in Europe*. Brussels: EURYDICE.

Zammuner, V. L., & Galli, C. (2005). The relationship with patience: Emotional labour and its correlates in hospital employees. In C. E. Hartel, W. J. Zerbe, & N. M. Ashkanagy (Eds.), *Organizational behaviour: An emotions perspective* (pp. 251–285). Mahwah, NJ: Lawrence Erlbaum Associates.

Zelditch, M., Jr., & Walker, H. A. (1984). Legitimacy and the stability of authority. In E. J. Lawler (Ed.), *Advances in group processes* (Vol. 1, pp. 1–27). Greenwich, CT: JAI Press.

Zikhali, J., & Perumal, J. (2016). Leading in disadvantaged Zimbabwean school contexts: Female school heads' experiences of emotional labour. *Educational Management Administration Leadership, 44*, 347–362.

INDEX

achieved capability(ies), 36–37, 194
Afghanistan, 2, 5
agency of women school leaders, 117–19
   diversity in school contexts, 132
   and education system, 119, 121–23, 126
   family support, 126–29, 132
agency, mediating, 7–81
American Association of School Administration (AASA), 34
anglo-Indian women teachers, 12
ascribed capability(ies), 36, 71
authority, 25–27
availability of opportunities, 38–43

Bangladesh, 5
Block Resource Centres (BRC), 36

capacity–agency interactions/relationship, 185–88
causal power, of social structures, 23, 182
chrono system, 20, 23
Cluster Resource Centres (CRCs), 36
College of Teacher Education (CTE), 36, 112
continuum of interaction for legitimacy
   leadership behaviour and gender perspective, interaction between, 180–81

   promotion and preventive-focused leadership behaviour, 144–48
   traditional and rational gender perspective, 179–80
democratic/participative leadership style, 9
determinants of school leadership, of successful women in India
   capacity–agency interactions/relationship, 112–13
   iterative steps, 115
   nature–magnitude relationship for structure, 113–14
   structure–agency interaction, 115
deterministic legitimacy women leaders
   backlash effect, 168–71
   illegitimacy effect, 171–73
distribution
   of school categories, in state and UTs, 75–77
   of teachers in different school at state level, 78–80
distribution of opportunities, 35
District Institutes of Educational Training (DIET), 36
District Primary Education Programme (DPEP), 11
domain specific capacity, 113, 123, 138, 145, 185, 188, 198, 201–202
domestic capacity, 113

Durga Bai Deshmukh Committee, 10

empowerment of women, in South Asia, 15
exo system, 20, 23, 114
expert power, 152

fitting-in opportunities, 3
Five Year Plan (12th), 235
formal education, 6, 126, 209
fundamental human capacity, 113, 116, 120, 122–25, 129–30, 133, 138, 142, 144–46, 148

gender and development (GAD), 1
gender difference, 9, 30, 137
giving-in opportunities, 3

head master (HM), 93, 109
head mistress, 91, 109, 127
head teachers (HTs), 33
heads of schools (HoS), 15
high legitimacy women leaders, 160–65
human development
   agency of women school leader and, 24–25
   and life-course approach, 20–21
   ecology of, sub-systems, 22–23
   methodological approach for study, 28–32
   methodology to study, 17, 27, 32
   quantitative and qualitative approach to study, 29–30
   and structure-agency interaction, 19–20
   whole and whole relationship for, 23–24

Jawahar Navodaya Vidyalaya (JNV), 161

Kendriya Vidyalaya, 66

ladder of school leadership of women, 82, 184
   aspiration from family members, 84, 101
   availability of opportunity, 184–85
   balancing resilience with determination, 94–98
   definition of, 82
   family support from parents and husband, 128–29
   family, social and educational background of, 83–84, 87–90
   gender as notion or experience, 81
   leading school administration, management and academic functions, 81, 83–84, 98–103
   school leadership positions in education system, 37–43
   steps in, 82
   zeal beyond school leadership, 81–83, 103–7
leadership position in different school categories, women representation in
   acting HMs, 38
   aggregate scenario of four regions of India, 56, 60
   aggregate trend among acting HM in regions, 56
   all-India scenario, 43–44
   capability as form of opportunity, 71–72
   head teachers, 46
   in eastern region, 48–49
   in northern region, 51–53
   in southern region, 53–56
   in western region, 49–51
   parallel positions as alternate choice, 35–36, 69–71
   principals, 47–48
   and recruitment policy and process, 62–63, 66–69
   state level representation, 61

vice principals, 46–47
legitimacy of school leadership of Indian women
  focus on behaviours, 159
  and gender perspective, 154–56
  process of, 160–76
  use of power by women, 25
legitimization process, of women school leaders
  deterministic legitimacy, 168
  high legitimacy, 160–66
  moderate legitimacy, 166–68
  no legitimacy, 174–76
life-course theory, 20
location of work, 36, 71

macro system, 20, 114, 208
masculinity–femininity syndrome, 3–4
meso system, 20, 23
micro system, 20, 23
Millennium Development Goals, 1
moderate legitimacy women leaders, 166–68
morphogenesis, 183, 188, 199
morphostasis, 183

National Curriculum Framework for Teacher Education, 10
National Policy on Education, 10
Navodaya Vidyalaya schools, 104
Nepal, 5, 7
no legitimacy women leaders, 174–76

opportunity for agency, 115–16
organizational power, 153
outcome of opportunities, 37

Pakistan, 7–8
path-wise exposition of school leadership
  achieving status of leader in school, 199–201
  acquiring leadership position, 93–94, 127, 136, 149
  ascend path of success as leader, 201–3
  aspire for school leadership positions, 194–96
  availability of opportunities, 188, 194
  transcend leadership and limitations of education system, 203–5
perception of power differentials, 25, 28, 153, 156, 158–60, 165, 178–80, 186, 190–93, 198, 201, 203–4, 206
policy implications, on women participation
  to bridge gap between school leaders and community, 215–16
  enhancement of legitimacy, 216–17
  family support for inclusive approach, 209
  to increase provision and access to leadership positions, 212–13
  right of opportunity for career progression, 214–15
power, 25–27
practical evaluative agency, 112–13, 123
Programme of Action, 10
projective agency, 112–13, 129
proximal process, 21–22
public patriarchy, 6
Public Service Commission (PSC), 62, 91

quantitative narrative analysis (QNA), 28
quest for success, as school leader characteristics features of structures and women leaders agency, 207–10

to adopt different leadership
behaviour, 206
zeal to achieve, 137–38, 205

Rashtriya Madhyamika Shiksha
Abhiyan (RMSA), 36, 69–70,
121, 163, 214
recruitment policy, 62–63, 66–69
referent power, 152

Sarva Shiksha Abhiyan (SSA), 36,
69–70, 121, 124, 163, 169,
214
school and agency of women school
leaders
achieving excellence, 136
crossing gendered barriers, 137
and interaction with different community, 163
need to improve teaching-learning
process, 135–36
negotiation and navigation for
school leadership, 138–39
people-centred approach, 132,
135
school management and administration, 136
zeal beyond norms, 137–38
school leadership development programme (SLDP), 30, 169, 215
school leadership in developing countries, factors influencing
conversion of compulsions, 4
drawuing parallel line between
home and school, 6–8
masculinity-feminity syndrome,
3–4
mediating agency, 7–8
patriarchy, 6
socio-cultural effect, 4–5
thwarted opportunities, 5–6
use of parallel strategies by women
school heads, 69–71

school leadership of women in India,
10–12
defining in Indian context, 210–11
theorization process, 184–88
school leadership positions in
developing countries, women
representation in, 32–34
equal opportunities and outcome
of participation, 34–37
examining opportunities in education system, 37–38
matching of school categories, 38
opportunities availability in different categories, 38–43
School Management Committee
(SMC), 20, 97, 105, 134, 136,
140, 142, 163, 175
silent cries, 3–4
social ontology
framework for constructing, 183
principles applied to theorise
school leadership of women,
182
social practices, 182
State Council of Educational Research
and Training (SCERT), 36, 122
structure–agency interaction, 19
and human development, 20
success path of women school heads,
in India
capacity–agency interaction/relationship, 145
determinants of, 149
influence of nature and magnitude
of structures, 148
mediating deterministic education
system nature, 148–49
Sustainable Development Goals, 1

teaching occupation, 6

Union Public Service Commission
(UPSC), 64, 66, 85, 93

Universalisation of Elementary Education (UEE), 39

whole school leadership of women, 24

women in development (WID), 1, 2, 212, 215

women participation
in secondary education, 10, 33
UNESCO emphasis on, 2

working women in India, involvement and renegotiation of, 21

ABOUT THE AUTHOR

N. Mythili is an expert in school education with 16 years of professional experience. She began her career as a trained graduate teacher in a government-aided institution and taught mathematics and physics at secondary level for six years in Bengaluru, Karnataka. She secured the third rank at the university level in her MEd degree. Later, she obtained national scholarship to do her PhD at the Institute for Social and Economic Change, Bengaluru. She undertook research to know the causes for the burning issue of the education system even today, that is, lower levels of learning among students, for her PhD degree under the title 'Determinants of Quality of Schooling in Rural Primary Schools in Karnataka'. In her thesis, she carried out an in-depth study on time-on-task in teaching-learning process, an unexplored area in the year 2000, leadership at block or sub-district level and community participation for children's schooling. Soon after she completed her PhD, she worked as Research Associate at the Centre for Multidisciplinary Development Research at Dharwad, Karnataka and engaged in the project of developing education data banks.

Dr Mythili joined the National Institute of Educational Planning and Administration (NIEPA), New Delhi in 2013. Since then she has been working as Assistant Professor at the National Centre for School Leadership Development. Here, she led the team for developing Curriculum Framework for School Leadership. Besides, she also led the starting of Post Graduate Diploma in School Leadership and Management, first of its kind in India.

About the Author

Before joining the NIEPA, New Delhi, Dr Mythili worked at the Tata Institute of Social Sciences, Mumbai as Project Officer for research on the topic 'Strengthening and Empowering State Education Resource Institutions in Karnataka under 12th Five Year Plan'. Prior to this, she worked as Specialist, People Development in the unit of Educational Leadership and Management at Azim Premji Foundation, Bengaluru and was also briefly involved in curriculum development for the Educational Leadership programme for the then forthcoming Azim Premji University at Bengaluru.

Dr Mythili's research articles on the community pressure for achieving higher quality, effective use of time and quality education are published in well-known journals in India. Besides quality of schooling and education, her other areas of research interest include school leadership, teacher education and its regulatory mechanisms, governance and leadership.